CLASSICAL PRESENCES

General Editors

LORNA HARDWICK   JAMES I. PORTER

CLASSICAL PRESENCES

Attempts to receive the texts, images, and material culture of ancient Greece and Rome inevitably run the risk of appropriating the past in order to authenticate the present. Exploring the ways in which the classical past has been mapped over the centuries allows us to trace the avowal and disavowal of values and identities, old and new. Classical Presences brings the latest scholarship to bear on the contexts, theory, and practice of such use, and abuse, of the classical past.

China from the Ruins of Athens and Rome

Classics, Sinology, and Romanticism, 1793–1938

Chris Murray

OXFORD
UNIVERSITY PRESS

OXFORD

UNIVERSITY PRESS

Great Clarendon Street, Oxford, OX2 6DP,
United Kingdom

Oxford University Press is a department of the University of Oxford.
It furthers the University's objective of excellence in research, scholarship,
and education by publishing worldwide. Oxford is a registered trade mark of
Oxford University Press in the UK and in certain other countries

First Edition published in 2020

Impression: 1

Published in the United States of America by Oxford University Press
198 Madison Avenue, New York, NY 10016, United States of America

British Library Cataloguing in Publication Data

Data available

Library of Congress Control Number: 2020941927

ISBN 978-0-19-876701-5

Printed and bound by
CPI Group (UK) Ltd, Croydon, CR0 4YY

For
Michael O'Neill:
a mandarin of the first order

Acknowledgements

Work for this book started in Singapore, progressed in Durham, and concluded in Melbourne, by way of a short period as a visiting researcher at LongRoom Hub, Trinity College Dublin. I presented parts of the research in guest lectures for Northumbria University, the nineteenth-century seminar at the University of Sydney, Romantic Realignments at the University of Oxford, and as conference papers in Hampstead, Hong Kong, Sheffield, and Tokyo. Thanks to all who have listened and responded to my work in progress. Above all—amidst much upheaval—love to Claire, and new recruits Maddy and Pearse, for teaching me that home is where the heart is.

The main course of this research was prepared as an IAS Junior Research Fellow at Durham University. Thanks to the European Union's Seventh Framework Programme for funding the DIFeREns project, which made this possible. The Institute of Advanced Study housed me for a time in a beautiful office overlooking Palace Green and Durham Cathedral. In this august setting Audrey Bowron, Linda Crowe, and Simon Litchfield endured my working-day idiocy and occasionally fed me. I had gallant allies in the Department of English Studies. My gratitude for companionship and collegiality go to Marco Bernini, Eleanor R. Barraclough, Mark Campbell Chambers, Robert Carver, Megan Cavell, Daniel Derrin, Vicky Flood, Peter Garratt, Daniel Grausam, long-suffering Wolverhampton Wanderers fan Jason Harding, Jenny Holden, Time Lord Simon James, Roisin Laing, Marina Mackay, Arthur Rose, Mark Sandy, Will Viney, and Sarah Wootton. Appreciative noises towards the dynamic Bennett Zon and all involved in the Centre for Nineteenth-Century Studies. In the Department of Classics and Ancient History, my especial thanks to Barbara Graziosi and Edmund Richardson.

At Monash, thanks to my students for being brilliant and interesting, and for bringing me doughnuts. In Literary Studies and the wider domain of Arts, I am grateful for the support of Ali Alizadeh, Gloria Davies, Kevin Foster, Robin Gerster, Peter Groves, Melinda Harvey, John Hawke, Sue Kossew, Chandani Lokuge, Sascha Morrell, Simone Murray,

Michelle Smith, Patrick Spedding, Beatrice Trefalt, and, across the precinct in Music, Paul Watt.

Karen O'Brien, Vidyan Ravinthiran, and Nicholas Roe were kind enough to comment on particular chapters of this book in progress. John Barnard, Jenny Day, and Noël Golvers assisted with queries. Elsewhere in the field I've been glad to have the advice and friendship of Maddy Callaghan, Ant Howell, Peter J. Kitson, Seamus Perry, Heidi Thomson, and Tim Webb. My gratitude to all at Oxford University Press and the Classical Presences series, and to my anonymous referees for patient and constructive criticism.

This book is dedicated to the great Michael O'Neill (1953–2018). I wish I could hand him a copy down the Half Moon Inn over a glass of cabernet sauvignon and a packet of Mini Cheddars. Michael was instrumental in bringing me to Durham. He advised me on the proposal for this book, and read one of the chapters. He shared his considerable wisdom on every aspect of scholarly life, and he held intelligent opinions about football. There was the time, after some administrative annoyance, he said, 'We can't end the week like this', so we talked about Baudelaire instead. When I was offered my position at Monash, we met over coffee at the Marriott Hotel to discuss the prospect, alongside the year-old Maddy. With the job contract in one hand and animal biscuits in the other, Michael helped me make the decision to move to Australia. And so much else. Thanks, old sport—I'll miss you.

Contents

List of Figures

1

A Classical Cathay and a Real China

Open *An Historical Account of the Embassy to the Emperor of China* (1797) and you'll see a vision of Asia embellished with Graeco-Roman motifs (Figure 1.1). In Thomas Stothard's frontispiece, British ambassador Earl George Macartney (1737–1806) enjoys a prospect of a Chinese landscape dotted with pagodas and arched bridges. Immediately under the window stand imperial soldiers, intimating that our scene is a royal domain such as the Forbidden City in Beijing. Facing Macartney, a mandarin gestures through the casement. This is an invitation for the reader, like the ambassador, to enjoy the splendour of China. Yet the experience is facilitated by a Grecian figure, at the left of the illustration, who holds the curtain aside. This woman wears a Greek headband and a diaphanous dress. In one hand she has a caduceus, the implement of Hermes that is associated with diplomacy. Overhead float three cupids, one of which bears an olive branch. The list of illustrations describes the woman as 'the Female representing Commerce'.

Stothard's symbolism becomes clearer in light of his caption. From the cupids we infer hope that relations will blossom between Britain and China. Their olive branch is a sign that grievances must be redressed: the Britons are unhappy about trading conditions at Canton. Commercial interests motivated the Embassy, so Commerce personified provides the opportunity to see China by opening the curtain. If classical flourishes seem unusual for a treatment of the Macartney Embassy, it is perhaps more surprising for a modern reader to learn that they were not inappropriate. Granted the opportunity to transcend time and witness Macartney's meeting with the Emperor of the Qing Dynasty in 1793, a spectator might wonder, 'Why are they speaking Latin?'

China from the Ruins of Athens and Rome: Classics, Sinology, and Romanticism, 1793–1938.
Chris Murray, Oxford University Press (2020). © Chris Murray.
DOI: 10.1093/oso/9780198767015.001.0001

Figure 1.1 Thomas Stothard embellishes Macartney's vision of China with Graeco-Roman motifs.

These classical presences have both practical explanations and greater significance. Macartney was allowed to bring only a select retinue to Yuanmingyuan, the Garden of Perfect Brightness. The official sketch artist, William Alexander, had travelled all the way to China but was excluded from the diplomatic encounter with the Qianlong Emperor (r. 1735–96). Hence Alexander's set of pictures omits the dramatic moments at which Macartney first saw the Forbidden City in the distance, and his reception nearby at Yuanmingyuan. Stothard, a professional illustrator who had seen no more of China than in Alexander's pictures, supplied the necessary image from his imagination. Classical motifs enable Stothard to tell readers a great deal about the issues at stake in the Embassy. His picture is laden with information, like a satirical cartoon of the period. However, publisher John Stockdale appears to have lacked confidence that Stothard's illustration was a sufficient introduction to the subject of the book. It is telling that Stothard's arrangement of cupids and a Grecian Commerce faces, on the recto, a matter-of-fact title page, which features an 'English Merchant showing some fine broad cloth to a Chinese'.

The dissimilarity between Stockdale's two pictures befits the matter illustrated. For a long time the British government struggled to decide precisely how it should deal with China. This uncertainty pervaded the diplomatic effort, which muddled purposes and was discernibly neither one thing nor the other in execution. The Macartney mission was an uneasy collaboration between the British government and the East India Company; hence the gunboat HMS *Lion* sailed to China alongside an East Indiaman, the *Hindostan*. Trade agreements and diplomatic relations were not mutually exclusive matters in European diplomacy, but they were in the Chinese imperial mindset: it would be inappropriate to discuss the coarse topic of commerce with the Emperor. Thus the British approach was not viable from the Chinese perspective. In the *Historical Account*, Macartney declares that China is 'one of the sublimest objects for human contemplation', but he admits that the Embassy was motivated by 'commercial intercourse'.[1] Appropriately, the effect of juxtaposing the first illustrations is to hover between imaginative and literal modes of representation. Confusion abounded in Anglophone engagements with China. *An Historical Account of the Embassy to the Emperor of China*, excerpted by Secretary George Staunton (1737–1801) from the papers of Macartney and companions and published in 1797, should not be mistaken for *An Authentic Account of an Embassy from the King of Great Britain to the Emperor of China*, also excerpted by Staunton

---

[1] George Staunton, *An Historical Account of the Embassy to the Emperor of China* (London: J. Stockdale, 1797), 1 and 20.

from the papers of Macartney and companions and published in 1797.[2] Furthermore, Stockdale published an *Abridged Account* the same year, which reproduces Stothard's frontispiece although reversed from right to left.

The number of languages in use during the Macartney Embassy constituted cacophony rather than harmony, and was symptomatic of complication. The problem was not simply for one side to understand the other, but for the British delegation to comprehend *itself.* Macartney's reception by the Emperor was not a gathering of polyglots. The British representatives, and those whom they required to relay their speech in Mandarin, struggled for a common language. It had been difficult to find interpreters for the Macartney Embassy. The Chinese were forbidden to leave their country on pain of death by strangulation, and faced public decapitation if they taught their language to foreigners. These proved considerable deterrents. Plans for the Embassy appeared to be at an impasse until intelligence reported the existence of two native Mandarin-speakers at the Chinese College in Naples. This institution was a legacy of the sixteenth- and seventeenth-century Jesuit mission to China. The two converts to Christianity had fled probable persecution in China, where their religion was likely to earn them three months wearing the cangue followed by a lifetime of slavery. Offered the opportunity, Ke Zongxiao and Li Zibiao professed that they were sufficiently homesick to accompany the Embassy, so risking death (on two counts, as they had not only left China, but taught Mandarin to Staunton's son, Thomas).[3] To fool the Qing officials, the interpreters adopted British dress and used their Christian names, Paul and Jacobus. These scholars had studied Mandarin, Italian, and Latin, but not English. For the British delegates to communicate with their interpreters, they needed either to have learned Italian or to remember their schoolboy Latin. As it happened, few of them had good Latin. At one point Macartney even forbade the delegates from speaking Latin so that their poor standard would go unnoticed by the Portuguese missionaries, whom the mandarins had

---

[2] The *Historical Account* is a shorter text and, as Stockdale brags in his preface, is much cheaper. One volume of the folio *Authentic Account*, which cost as much as £6, 6s in boards, comprises plates.

[3] It is fitting that Thomas Staunton is the source of information on these punishments in his *Ta Tsing Leu Lee: Being the Fundamental Laws and a Selection of the Supplementary Statutes of the Penal Code of China* (London: Cadell and Davies, 1810), 232 and 533.

drafted in as interpreters.[4] Fortunately he had brought a German scholar, J.C. Hüttner, to undertake most of the translation from English to Latin. In turn Ke and Li rendered Latin as Mandarin, which Qing officials recorded both in Chinese characters and in Manchu.

Did Macartney kowtow to the Emperor? The British party found the process undignified, and noted that the Qing court had allowed the Russians to abstain from the kowtow in 1720. Protocol was important in 1793 but probably did not affect the outcome of the Embassy. The kowtow was not so crucial as British commentators would claim during the nineteenth century when they, like their Chinese counterparts, became fixated with national humiliation. The Protestant missionary and Sinologist Robert Morrison (1782–1834), interpreter on the Amherst Embassy of 1816, realized that the kowtow gained significance to Britain because so much was being lost in translation: 'ceremonies ... speak a language as intelligible as words'.[5] The Macartney delegates explained their aversion to the kowtow with erudition:

The Mandarines ... were astonished when they heard that, for a similar act done by an European, Timagoras, in the character of Embassador to a powerful monarch of the East (of Persia), was condemned to suffer death by his country-men, the Athenians, as soon as he returned home, for having degraded the nation who deputed him.[6]

In Plutarch's *Life of Artaxerxes*, the Persian emperor's visitors attempt to convince him that they have performed *proskynesis*, then pass off the prostrations as insincere among their own people. The allusion proves apt. English sources claim that Macartney did not kowtow; imperial Chinese records say he did.[7]

Naturally, the Macartney Embassy was a disaster. British commentators expected it to be a disaster beforehand, and reported it as one afterwards despite the ambassador's efforts. Macartney controlled the publication of accounts by himself and his most important delegates. He appointed Staunton as editor, and ensured there was a text from the

    [4] William Jardine Proudfoot, *Biographical Memoir of James Dinwiddie* (Liverpool: Edward Howell, 1868), 45–6. Dinwiddie was Astronomer to the Embassy.
    [5] George Thomas Staunton, *Miscellaneous Notices Relating to China*, rev. (London: John Murray, 1850), 121.
    [6] Staunton, *Historical Account*, 309.
    [7] Ssu-yü Teng and John Fairbank ed., *China's Response to The West: A Documentary Survey, 1839–1923* (Cambridge, MA: Harvard University Press, 1954), 20.

official record to suit every budget. In these books the diplomats attempt to dignify the affair. Unfortunately they were beaten to the post by Macartney's butler, Aeneas Anderson, whose memoir was published in 1795. Anderson's book proceeds, as *The Monthly Review* observes, 'in a manner not calculated to enhance our ideas of the business'. In light of the ill-planned mission to China, this journalist intimates that Britain has had enough of experts. Although concluding with a polite assurance that the imminent, official accounts will add much to British comprehension of China, the reviewer assumes that Anderson's 'must be an accurate narrative' because of his very ignorance of the arts and sciences.[8] Anderson makes it clear that the British embassy was 'dismissed . . . without the least ceremony'.[9]

Embarrassment in China did not surprise the British public. Peter Pindar's satirical *Lyrical Epistles*, published before their departure in 1792, envisions Macartney and delegates flogged by Qing officials for begging:

> Stripp'd, schoolboy-like, and now I see his Train,
> I see their lily bottoms writhe with pain.[10]

After the event appeared another satire, which purports to be the Emperor's edict to George III. Here the Emperor expresses regret that William Pitt and various other, prominent politicians were not dressed as Tartars and dispatched to China instead of the Macartney delegation. Thomas James Mathias's *Imperial Epistle from Kien Long* (1794) is most concerned with character assassinations, but it makes a canny point: that news of Britain's war with France has reached the Emperor, who sees the visitors hence as troublemakers. This Emperor of China commands knowledge of Roman culture, as evident in his account of Edmund Burke's career, which includes explicit comparison to Cicero and subtler allusion to Virgil's *Georgics*:

> Onward with more than Tully's force he prest,
> With more than all, but Tully's judgment, blest:

---

[8] *The Monthly Review* 2, no. 17 (1795): 72–8.

[9] Aeneas Anderson, *A Narrative of the British Embassy to China, in the Years 1792, 1793, and 1794* (London: J. Debrett, 1795), 222.

[10] Peter Pindar [John Wolcot], *A Pair of Lyric Epistles to Lord Macartney and his Ship* (London: H.D. Symonds, 1792), 18.

High truth in large discourse with wisdom fraught,
Not better heard in Tusculum, he taught;
In every realm of every science found,
Plain are his steps in all—but Grecian ground.
A temple last he rear'd by art divine,
And plac'd his Caesar in the central shrine.

(119–26)

Cicero is a means for the poem's Qianlong Emperor to question British intentions in China. Burke (1729–97) alluded to the Roman's Verrine orations frequently during the trial of Warren Hastings (1732–1818), former Head of the Supreme Council of Bengal. Hastings was charged with corruption. His trial had already run for six years when Macartney met the Emperor. Hastings would not be acquitted until 1795. The vision of Macartney beaten for begging, like the Verrine trial of Hastings, demonstrates domestic scepticism towards British actions overseas. Thus classical allusion in *The Imperial Epistle from Kien Long* encodes an anxiety, also articulated in the *Lyrical Epistles*, that Britain's wish to enrich itself in China was transparent and shameful.

The point of this book is that you can't understand how Anglophone ideas of China formed without paying attention to classics. With focus on the period from the Macartney Embassy to the conclusion of the second Opium War in 1860, I consider how classics informs literary engagements with China. The result is a classical Cathay, a vision of China which is explicitly informed by Greek and Roman ideas and serves as an imaginative substitute for the real China. The examples of the Stothard illustration and the Latin-speaking interpreters demonstrate how classical culture might constitute a lens through which Anglophone thinkers viewed China. Stothard represents such an apparatus almost literally: the casement that opens onto China is framed by symbols sourced in the Graeco-Roman tradition. He uses a familiar visual-shorthand to tell us that the Macartney Embassy is an opportunity for new friendships to flourish and for old wrongs to be righted. Comparably, Latin was the medium through which Macartney's delegates could communicate with their interpreters; they accessed China via Graeco-Roman culture. In turn, the early accounts of the Macartney Embassy assume a readership learned in classical antiquity, and that this offers the best way to introduce the unfamiliar culture. John Barrow, Private Secretary to the Macartney Embassy, often alludes to classics in his own book, *Travels in China* (1804). Usually these references serve as yardsticks by which Barrow finds China inferior. He complains that China has no architecture to rival Greek and Roman ruins, and that Beijing lacks ancient Rome's 'conveniencies of common sewers'.[11]

That classics offered a lens through which Britain could view China is useful as a starting-point for this book, but it would be unwise to apply the hypothesis too broadly. Every concept within the formulation is unstable. First, we might elaborate on the idea of a lens. Classics could help outsiders who adopted unilateral perspectives on China, but could also affect gazes in the opposite direction, and even facilitate back-and-forth exchanges between east and west. 'Mirrors within mirrors' is a phrase with which Jerry Toner typifies the relationship between classics and Orientalism (a term to which I shall return).[12] Such reflections did occur from the Chinese side, where literati were not utterly ignorant of the Western classical tradition. For example, Jesuit Sinology applies Aristotelian notions of causation to Confucianism in *Confucius Sinarum Philosophus* (1687), which includes a Latin version of *Analects*. On the other hand, the missionaries also introduced classical texts to China. To disseminate Christianity in China, the Jesuits needed first to overcome the insularity prescribed by Confucianism, which prioritizes duty towards the family and depicts the ruler as a kind of parent. Matteo Ricci (1552–1610) translated Cicero's *Laelius on Friendship* into Chinese to address this problem. He hoped to convince Chinese readers that Cicero's ideas on friendship were compatible with Confucius' reflections on the delight of receiving guests (*Analects* 1.1). There is no evidence of serious Chinese attention to Cicero in light of Ricci's booklet, but the missionary himself was received warmly. Chinese scholars were open to many of the foreign ideas Ricci brought. In particular, mathematicians were interested in Euclid, whose *Elements* was translated into Chinese in 1607. Cicero's text can partly be credited for bringing about these exchanges. Thus, the *Historical Account*—most probably unwittingly— applies classical concepts to a China that had already assimilated aspects of Europe's classical tradition. Furthermore, some of the classical works cited in this monograph have Asian concerns, as in the *Iliad*, Aeschylus' *Persians*, and the Neopythagorean thought influenced by

---

[11] John Barrow, *Travels in China* (London: T. Cadell and W. Davies, 1804), 5 and 98.

[12] Jerry Toner, *Homer's Turk: How Classics Shaped Ideas of the East* (Cambridge, MA: Harvard University Press, 2013), 13.

Hindu philosophy. This ancient Orientalism complicates the hypothesis that Graeco-Roman antiquity offered a set of paradigms to evaluate unrelated cultures, as the paradigms themselves were touched by inter-actions with Asia. Classics and Orientalism are accretions, and each contains the other to an extent (much as, in the *yin-yang* binarity, *yin* contains *yang* and vice versa).

A second and significant difficulty in the triangulation of classics, Anglophone literature, and China arises from the elusiveness of the key terms. I reserve 'Sinology' for scholarship on China, much as 'classicist' is conventionally used to denote professional dedication to classics. For clarity, I use the term 'classics' in reference to ancient Greek and Roman culture, but I do not adopt the modern convention of referring to works by Confucius, Laozi, and Zhuangzi as 'classical' Chinese texts. My usage does not communicate a qualitative judgment, but rather an attempt to delineate disciplinary boundaries at the outset (although those bound-aries prove to be permeable). Further explanation is required as there are texts discussed in this book that would not be considered canonical today. The authors who discuss China herein frequently do so with consideration of the old reliables—Homer, Plato, the Greek tragedians, Lucretius, and Virgil—but also with reference to texts that would be unlikely to appear on a university's classics syllabus, or to be translated for a trade paperback. For instance, I argue that Porphyry is the primary source for Charles Lamb's comical account of the Chinese discovery of cooking, 'A Dissertation upon Roast Pig' (1822), and that a copy of Philostratus' works in a Beijing library might account for similarities between John Keats's *Lamia* (1820) and Chinese tales of the White Snake. This book examines a period in which deepening knowledge of Asia coincided with new classical interests.

Encounters with classical culture in Britain of the long nineteenth century were often idiosyncratic, and resulted from a commitment to Greek and Roman antiquity that might have no relation to formal study. Edward Shils terms this mode of reception 'substantive traditionality' to mean not merely an appreciation of ancient wisdom and accomplish-ment, but belief that patterns of past occurrences can be used to derive guidance on the present.[13] Shils distinguishes this kind of reception from 'a tradition' considered as an unchanging canon passed on from one

---

[13] Edward Shils, *Tradition* (Chicago: University of Chicago Press, 1981), 21.

generation to the next in the (theoretical) unbroken line. Even allowing that there was no monolith known as 'classics', the privilege that authors granted to certain aspects of classical culture rather than others might seem incoherent, illogical, or inconsistent to later readers. Classical Rome became increasingly relevant to nineteenth-century Britain as a model of empire and cultural hegemony and, indeed, as a society that assimilated the best aspects of a predecessor. Yet it appears to have been a step too far for Victorian Britain to remember that the greatest Roman epic traces the founder of its civilization to Asia. Prefacing his 1867 translation of the *Aeneid*, John Conington defends his use of Sir Walter Scott's verse-form as opposed to the *ottava rima* that Byron popularized in his Turkish Tales: 'Unlike as the spirit of Border warfare may be to the spirit of the *Aeneid*, the spirit of Oriental passion is still more unlike.'[14] Furthermore, if ideas from the ancient world loomed more prominently in eighteenth- and nineteenth-century discourse than in today's, reverence for classical culture was not universal among intellectuals of the time. In his satirical poem *Of Taste* (1756), for instance, James Cawthorne attributes Britain's enthusiasm for Chinese architecture to boredom with the prevalent classical influences, which are seen as rigid:

> Of late, tis true, quite sick of Rome, and Greece,
> We fetch our models from the wise Chinese:
> European artists are too cool and chaste,
> For Mand'rin only is the man of taste;
> Whose bolder genius, fondly wild to see
> His grove a forest, and his pond a sea,
> Breaks out—and, whimsically great, designs
> Without the shackles of rules, or lines.
>
> (99–106)

A practice emerged of adopting Chinese aesthetics simply for a change from classical models. William Garrick's 1755 production of *A Midsummer Night's Dream*, following a 1692 operatic adaptation, set Theseus and Hippolyta's feast in a Chinese garden. Such a move is a rejection of classical inheritances, but one in which the encounter with China is nonetheless oriented in relation to 'Rome, and Greece'. Explicit rejection can be considered among the myriad forms of reception.

---

[14] *The Aeneid of Virgil*, trans. John Conington (New York: W.J. Middleton, 1867), xix.

For those who loved knowledge of the ancient world, the means to cultivate a formal interest in the subject were not obvious. Authors such as Edward Gibbon, Samuel Taylor Coleridge, and Keats either attended university before the introduction of the classical Tripos at Cambridge in 1822, or did not attend at all. Some had inspirational school-teachers, but these authors often navigated their own paths through Graeco-Roman culture. Moreover, previous works of classical reception were at least as influential as direct exposure to ancient works. A person's image of the last days of Rome might be derived from a performance of Shakespeare's *Titus Andronicus*. Family, and not formal instruction, appears to have been most frequently responsible for inculcating a love of classical culture among the authors discussed in this book. Sara Coleridge's classical studies offered, amongst other benefits, a way to know her distant father though his favourite literature. The Tennyson household was one in which young Alfred and his brothers not only pored over ancient texts at their father's behest, but also transcribed commentaries in Greek and Latin. Where I consider particular authors' writings on China in depth, I characterize their modes of classical reception.

At times, classical reception had nothing to do with reading old books. The current of Philhellenism in late eighteenth-century Britain appears to have gained momentum from the French revolutionaries' assumption of Roman exempla. What was emblematic of Republican France could not respectably be adopted in Britain. Controversy erupted in 1811 over a physical act of classical reception, the arrival of the first of the Parthenon Sculptures in Britain, acquired by Lord Elgin. Another kind of transmission altogether is evident in Macartney's record of the journey to China, on which the sailors demonstrated their own classical inheritance, in a form that incurred the ambassador's disapproval:

They arrived under the equator, about eleven o'clock, on Sunday the 18th of November; and Sir Erasmus Gower permitted the ship's company to indulge themselves in the ludicrous ceremony commonly observed when crossing the line. . . . A sailor was dressed up in a manner to imitate the God, Neptune, holding in his hand a trident, his garments dripping wet with the element he is supposed to command. He stood at the ship's head; the Embassador, Sir Erasmus Gower, officers, and passengers, being all assembled on the quarter-deck, and demanded in an audible voice, the name of the vessel thus encroaching on his dominions. An answer being given from the quarter-deck, Neptune, with his attendants, fantastically accoutred, advanced with solemnity towards them, and presented his Excellency with a fish, recently caught, as part of the produce of the deity's domain. His godship was treated with respect, and received, for himself and companions, the accustomed silver offerings from those who had before crossed the line, but which were rigorously extracted from others who had not, under the penalty of going through a ceremony more ludicrous than agreeable.

To keep up the charter, however, some noviciates are always marked out as victims for the ceremonial. It consisted of an ablution; generally performed in one of the ship's boats, filled with water, into which the party is souced, blindfolded; and after he has received a good ducking, he is lathered, not too cleanly, and shaved, not very tenderly, by Neptune's tonsor, with a wooden razor; and that in so solemn, and, apparently, scientific a manner, as to excite, in the by-standers, broad grins, and convulsive laughters. A hearty meal, accompanied with music and exhilarating libations to Bacchus concluded the amusement.[15]

In Chapter 2, I discuss some of Macartney's own allusions to classics as he contemplates China (it would have been hard for him *not* to think of Virgil, his valet being named Aeneas). Here his snobbishness and Commander Sir Erasmus Gower's condescension intimate a sense that there are 'high' and 'low' forms of classical reception. In his journal Macartney is an empiricist, whose references to Graeco-Roman antiquity serve classification by statement of likeness or difference. His use of classics is scientific; the sailors' he deems superstitious and is not, to Macartney, a legitimate revival of antiquity. Yet the ceremony left an impression on Alexander who—presumably as an affectionate gesture towards the crew—sketched a 'Chinese Neptune' on visiting a temple to Yu Qiang, god of seafarers. 'Low' classical reception is crucial to portrayals of China that were disseminated far more widely than Macartney's scientifically toned notes. Classics and China intersect in the works of quite scholarly authors, but also in popular forms such as musicals, and the tales that circulated orally about Willow crockery. The thinkers studied in this book share a belief in Graeco-Roman antiquity as a source of aesthetic paradigms, historical precedents, and literary analogues that would benefit considerations of China. To approach their works requires knowledge of what kind of Sinology was available to the Anglophone reader.

Knowing China in English

Before books that narrated and responded to the Macartney Embassy were published, Britain's primary source of information on China

---

[15] Staunton, *Historical Account*, 74–5.

was Jean-Baptiste du Halde's *General History of China* (1735) in four volumes. Samuel Johnson reviewed the publication enthusiastically in 1738. Du Halde credits twenty-seven Jesuit missionaries from whose scholarship his text has been excerpted and translated from Latin into French. The first English version of du Halde's text appeared in 1736, with a third edition published in 1741. The scope of the *General History* is encyclopaedic. It contains literary and scientific works in translation, historical accounts, and the missionaries' essays on Chinese life. Consult it for topography, the layout of a Chinese city, the structure of the thirteen-thousand-strong mandrinate, twenty pages on ginseng, and a hundred pages on medical diagnoses from the pulse. The Jesuits used Latin as the language of scholarship; otherwise there is little that is classical about the *General History*. It provided readers with a factual basis for thinking about China, not an imaginative one.

Alongside rigorous and conscientious Sinology, some of the information on China that du Halde made available to European readers was unreliable. Although the Jesuits were distinguished from subsequent European visitors to China by their indifference to commerce, they were subject to particular pressures which distorted their scholarship. The wilful fudging of Catholicism with Chinese traditions brought about the end of the Society of Jesus in 1773. The Jesuit Sinology assembled by du Halde illustrates the same forces that would instigate the Rites Controversy. To secure domestic support for their mission, the Jesuits were required to portray China as wise in some contexts, and as absurd in others. They needed China to appear spiritually deficient, but worthy of the gospel.

The concurrence of worthiness and ignorance receives prolonged attention in Volume the Third. Du Halde depicts Chinese astronomers as dedicated observers who lacked comprehension. They were so impressed by the Jesuit fathers' revelations that these scientists allegedly 'began to look upon the *Europeans* as their Masters'.[16] Du Halde reports that the missionaries gained the Kangxi Emperor's favour by their sophisticated astronomy, which he put to the test on several occasions. In this way the Jesuits gained a foothold at court at the expense of the suspicious and superstitious mandarins, whom du Halde portrays

---

[16] Jean-Baptiste du Halde, *The General History of China*, trans. R. Brookes, 3rd ed., 4 vols (London: J. Watt, 1741), 3:78. Hereafter cited parenthetically by page numbers in text.

muttering about the foreigners in the shadows. Readers infer that the Qing Emperors might be open to higher truths. Du Halde accentuates this possibility. He cites ancient Chinese records that appear to document the Biblical flood, and mentions a European theory that the Chinese are 'immediate Descendants' of the 'primitive *Hebrews*' (3:79). On several occasions, du Halde alludes to the 'common opinion' that the Chinese are 'sons of Noah' without committing to it as fact. Whether historically sound or not, the theory that the Chinese deviated long ago from Hebraic monotheism is useful for du Halde to intimate that they might be retrieved spiritually (3:18–19). Meanwhile the Jesuits' plan failed: missionaries remained at Qing court to teach European sciences and art, but the Dynasty's attitude to Christianity turned from wariness to hostility.

One consequence of the missionaries' biases is that du Halde's readers could access respectful treatments of dynastic history, wildlife, and the examination system, but little on metaphysics. Du Halde scorns Buddhism and Daoism, while praising Confucianism as an ideology that could accommodate Christianity. He tells us that the business of Buddhism is to sell indulgences. Du Halde says that the public bribe monks for better reincarnations. Meanwhile the monks do not believe in metempsychosis at all but, we are told, the 'Demon' Buddha gave them an 'Interior Doctrine' of 'Indolence', with the aim 'to desire nothing, to perceive nothing', and so to become 'like a Stone' (3:35–50). Du Halde describes Daoism comparably as 'a Web of Extravagance and Lies' which preys upon ignorance with exorcism services and promises of immortality. Daoists 'affect a calm' but are most concerned with 'Magical Forms of invoking Demons' (3:14–33). In journals Ricci alludes to the syncretism of Confucianism, Daoism, and Buddhism, which was instituted as official spiritual practice during the Ming Dynasty (1368–1644): 'these three laws or cults coalesce into one creed and all of them can and should be believed'.[17] Yet du Halde's pages omit syncretism, and lack serious considerations of Buddhism and Daoism as philosophies of self-cultivation. His critiques of these traditions neglect their major texts, and refer instead to the de facto spiritual practice that dominated

---

[17] *China in the Sixteenth Century: The Journals of Matteo Ricci, 1583–1610*, trans. Louis Gallagher (New York: Random House, 1953), 105.

China—a folk religion derived from syncretism—which the *General History* represents as idolatrous.

Swayed by Jesuit prejudices, later visitors were slow to examine Chinese spirituality. Habits die hard; negative references to Buddhism and Daoism in eighteenth- and nineteenth-century Anglophone texts demonstrate that the authors relied on du Halde despite their own, first-hand exposure. Either Macartney's delegates inferred from du Halde that aspects of China were not worth reinvestigation, or they needed his text to interpret the foreign culture. Hence in Barrow's cynical description of Laozi (sixth century BCE), Daoism is an ingenious fabrication which the sage concocted as 'the means of raising his reputation'. Ridiculing the quest for immortality and the doctrine of reincarnation, Barrow misrepresents Laozi entirely by quotation from Horace's 'Ode to Leuconoe':

> He maintained, like Epicurus, that to live at his ease and to make himself happy were the chief concerns of man: that, to seize the present moment, regardless of the past and of that to come, was the business of life,
>
> 'Carpe diem, quam minimum credula postero.'
> '— Swift the fleeting pleasure seize,
> Nor trust tomorrow's doubtful light.'[18]

Adding the quotation from Horace, Barrow culled his summary of Daoism from du Halde (3:30). Gradually in the period covered by this book, Anglophone scholars recognized spirituality as a lacuna in their studies of China. It was several decades after Barrow's contemptuous account that Anglophone versions of Buddhist and Daoist texts first appeared. Perhaps ironically, a great leap forward in Anglophone Sinology resulted from the greater access to China that missionaries obtained from the Treaty of Nanjing (1842). These visitors saw that their task necessitated true comprehension of Chinese spirituality rather than derision. In later chapters I examine Tennyson's and Yeats's interests in Daoism, which were facilitated by conscientious translations for which earlier readers had no equivalent. The diverse roles of Christianity in advancing Sinology form one of the threads that run through this study.

The focus of this book lies after the mid-eighteenth-century heyday of what we now call (anachronistically) *chinoiserie*. Yet China was not

---

[18] Barrow, *Travels in China*, 463–4.

simply in vogue one decade and out the next. Chinese aesthetics went in and out of fashion repeatedly. Joanna Baillie considers such vacillations in her 'Lines to a Tea-Pot' (composed 1790, published 1840). The cycle had happened again by the time Lamb wrote 'Old China' in 1823. Certain spells of popular enthusiasm or contempt for China accorded with developments in international relations. The widespread fascination with China prompted by the Macartney Embassy had been replaced with aversion by the time of the Amherst Embassy (and because this book is primarily concerned with literature, I say relatively little about the latter). However, at times it is impossible to see how surges of interest in *chinoiserie* corresponded to politics or indeed to anything beyond aesthetic fads. A penny for the thoughts of the Prince Regent who, having authored a missive to the Jiaqing Emperor for the humiliating Amherst Embassy of 1816, nonetheless had Brighton Pavilion's Music Room decorated after Alexander's images from the Macartney expedition in the following years.[19] Amid these fluctuations in taste, we can assume that all literary thinkers considered in this book had been exposed to popular iterations of Chinese culture in *chinoiserie*. As with classics, notions of China reached people through a variety of media. For all their eclectic reading, Keats and Lamb also encountered the exotic produce of China in apothecaries' windows and East India Company ledgers respectively.

China itself was a nebulous idea in eighteenth- and nineteenth-century Britain. To an extent it remains so to outsiders. As late as 1792, Monboddo cited de Guignes's claim that the Chinese language originated in Egypt, but this attempt to connect China to the Hellenistic world gained little attention.[20] Attempts to transfer European paradigms onto China have proved inadequate, even in so simple a matter as delineating the location of the country. The debate over whether China and what the Persians named Cathay were the same place is evidence that precisely where China *was* caused much uncertainty. Chinese territories were disputed in the period covered by this book much as they are today. The Qing Dynasty claimed Taiwan as a Chinese possession only

[19] The Emperor's response imagines that the Regent 'sighed after happiness' from regret that he could not pay tribute in person. Quoted in Staunton, *Miscellaneous Notices*, 208.

[20] [James Burnett, Lord Monboddo], *Of the Origins and Progress of Language*, vol. 6 (London: T. Cadell, 1792).

in 1683. When the adventurer Thomas Manning (1772–1840) met the Dalai Lama in 1811, the Tibetans were rioting to protest foreign rule. Qing officials had arranged mass settlement of the region by newcomers of Han ethnicity, in an attempt to assimilate Tibet.

If demarcations of China's borders proved difficult, Sinologists identified a quintessential Chineseness both in Chinese natives and those who had carried Han culture to places such as Indonesia and the Malayan peninsula. This essentialism remains key to discussions of China. In a modern study, journalist and Sinophile Martin Jacques suggests that China should be understood as a 'civilisation-state', which he distinguishes from the Westphalian system of supposedly equal 'nation-states' in Europe.[21] European nations came to acknowledge each other's sovereignty, borders, and (in a legal sense) equality following the Peace of Westphalia (1648). By contrast, the essentialist-Chinese argument posits that China was, for two millennia, the undisputed Asian hegemon, and that it has long defined itself by its dominant cultures ahead of physical boundaries. The term 'civilisation-state' invites us to associate China with the preeminent Han ethnicity, and the cultural stability said to have prevailed since the institution of Confucianism at the heart of state education during the Qin Dynasty (221–206 BCE). Confucius was not only a philosopher of conduct, but an editor of history and poetry. Therefore Confucian education contains a canon of ancient history and literature, a distillation of Han culture.

International commentators have not reached consensus on whether the persistence of Confucian education substantiates the popular idea of a single culture that has endured the rise and fall of dynasties and even foreign rule (at which points the newcomers tended to adopt Chinese customs). Peripheral regions of China adopted the Confucian system belatedly and, in certain cases, not by choice. It was, and is, useful for China's rulers to look back to a homogenous Han-Confucian state, but the historical reality is more complex. While the authors on whom this book focuses made and read comparisons of China to individual European nations, a truer resemblance in development might be derived by juxtaposing the Qing Empire with Europe considered as a fragmented continent whose domains were often in conflict.

[21] Martin Jacques, *When China Rules the World: The Rise of the Middle Kingdom and the End of the Western World*, 2nd ed. (London: Penguin Books, 2012), 557.

Of the Sinology available in the late eighteenth century, du Halde does believe in a durable, Chinese culture: 'for almost 4,000 Years, and upwards, it has been govern'd, almost without Interruption, by its own Native Princes, and with little Deviation either in Attire, Morals, Laws, Customs, or Manners, from the wise Institution of its first Legislators' (2:1). Some British commentators were awestruck at Chinese claims to cultural longevity, while others doubted that the line was unbroken. There were those who thought it a bad thing. The obverse of China's alleged longevity was its supposed stagnation. The latter would become a consensus view in late-eighteenth- and nineteenth-century Britain because it was obvious that—while the two countries had similar economies at the start of that period—China was being left behind for want of an industrial revolution. Historians now consider the eighteenth century the golden age of the Qing Dynasty. The Qianlong Emperor's monuments to his family's success at Chengde have prompted comparisons to Louis XIV's Versailles.[22] The length and prosperity of his reign could be likened to Queen Victoria's. However, nineteenth-century Anglophone commentators did not acknowledge that Europe's economies had overtaken China's quite suddenly. The precise reasons why Europe advanced economically while China became poor remain uncertain.[23] In his influential study *The Great Divergence* (2000), Kenneth Pomeranz observes that the Industrial Revolution resulted from factors such as the availability of coal in Europe, the possession of colonies which could supply commodities, and high wages which prompted machination. China had relatively low wages and limited resources.[24] What is obvious is that the cliché of a changeless China became commonplace in European discourse, and it predicated broad assumptions. Montesquieu's vision of unvaried Chinese despotism in *The Spirit of the Laws* (1748) is based only on du Halde's account of Qing governance. British incredulity that China did not want free trade, where foreign merchants had once

---

[22] Ruth W. Dunnell and James A. Millward, 'Introduction', in *New Qing Imperial History: The Making of Inner Asian Empire at Qing Chengde*, ed. James A. Millward et al. (London and New York: Routledge, 2004), 1–4.

[23] See for example Jean-Laurent Rosenthal and R. Bin Wong, *Before and Beyond Divergence: The Politics of Economic Change in China and Europe* (Cambridge, Massachusetts: Harvard University Press, 2011).

[24] Kenneth Pomeranz, *The Great Divergence: China, Europe, and the Making of the Modern World Economy* (Princeton, New Jersey: Princeton University Press, 2000).

enjoyed greater access, failed to consider that a significant alteration had taken place with the rigid imposition of isolationist policies during the Qing Dynasty (1644–1911).

The Chinese term for China is *Zhongguo* (中国), usually translated as 'The Middle Kingdom'. To think instead of *Zhongguo* as 'The *Central States*'—closer to the original meaning of the name—might better introduce the political perspective that frustrated the Macartney delegation in 1793 and the Amherst Embassy in 1816. The Qianlong Emperor dispatched Macartney without a trade deal, but with a letter for George III. Here he thanks the King in terms that suppose China's centrality, in the sense of it being a site of international focus and pre-eminence:

> Inclining your heart towards civilization you have specially sent an envoy respectfully to send a state message, and sailing the seas he has come to our Court to kotow and to present congratulations for the Imperial birthday, and also to present local products, thereby showing your sincerity.[25]

The Emperor cites the traditional belief that the Celestial Kingdom was at the centre of the universe. Supposedly, China exerted a gravitational pull on other peoples, who were drawn to *Zhongguo* in order to pay tribute and to be improved by Chinese culture. In practice the Manchus employed different diplomatic tactics to interact with the diverse people in their sphere. They had not entirely Sinicized, but projected Chinese essentialism when it suited. Hence the Qing officials' tactic to rid themselves of the British visitors was to accept at face value the explanation that George III wished to congratulate the Emperor on his birthday, and to rebuff indecorous talk of trade.

Centrality could also occasion anxiety. Placing his own diplomatic exchanges with China within a historical assessment of the country's international relations, Henry Kissinger identifies the ancient board-game *weiqi* (围棋) as an encapsulation of Chinese foreign-policy.[26] Defeat occurs in *weiqi* when one player's pieces are entirely surrounded by the opponent's. The first appearance of the British delegation in Beijing prompted new concerns about China's security. The Qianlong

---

[25] *An Embassy to China: Being the Journal kept by Lord Macartney*, ed. J. L. Cranmer-Byng (London: Longmans, Green, and Co Ltd, 1962). Cranmer-Byng provides a modern translation from the Emperor's Chinese. The most commonly cited translation of the letter is based on the Jesuits' Latin version, which softens the Emperor's supercilious language.

[26] Henry Kissinger, *On China*, repr. (London: Penguin Books, 2012), 23–5 and *passim*.

Emperor may have seemed aloof and ignorant to British commentators, but immediately on Macartney's departure the ruler ordered extensive fortifications along China's coasts. His fears were validated: during the nineteenth century, China proved vulnerable to foreign attack, and susceptible to encirclement by hostile powers.

Given that considerations of its centrality were at one time a source of Chinese pride but later connoted fear, and the dispute over claims to a persistent Chinese culture, it is not surprising that British writers struggled to comprehend China. This is not to say that they supplemented their knowledge of China with classics only because they were ignorant of China, or because strictly relevant information was not available. It is true that misconceptions of and generalizations about Asia were common, yet British authors who had never been to China could also display impressive knowledge about life there. For example, in correspondence Robert Southey draws a shrewd comparison between the United Irishmen and the Eight Trigram rebels of 1813.[27] In one essay, Thomas de Quincey wonders whether the *Tiandihui* (天地會, the Heaven and Earth Society or 'triads') might collaborate with the British against the Manchu officials, an interpretation of Chinese politics at odds with the broad statements he makes about Orientals elsewhere.[28] Readers such as Coleridge delved deeper by consulting Dominican Sinology which, although much less widely disseminated than the Jesuit scholarship, attempts a rigorous engagement with Chinese metaphysics.

Undoubtedly Sinology changed in the period studied by this book. In later chapters, we see that translations of Chinese texts became increasingly prominent in the Anglophone literary world. Yet readers did not always avail themselves of the best information on Asia. The status of classics as a master-knowledge was partly accountable for the neglect of scholarship on foreign cultures. Johann Joachim Winckelmann wrote influentially of Periclean Athens as the supreme culture that either invented paradigms entirely or improved on exogenous models: it was unnecessary to learn about other cultures because the Greeks had

---

[27] *The Collected Letters of Robert Southey*, ed. Lynda Pratt, Tim Fulford, and Ian Packer, 9 vols (Romantic Circles, 2009–), 4:2496. https://romantic-circles.org/editions/southey_letters/Part_Four/HTML/letterEEd.26.2496.html (accessed 4 July 2019).

[28] *The Works of Thomas de Quincey*, ed. Grevel Lindop et al., 21 vols (London: Pickering & Chatto, 2000–03), 11:562. Hereafter cited parenthetically.

assimilated what was worthwhile from elsewhere.[29] Charles Dickens was one commentator to identify the pitfalls of transposing knowledge from one field to the other. In *The Pickwick Papers* (1836–37), our hero encounters Pott, editor of the *Eatanswill Gazette*. Pott rebukes Pickwick for his failure to read 'a copious review of a work on Chinese metaphysics' in articles which, he says, 'have excited...universal attention and admiration'. The editor explains how his critic produced this Sinology:

> He read up for the subject, at my desire, in the *Encyclopaedia Britannica*...He read, Sir...for metaphysics under the letter M, and for China under the letter C; and combined his information, Sir![30]

Neither Dickens's satire nor international developments persuaded everyone that the most useful writing on Asia should be based on first-hand experience of its places or intimate study of its cultures. James Mill claims that not having visited Asia ensures his objectivity in *The History of British India*, first published in 1817 and with a final revision published in 1858 in light of the Indian Mutiny. He names Tacitus, who never went to Germany, as a comparable authority.[31] In particular nineteenth-century contexts, the status of classics was elevated for political reasons; for example, to disadvantage native applicants to the Indian Civil Service, who would be required to take an entrance exam that focussed on Greek and Latin.[32] Anglophone contemplation of China was not a chronological journey from ignorance to knowledge, and the role of classics therein did not recede at the same rate that scholarly information on China was published. On the contrary, deepening knowledge of China offered new opportunities to consult classical analogues. Such shifting sands thwart attempts to offer a succinct theory for treatments of China informed by classics. However, elements of critical theory are useful to an extent, even if only to demonstrate that classics performs a number of functions in Anglophone visions of China that are irreducible to one conceptual model.

---

[29] Johann Joachim Winckelmann, *Reflections on the Painting and the Sculpture of the Greeks*, trans. Henry Fuseli (London: A. Millar, 1765), 1–2.

[30] Charles Dickens, *The Pickwick Papers: The Posthumous Papers of the Pickwick Club*, ed. Mark Wormald (London: Penguin Classics, 2000), 679–80.

[31] James Mill, *The History of British India*, 3rd ed., 6 vols (London: Baldwin, Craddock, and Joy, 1826), 1:x.

[32] Toner, *Homer's Turk*, 10, and Phiroze Vasunia, *The Classics and Colonial India* (Oxford: Oxford University Press, 2013).

Theorizing a Classicized China (or Not)

In his 1837 essay on Francis Bacon, Macaulay describes the 'incalculable...
debt' that 'a man of liberal education naturally entertains towards the great
minds of former ages': 'They have filled his mind with noble and graceful
images. They have stood by him in all vicissitudes—comforters in sorrow,
nurses in sickness, companions in solitude.'[33] Venturing into new
realms, either physically or imaginatively, one might turn to the classical tradition as to a friend. One's idea of classics can be consolatory
because it is familiar and stable, a repository of timeless paradigms to be
consulted when confronted with new information. There are parallels
in the fascination that China exerted over Anglophone literature in the
long nineteenth century. Obviously this related to the practical matters
of trade and war. Yet the spell that China cast over British writers
gained its imaginative force from one of the most potent childhood
influences, *The Arabian Nights Entertainments*, first translated from
Antoine Galland's French text in 1706:

> In the capital of one of the largest and richest provinces of the kingdom of China,
> there lived a tailor, whose name was Mustapha.... His son, whom he called
> Aladdin, had been brought up after a very careless and idle manner.[34]

Such commitment to favourite texts has twofold importance. First,
Arabian Nights situates China in the Orient, a generalized view of the
East that includes Egypt and the Holy Land. Consequently, China has
long been associated with clichés of despotism, luxuriance, and effemin-
acy which European thinkers attributed broadly to the Orient. This
vague idea of the Orient competed with the more scholarly Sinology
exemplified by du Halde and the Macartney Embassy narratives, but
neither vision pushed out the other. The writers discussed in this book
read serious treatments of China without relinquishing the fantastic
Orient portrayed in *Arabian Nights* and at times, in their own works,
flit between one and the other way of representing China. Secondly,

---

[33] Thomas Babington Macaulay, 'Lord Bacon', in *Critical and Miscellaneous Essays:
Contributed to the Edinburgh Review* (London: Longman, Brown, Green, and Longman,
1843), 2:287–8.
[34] *The Arabian Nights Entertainments: Consisting of One Thousand and One Stories,
Told by the Sultaness of the Indies*, 4 vols (Edinburgh: D. Schaw, 1802), 3:282.

I emphasize the love of literature to approach how a China informed by the study of classics might be theorized.

No single theory for how Western literature examines Asia fits every writer mentioned in this book. Authors such as de Quincey conform neatly to the model for thinking about Asia that Edward W. Said outlines in *Orientalism* (1978). De Quincey, as I discuss in Chapter 6, wields classics as a master-knowledge against those sympathetic to China. His portrait of a frightful Oriental Other is a projection of his own worst qualities. De Quincey's warmongering rhetoric in favour of the Opium Wars manifests the kind of imperial wish to structure and control Asia which, to Said, underlies Orientalism. However, many Anglophone writers on China opposed empire: this book ends with a study of Yeats. Some authors dreamed of Asia as an escape from the realities of Britain. Gibbon and Coleridge feared that over-expansion would weaken Britain as it had weakened Rome. Reimagining the subject in the world of Homer, Tennyson and Sara Coleridge contemplated British opium smuggling in China, which weakened the Chinese population while it strengthened Britain's foothold in Asia. These writers viewed imperialism negatively; others, such as Lamb and Joanna Baillie, contemplated international trade and globalization in light of Chinese produce, but indicated no particular opinion of empire per se. Therefore Said's pathbreaking study is helpful to an extent; its limitations, as Said himself explains, result from his concentration on nineteenth-century European treatments of the Middle East.

Later theorists elaborate on Said's model in ways that illuminate certain responses to China. In *Sinologism* (2013), Ming Dong Gu's eponymous coinage refers to the 'bilateral construction' of China. By this he means that the assembly of China in the Western imagination is a dialogue in which China itself participates.[35] One form of evidence for Gu's theory, pertinent to this book, is the eighteenth-century Chinese crockery which took on the aesthetic qualities of British *chinoiserie*: Chinese manufacturers designed their wares for export, to compete with domestically produced crockery on the British market. With the dominance of Western imperial-powers from the mid-nineteenth century, Gu argues, Sinologism developed into an unconscious fetishization

---

[35] Ming Dong Gu, *Sinologism* (London: Routledge, 2013), 6.

of the West by a China that felt inferior.[36] Thus Gu corroborates Zeng Jize's response to the Anglo-French campaign of 1860: as I discuss in Chapter 7, Zeng deplores European aggression, but writes in English and articulates China's condition using Keatsian classicism. Other Anglophone writers on China are unsuited to Gu's hypothesis. To this end it is useful to think of Saree Makdisi's discussion of Orientalism as fluid, as an 'endless *becoming*'.[37] In that spirit, Peter J. Kitson makes several kinds of useful contribution in *Forging Romantic China* (2013). His verb denotes epistemology viewed in the light of common sense. Kitson points out that a considerable amount of what would be adopted as knowledge of China was forged on the spot as a working hypothesis that enabled visitors to negotiate the unfamiliar. He stresses too that Sino–British relations should not be viewed bilaterally, but must be assessed in a multi-polar context. India, for example, had a significant place in Sino–British relations within an 'already "globalized" eighteenth-century world order'.[38] Of writers who never visited Asia, I agree with Robert Irwin's suggestion that Orientalism was commonly 'academic drudgery' impelled by imaginative interest in Asia, and—although Irwin carries his apology for Orientalism to an extreme—that we need not always suspect imperialist motives.[39] The memoirs of the Macartney Embassy show that the same author could be an academic drudge *and* forging on the spot. What unites the writers discussed in this book is that they loved literature and that Asia captured their imaginations. When we attempt to find a common denominator for the theories and writers we end up back at Macaulay and the beloved texts that stand by us.

I say too that the mode of regarding China covered by this book is Romantic; 'mode' in the singular because this is the capacious genre of discord and the struggle towards ideals, the genre of mysteries, doubts, uncertainties, and endless becoming. Where Macartney compares Chinese offerings to passages by Virgil and Ovid, his empiricism is tempered

---

[36] Gu, *Sinologism*, 39.

[37] Saree Makdisi, *Romantic Imperialism: Universal Empire and the Culture of Modernity* (New York: Cambridge University Press, 1998), 118.

[38] Peter J. Kitson, *Forging Romantic China: Sino-British Cultural Exchange 1760–1840* (Cambridge: Cambridge University Press, 2013), 3. The book is a key resource on the scope of Romantic engagements with China.

[39] Robert Irwin, *For Lust of Knowing: The Orientalists and their Enemies*, repr. (London: Penguin Books, 2007), 8.

by an imaginative element that he did not find in du Halde.[40] In the wake of the Embassy narratives came texts on China that amplify the classical and even reimagine Chinese topics in Graeco-Roman settings. There are other works of classical reception that themselves have little to do with Sinology, but in which later writers found aspects that aided their attempts to understand China. Classics and Sinology mingle to greater and lesser extents. I argue that Coleridge's 'Kubla Khan' (1797/98) and Lamb's 'Dissertation upon Roast Pig' are vital to how English speakers perceived China, but I ascribe similar status to Keats's 'Ode on a Grecian Urn' (1819) and de Quincey's 'Theory of Greek Tragedy' (1840) too. I propose Yeats's 'Lapis Lazuli' (1938) as the terminus for the classicizing, Romantic treatment of China, which also allows the historical scope of the book to include the fall of the Qing Dynasty, once foretold by Macartney.

Classics assumes various guises in Anglophone treatments of China. Frequently it occurs to supplement the unfamiliar, to render the strange knowable. Graeco-Roman inheritances offer interpretative paradigms for foreign ideas, and lend narrative shape to fragmentary information. Classics also provides historical precedents used to assess Britain as an international power in light of events in China. This self-reflective usage corresponds to the primary significance of this book, which is what it tells us about the Anglophone reader of the long nineteenth-century. It should become clear from the following investigations that the old and the exotic were not separate interests, that antiquity and Asia were of equal and interrelated importance as components of the Anglophone intellect. This mindset is forward- and outward-looking, but gets its bearings in relation to the ancient past. Consequently, the coda to this book discusses a time by which Chinese and classical texts have become cohabitants in a world literature, a union which I think proceeds natur-ally from the cosmopolitanism which I portray in earlier chapters as wide temporally as well as regionally.

A further concern is to assess whether the transpositions I discuss helped or harmed the course of Anglophone Sinology. Classical pres-ences have the potential to colour views of China so that the results are inaccurate. Yet literature which made the Chinese more sympathetic to a

---

[40] George Staunton, *Authentic Account of an Embassy from the King of Great Britain to the Emperor of China*, 2 vols (London: W. Bulmer, 1797), 2:407.

British audience has importance irrelevant to the strict measure of fact. Interest impelled efforts for further knowledge, and I suggest that imaginative treatments of China benefitted Sinology rather than occluding it. Furthermore, I suspect that many copies of du Halde went unread. Visionaries captured the imagination to a greater extent than historians, although at times the two were more closely alike than might be expected. To that end Chapter 2, on Edward Gibbon and Samuel Taylor Coleridge, assesses the parallels that the two detected between the declines of Rome and Yuan Dynasty China, occurrences which appeared prescient to Sino-British relations. In Chapter 3, the many details shared by Keats's *Lamia* (1820) and Chinese texts on the White Snake legend indicate exchanges of influences, back and forth between Europe and Asia, over a prolonged period. Chapter 4 studies ekphrastic writing on porcelain—with focus on Lamb and reference to Baillie—and the emergence of narratives based on the Willow pattern, in which the characters are more Ovidian than Chinese. As the primary subject of Chapter 5, Tennyson's poetry demonstrates that a setting in mythical Greece might enable an creative work to challenge the narratives of national progress that surrounded Britain's interactions with China. Coleridge's children, Hartley and Sara, composed works cognate with the treatment of the opium crisis in Tennyson's 'Lotos-Eaters' (1833). De Quincey's less sympathetic perspective on China is the focus of Chapter 6. His journalism in favour of the Opium Wars cites notions of beneficial sacrifice sourced in his reading of Greek tragedy. Yet his classical allusions, deeply personal material to de Quincey, betray his self-identification with the Chinese: this jingoistic journalism should not be taken at face value. Chapter 7 returns to Yuanmingyuan, where the Summer Palace was sacked and looted by British and French soldiers in 1860. To commentators, the incident risked a national identity-crisis. Was Britain civilized or barbaric? Furthermore, the removal of artefacts from the Summer Palace instigated a repatriation debate that has become entwined with the Parthenon Sculptures controversy. Finally, Chapter 8 addresses William Butler Yeats's 'Lapis Lazuli', an ekphrastic account of a Chinese stone. The poet consults diverse cultures in search of the correct response to catastrophe. Yeats interprets the lapis, a relic of the Qing Dynasty, as material evidence of a universal wisdom which he finds also in Greek tragedy and Lucretius.

But if universal wisdom exists, surely there is universal folly too. That suspicion lurks beneath the surface of Coleridge's famous vision in a dream. As much as it articulates the powers of the Romantic Imagination, 'Kubla Khan' is also a response to the Macartney Embassy in which Coleridge, drawing on his reading of Gibbon, wonders whether Britain or China will re-enact the errors of imperial Rome.

2

'Ancestral Voices Prophesying War'

Samuel Taylor Coleridge, Edward Gibbon, and the Warnings of History

'How more than Homerically . . . is the character of Jacob sustained and unfolded,' Samuel Taylor Coleridge (1772–1834) muses in a private notebook.[1] In *Genesis*, Jacob toils under the man who is both his father-in-law and uncle, Laban. To retain his nephew's service, Laban deceives Jacob. After Jacob has worked for seven years, with the agreement that he would marry Laban's daughter Rachel as reward, Laban substitutes Leah for Rachel in the wedding ceremony. The men make a new agreement, by which Jacob toils another seven years to win Rachel's hand. Yet the family is disrupted by Laban's efforts to advance its interests. Jacob flees with Rachel. The discovery that Rachel has stolen the teraphim—the idols—from Laban's house influences Coleridge to enrich his comparisons to classical literature by reference to Chinese culture. Embedded in Coleridge's rumination on primitivism, treachery, and conflict, this allusion communicates Britain's growing hostility towards China during the nineteenth century.

At the heart of this chapter are kinds of re-enactment. These range from questions of literary influence to historical role-play. Ambassadors to China self-consciously repeated the behaviour of predecessors. They

---

[1] *The Notebooks of Samuel Taylor Coleridge*, ed. Kathleen Coburn and Anthony John Harding, 5 vols in 10 parts (London: Routledge & Kegan Paul, 1957–2002), §6191.

China from the Ruins of Athens and Rome: Classics, Sinology, and Romanticism, 1793–1938.
Chris Murray, Oxford University Press (2020). © Chris Murray.
DOI: 10.1093/oso/9780198767015.001.0001

sought to replicate earlier successes and correct failures. Traits he shared with Edward Gibbon led Coleridge to fear a similar reputation, yet his great poem on Chinese history is decisively marked by the historian's account of Kublai Khan. The historian and poet suspected that the new British Empire would rehearse processes familiar from annals of China and Rome. In political engagements with China, British protagonists and commentators identified various textual precedents to help them understand the current state of affairs, choose courses of action, and predict consequences. In this nexus, memoirs of Marco Polo and the Macartney Embassy acquired a prophetic value that Coleridge usually reserved for classical history and the Old Testament.

Coleridge's notebook entry, dated 1829, typifies his responses to the Bible. While he celebrates the Old Testament as poetry comparable to Greek epic, Coleridge upholds the Bible simultaneously as an authentic—if often symbolic—historical narrative of humanity's relationship with God. Hence, Coleridge feels obliged to account for Laban's religious practices. Using the teraphim, which commemorate deceased relatives, Laban pays reverence to his ancestors. Coleridge cites 'Chinese Ancestral Superstition' as a concept that might illuminate the place of family duty in primitive religion. This connection, to Coleridge, is central to the tale of Jacob and Laban:

But the 'Gods'/—I conjecture, the Lares, or Provi Penates—& I question, whether we are warranted in attributing more than a sort of Chinese Ancestral Superstition (Manes Superstites Patrum) to Laban, or to infer that it had already ripened into Idolatry—at least, not into a Polytheism countervening or superseding the Faith in <u>God</u>, the Creator.[2]

Coleridge blurs together the Lares and the Penates, and identifies Chinese ancestral tablets with these Roman household gods. This conflation was typical during Coleridge's lifetime, and corresponds to various attempts to establish common origins of monotheism, in which scholars often identified classical gods with particular Asian figures. In his record of the Macartney Embassy, Staunton's son George Thomas Staunton ('Thomas', 1781–1859) notes that the Chinese have 'their *Lares* and *Penates*', duplicating a phrase that his father uses in the *Authentic*

---

[2] *Notebooks of Samuel Taylor Coleridge*, §6191.

Account.[3] Thereafter, Chinese family tablets were frequently identified as equivalent to Roman household deities, and possibly confused with Zao Jun, the Kitchen God. This association was perpetuated in works such as the missionary Robert Morrison's *A View of China for Philological Purposes* (1817). Despite prolonged residence in China, Morrison introduces the Chinese concept by reference to the prevalent cultural touchstone, sourced in ancient Rome.[4]

Coleridge continues the line of thought in his next notebook entry, which elaborates on the classical overtones that Chinese ancestor worship had acquired:

Was there not a period in the simple states of pastoral Clans when religious Images had not disclosed the evil tendency, & were no worse than *tolerabiles ineptiae*? . . . The God of Isaac was imaged in Isaac . . . . The dread of meeting the Heroes in their nightly Rounds—blindness, the supposed penalty, among the Greeks. To consult Eschylus, and Lycophron.[5]

Because it poses no threat to monotheism, Laban's 'Chinese Ancestral Superstition' is 'no worse than *tolerabiles ineptiae*' in Coleridge's view. So to align a custom that endures in contemporary China with the primitive origins of Christianity is a condescending sentiment (in the next chapter I comment further on this Hegelian type of relation). Ostensibly, Coleridge's language makes the exotic China familiar, and thus China is safely contained as a distant relative, backward but recognizable. Yet the identification of Chinese family tablets with Roman household gods is problematic. Chinese tablets simply commemorate the dead, who are considered to exert continued presences in the home. Coleridge's phrase, 'Manes Superstites Patrum'—'Surviving Ghosts of the Fathers'—captures the belief that the Chinese associated with these artefacts. By contrast, the domestic Roman deities have a more active function as protectors. To combine Chinese tablets with household gods infuses the Asian artefacts with the potential for violence. Coleridge indicates this threat by reference to Aeschylus. Antony J. Harding detects an allusion to an exchange in *Seven Against Thebes*, in which Antigone and Ismene reflect on their

---

[3] George Thomas Staunton, *A Complete View of the Chinese Empire* (London: G. Cawthorn, 1798), 384; Staunton, *Authentic Account*, 2:350.

[4] Robert Morrison, *A View of China for Philological Purposes* (Macao: East India Company Press, 1817), 111.

[5] *Notebooks of Samuel Taylor Coleridge*, §6192.

personal losses.[6] Both of their brothers háve perished in an attack on Thebes led by Polyneices and opposed by forces under Eteocles. The Chorus perceives that that the shade of the father, Oedipus, has become an Erinys, and hands on the family curse to his descendants (886–87, 977–79 and 991–93). The Biblical Laban's mistreatment of his nephew is comparable to the tragic inversion of responsibility in *Antigone*, in which Creon inhumes the living heroine and leaves dead Polyneices unburied. A forefather's ghost looms over Jacob and Laban too. Their history in *Genesis* culminates with a vow to respect each other's territories, an oath secured by their mutual fear of Isaac.

Although Coleridge's overt suggestion of Chinese ancestor worship is fleeting, the themes that emerge in his analysis of Jacob and Laban are central in the course of Britain's interactions with China. Whether Britain would recognize the national boundaries of the Qing Empire was a persistent issue. Were Coleridge to 'consult Lycophron' one more, he would encounter a text that interweaves war narrative and prophecy of future misfortune to ominous effect. The eponym of Lycophron's dramatic monologue *Alexandra*, a version of Cassandra, laments the internecine consequences of conflict as she relates the fall of Troy. Alexandra foretells the ordeals both of Aeneas' and Odysseus' parties, and relates her own unhappy history.[7] Rachel's flight with the family idols, when juxtaposed with the Roman household gods, evokes Aeneas' flight from the burning Troy, with Penates in hand; an image that foreshadows the aftermath of the Second Opium War (1856–60), in which British and French soldiers looted the Summer Palace.

Greek tragedy, the Old Testament, Roman household gods, and ancient epic mingle in Coleridge's notebook entry. To situate Chinese effigies amongst these ideas in 1829 illustrates the apparent inevitability of conflict between Britain and China. Yet the potential for violence was evident to Coleridge and other commentators some decades prior to the outbreak of the First Opium War in 1840. In 'Kubla Khan; or, A Vision in a Dream', drafted in the 1790s and first published in 1816, the Emperor of China hears 'ancestral voices prophesying war' (30). Coleridge's poem

---

[6] *Notebooks of Samuel Taylor Coleridge*, §6192n.

[7] Attributed contentiously to Lycophron of Chalcis (285–247 BCE). Interest in *Alexandra* was revived in Coleridge's lifetime by Henry Meen's *Remarks on the Cassandra of Lycophron* (1800).

as one of several texts to cite the Mongols as a precedent for British and Manchu imperialism. Accounts of the Macartney Embassy make similar associations. Where they allude to the Mongol Khans, these diplomatic accounts display the influence of Edward Gibbon (1737–94), as does Coleridge's poem.

To connect the British embassies to China with the Mongol Khans was somewhat obvious. The Khans, originally Mongolian tribesmen, preceded the Manchus not simply as rulers, but as invaders who established a dynasty in China.[8] So doing the Khans, and later the Manchus, adopted Chinese customs, but favoured Tibetan Buddhism as their dynasties' spiritual practice. The Qing encouraged the association with the Mongols' Yuan Dynasty by claiming the Khans as their ancestors. Hence the distinction between the Tartars and the Mongols was unclear by the advent of the Qing Dynasty. In his journal, Macartney reports the belief that 'the emperor was descended from Co-be-li, or, as we call him, Kublai Khan'.[9] Macartney was not to know that this claim was credible but hardly exclusive, as Genghis Khan had fathered hundreds of children. While the place name 'Rehe' had also been in use for some decades, in 1778 the Qianlong Emperor fixed the title of one residence as 'Chengde' for its evocation of the Khans' mountain retreat 'Shangdu' (Xanadu), a near homonym.[10] Mongol subjects knew the Qing as the 'great khans', *boghdo khaghan*.

When Macartney's delegation finally met the Qing Emperor at Yuanmingyuan, good omens seemed to lie in resemblances to *The Travels of Marco Polo* (*c.* 1300), the memoir of the Venetian visitor who befriended Kublai Khan (1215–94). The *Travels* was emerging from an uneven reception history to be adopted by Sinologists as a reliable narrative. William Marsden (1754–1836) explains that he undertook his translation 'with the view of removing . . . any doubts of the honest spirit in which the original was composed': 'the authenticity and importance of these travels have found enlightened advocates, and in modern times have been generally acknowledged by the most eminent historical and

---

[8] As this chapter explores the imaginative world of Coleridge and Gibbon, I refer to the Mongols as the 'Khans'. Gibbon uses this term ahistorically in reference to leaders of nomadic groups between which modern historians distinguish more carefully.

[9] Cranmer-Byng, *An Embassy to China*, 130.

[10] 'Shangdu' was transliterated as 'Ciandu' by Marco Polo, and 'Xamdu' in Jesuit scholarship.

geographical writers'.[11] The British delegates cultivated similarities they perceived between Marco Polo's account and their own situation. The Qianlong Emperor received visitors in an enormous tent, in emulation of the Khans. Marco Polo reports that Kublai Khan gives audience in a tent 'so long and wide that ten thousand soldiers might be drawn up' therein.[12] Like the thirteenth-century Venetians—and unlike the seventeenth-century Jesuit missionaries, who were the last Westerners to be granted residence in Beijing—the British delegates were motivated to visit China by commerce. Marco Polo and his companions were pioneers as the first Caucasians to meet Kublai Khan. Macartney hoped that he too could make history by persuading the Emperor to open China to foreigners for the first time in a century and a half. Macartney also relies on Marco Polo in his descriptions of China. At one palace he visits en route to Yuanmingyuan, the British ambassador borrows from Marco Polo's account of Shangdu: 'a considerable palace, surrounded by a garden and pleasure grounds, inclosed within a wall. . . . It was said to belong to the Emperor.'[13]

Parallels between Macartney's arrival at the Qing court and Marco Polo's initial encounter with Kublai Khan continued to the level of interactions between the Emperor and particular delegates. This may be evidence of clever planning by the British party. It is pertinent to wonder why a schoolboy was brought all the way to China on a diplomatic mission that consumed two years. Yet one of the few British visitors to have learned any Mandarin was Thomas Staunton, the vice-ambassador's twelve-year-old son. The boy took the opportunity to impress his host:

His Imperial Majesty asked . . . if there were any persons in the Embassy acquainted with the Chinese language; and being told that the Embassador's page . . . was the only one who had any proficiency in it, the Emperor desired he might be brought up to him; and he asked him to speak Chinese. His Imperial Majesty was so charmed with the converse and elegant manners of this

---

[11] *The Travels of Marco Polo*, trans. William Marsden (London: Longman, 1818), xv.

[12] *The Travels of Marco Polo*, trans. William Marsden, rev. and ed. Manuel Komroff, repr. (New York: Norton, 2003), 149. For clarity I have used this corrected version of Marsden's 1818 translation.

[13] Staunton, *Authentic Account*, 2:77.

accomplished young gentleman, that he took from his girdle his areca-nut purse, which hung to it, and presented it to him with his own hand.[14]

The account of friendly interaction between Thomas and the Qianlong Emperor recalls Kublai Khan's instant affection for young Marco Polo, who was the junior member of his party:

Upon [Kublai Khan] observing Marco Polo, and inquiring who he was, Nicolo made answer, 'This is your servant, and my son'; upon which the Great Khan replied, 'He is welcome, and it pleases me much,' and he caused him to be enrolled amongst his attendants of honour. . . . As long as the said brothers and Marco remained in the court of the Great Khan, they were honoured even above his own courtiers. Marco . . . learnt in a short time and adopted the manners of the Tartars, and acquired a proficiency in four different languages, which he became qualified to read and write. Finding him thus accomplished, his master was desirous of putting his talents for business to the proof.[15]

Beyond Thomas Staunton's favourable reception at court, the British visitors of 1793 failed to emulate the success of the Venetian model. Soon after Thomas encountered the Emperor, Macartney recalled Marco Polo's narrative in a very different spirit. Memoirs of the Macartney Embassy refer to the construction of Kublai Khan's pleasure gardens because the British delegates visited the Qianlong Emperor's palace at Chengde after their unproductive reception at Yuanmingyuan. Although the Qing Dynasty's Chengde was several hundred miles from the Khans' Shangdu, which had fallen into ruin in the fifteenth century, the residences were both mountain retreats which the royal families used to escape from the heat of summer. Once a modest hunting-lodge, Chengde had undergone extensive renovation between 1703 and 1790. In an assortment of palaces and temples, landscaped gardens and monuments, the site projected the Qing sense of their own identity: as rulers of an eclectic empire, as military conquerors, and as divine beings. Chengde emulated and probably surpassed the former magnificence of Shangdu. Hence Macartney gravitates towards Marco Polo's description of Shangdu in his own, brief account of Chengde, which reproduces the same details found in *The Travels of Marco Polo*. It is possible, given both the phonetic proximity of the two place names and the inexact topography of Marco Polo's China, that foreign visitors thought that Chengde

[14] Staunton, *Historical Account*, 348.   [15] *Travels of Marco Polo* (2003), 13–14.

actually was Shangdu. While Macartney's description of the pleasure gardens by recourse to Marco Polo is conventional, the placement of this episode in the approved memoirs of the 1793 Embassy is noteworthy. The evocation of Kublai Khan's building project follows almost immediately after the conclusion of the central narrative, on the ambassador's unsatisfactory interactions with the Manchu officials. Macartney mentions the construction of Kublai's palace amidst the dispute over the kowtow too.[16] In this context, the reference to Kublai Khan is veiled aggression, hinting that the current dynasty might be overcome by British force, as the Khans were by Chinese insurrection. The wish for violence is blatant in journal entries which were omitted from the earliest accounts of the Embassy, but published in 1807. As he departed, Macartney surveyed the Chinese fortifications on land, and recorded his astonishment at their fragility. Of the Manchu officials he wondered,

Can they be ignorant that a couple of British frigates would be an overmatch for the whole naval force of the empire, that in half a summer they could totally destroy all the navigation of their coasts and reduce the inhabitants of the maritime provinces, who subsist chiefly on fish, to absolute famine?[17]

With the benefit of hindsight, the British ambassador's aggression is significant.

Coleridge's initial draft of 'Kubla Khan', probably composed in 1797 or 1798, captures the hopes and tensions at work in the official accounts of Macartney's Embassy. Coleridge's apologetic Preface, which he composed in 1816 to coincide with the first publication of 'Kubla Khan', recapitulates the poem's inconclusive movement in a manner that parallels William Amherst's re-enactment of the Macartney Embassy the same year. In his Preface, Coleridge mentions reading *Purchas's Pilgrimage* (1613), a broad historical work that cannibalizes a range of travel narratives such as *The Travels of Marco Polo*. Yet Coleridge invites us to look beyond Purchas's book. He claims to have fallen asleep at a certain sentence in Purchas, which gives rise to the opening lines of Coleridge's poem: 'Here the Kubla Khan commanded a palace to be built, and a stately garden thereunto. And thus ten miles of fertile ground were

---

[16] Staunton, *Historical Account*, 316.

[17] John Barrow ed., *Some Account of the Public Life, and a Selection from the Unpublished Writings, of the Earl of Macartney*, 2 vols. (London: Cadell and Davies, 1807), 2:332.

inclosed with a wall.' However, Coleridge's poem displays knowledge of what happens next in the dynasty of Kublai Khan. Clearly, he had read other texts on the Khans. In addition to the poem's responses to accounts of the Macartney Embassy, this chapter explores the dialogue that 'Kubla Khan' sustains with a work that juxtaposes the fate of the Khan's Yuan Dynasty with the fortunes of Rome: the age's historical bestseller on the loss of a great civilization, Edward Gibbon's *History of the Decline and Fall of the Roman Empire* (1776–88).

Scholars have devoted considerable attention to textual influences on 'Kubla Khan'. John Livingston Lowes's *The Road to Xanadu* (1927) is the seminal text in studies of sources for particular phrases and images in the poem. John Beer's *Coleridge the Visionary* (1959) is equally foundational both for its examination of mythological origins, and the attention it draws to the Oriental despot theorized by Montesquieu, and how that figure corresponds to the speaker-poet of 'Kubla Khan'. E. S. Shaffer's *'Kubla Khan' and the Fall of Jerusalem* (1975) situates the poem amidst Coleridge's reaction to higher Biblical criticism, and his plans to compose an epic based chiefly upon Flavius Josephus' *Jewish War* (75 CE). These studies, and subsequent analyses that follow the examples of Lowes and Beer, cite many texts that might have inspired 'Kubla Khan'. Supplementary to these approaches, Coleridge's response to Gibbon facilitates the interpretation of 'Kubla Khan' as a prophetic work. The anxiety that 'Kubla Khan' articulates concerning British imperialism is informed by Coleridge's reading of Gibbon. The historian situates the Khans' story amidst the demise of Roman civilization, but simultaneously is mindful of Britain's contemporary affairs in Asia.

To an extent, Gibbon was also in Macartney's mind as the ambassador negotiated China. The diplomat had been elected a member of the Turk's Head Club in 1786, where he encountered the historian. Macartney had been a friend of Club members Edmund Burke, Joshua Reynolds, and founder Samuel Johnson for some decades prior to his election, and first encountered William 'Orientalist' Jones around 1770. It is likely that Macartney would have been elected a member sooner had he not spent time overseas as Governor of Granada (1776–79) and Madras (1781–85) respectively. Consequently, during his tenure Macartney was not in a position to converse with several of the Club's famous authorities on Asia other than Jones who, ending three years as Club president, had departed for Calcutta in 1783, and visited Macartney at Madras en route. Oliver

Goldsmith, who parodied Confucianism in *The Citizen of the World* (1760–61), died in 1774. Thomas Percy, who rendered notes on a classic Chinese novel as *Hao Kiou Choaan, or The Pleasing History* (1761), had been ordained Bishop of Dromore in Co. Down, 1782. Gibbon was the chief preserver of Jones's scholarship at the Club. Treatments of Asia in *The Decline and Fall* were indebted to Jones's works and advice. Like Gibbon, Macartney had spent time in Switzerland as a young man. The historian may have envied that Macartney struck up a friendship with Voltaire. Both Gibbon and Macartney had joined an intellectual milieu whose originator, if not an outright Sinophile, expressed a restrained respect for Chinese civilization in an essay on 'The Life of Confucius' (1742) and his brief introduction to William Chambers's *Designs of Chinese Buildings* (1757). Johnson's public response to du Halde's *General History*, in a pseudonymous letter to the *Gentleman's Magazine* (1738), captures his initial admiration for the mandrinate's recognition of learning. By the time Macartney encountered the Qianlong Emperor, Johnson had been dead for ten years. The critic would have welcomed the motivation for the diplomatic mission, as he had declared himself devoted to tea in response to Jonas Hanway's cautionary *Essay on Tea* (1756). James L. Hevia establishes the importance of the Club to Macartney's mentality at the time of the Embassy. In the nominally Orientalist setting of the Turk's Head Inn in Soho, discussion at the Club was typified by faith in empiricism, the tension between ideals and reality, and a desire to produce true knowledge.[18] These themes permeate *The Decline and Fall* and the narratives of Macartney's Embassy, and in turn shape Coleridge's treatment of the Khans. Additionally, when read as a response to Gibbon, 'Kubla Khan' illuminates a less assured persona than the one as which the historian would be known until the twenty-first century.

Coleridge, Gibbon, and Asia

'Gibbon's style is detestable,' Coleridge declared in 1833, 'but his style is not the worst thing about him.' So begins his most substantial

[18] James L. Hevia, *Cherishing Men from Afar: Qing Guest Ritual and the Macartney Embassy of 1793* (Durham, NC and London: Duke University Press, 1995), 64–5.

commentary on the work of Edward Gibbon. Towards *The Decline and Fall*, Coleridge is ruthless and dismissive:

> When I read a chapter in Gibbon I seem to be looking through a luminous haze or fog, figures come and go, I know not how or why, all larger than life or distorted or discoloured; nothing is real, vivid, true; all is scenical and by candle light as it were. . . . I protest I do not remember a single attempt made throughout the work to investigate the causes of the decline or fall of that Empire. How miserably deficient is the narrative of the important reign of Justinian! And that poor piddling scepticism—which Gibbon mistook for Socratic philosophy—has led him to misstate and mistake the character and influence of Christianity in a way which even an avowed Infidel or Atheist could not have done. Gibbon was a man of immense reading, but he had no philosophy, and he never fully understood the principle upon which the best of the old historians wrote. He attempted to imitate their artificial construction of the whole work—their dramatic ordonnance of the parts—without understanding that their histories were intended more as documents illustrative of the truths of political philosophy than as mere chronicles of events.
>
> The key to the declension of the Roman Empire is the Imperial Character overlaying and finally destroying the National Character. Rome under Trajan was an Empire without a Nation.[19]

Coleridge attacked Gibbon on other occasions. He finds Gibbon's rhetoric no less 'detestable' in an 1818 lecture 'On Style'. Here he places the historian alongside Johnson as proponents of an eighteenth-century fashion that 'creates an impression of cleverness by never saying any thing in a common way' (5.2:237). While Coleridge does not name Gibbon in *Lay Sermons* (1816–17), he sets out his belief that history should maintain a positive theological focus. Contrary to the Humean scepticism and Lockean empiricism that underpin *The Decline and Fall*, Coleridge insists that humanity's relationship with God should constitute the overall narrative of history. In a lecture 'On Corrupt Philosophy', delivered at the Crown and Anchor Tavern on the Strand in 1819, Coleridge accuses Gibbon of 'offences' against the 'most serious duties of an historian'. Gibbon exaggerates the importance of some early Christians' millennial prophecies, Coleridge claims. He is exasperated that Gibbon places undue emphasis on popular 'belief of the last conflagration' in place of a serious argument on the doctrine of the soul's

---

[19] *The Collected Works of Samuel Taylor Coleridge*, ed. Kathleen Coburn et al., Bollingen Series 75, 16 vols in 34 parts (1969–2002), 14.1:418–19. Hereafter cited parenthetically.

immortality (8.1:304–05). Most of Coleridge's specific criticisms of *The Decline and Fall* relate to the controversial chapters (15 and 16) that account for the advent of Christianity and the early fortunes of the Church.

At times Coleridge is unfair to Gibbon. For example, I shall return to his idea that 'the Imperial Character overlaying . . . the National' might undermine an empire because, rather than describing a dynamic that escaped Gibbon's notice, Coleridge's phrase captures the account of the Mongol Khans in *The Decline and Fall* rather neatly. Furthermore, there are reasons not to take Coleridge's criticisms of Gibbon at face value. The 1833 tirade occurs in Coleridge's *Table Talk* (1835), a collection of utterances selected precisely because they are forceful and therefore quotable. Some of the sentiments Coleridge expresses against Gibbon are commonplaces. The charge that Gibbon hides behind elaborate language is one that had been made already by critics such as Henry Edward Davis in his *Examination* of *The Decline and Fall* (1778). Where he protests too much, Coleridge's criticism of Gibbon belies his earlier dependence on the historian. Over his lifetime, Coleridge consulted at least four different copies of *The Decline and Fall*, in various editions.[20] Undoubtedly this was a matter of preference, as Coleridge could very capably read Latin and Greek books for himself. Either Gibbon was a favourite of Coleridge's youth, or he found it more convenient to return to *The Decline and Fall* than other texts. Moreover, the intellectual trajectories of the two men had certain similarities likely to have made the older Coleridge uneasy.

As children, both Gibbon and Coleridge were absorbed by *Arabian Nights*, which they first read in an English version of Antoine Galland's twelve-volume French text (1704–17). In his memoir, Gibbon recalls that, 'Before I left Kingston school I was well acquainted with Pope's Homer and the Arabian Nights Entertainments, two books which will always please by the moving picture of human manners and specious miracles.'[21] In time he acquired three different editions of *Arabian Nights*, including the French text. This formative influence probably

---

[20] Ralph J. Coffman, *Coleridge's Library: A Bibliography of Books Owned or Read by Samuel Taylor Coleridge* (Boston: G.K. Hall & Co., 1987), 88.

[21] *Miscellaneous Works of Edward Gibbon*, ed. John Holroyd, Earl of Sheffield, 3 vols (Dublin: P. Wogan, 1796), 1:25.

motivated, to an extent, Gibbon's intention to study Oriental languages at Magdalen College, Oxford. Dissuaded from this field by the dons, Gibbon turned his attention to theology instead and—swayed by his findings—became a Catholic.

Arabian Nights made so great an impression on Coleridge that his father confiscated and destroyed the volumes. As recalled in a letter of 1797, the young Coleridge's loss of this Orientalist fantasy anticipates 'Kubla Khan'. With his *Arabian Nights* volumes consigned to flames, the boy relied upon poetic imagination to retrieve his vision of Asia:

At six years old I remember to have read . . . the Arabian Nights' entertainments—one tale of which . . . made so deep an impression on me . . . that I was haunted by spectres, whenever I was in the dark—and I distinctly remember the anxious & fearful eagerness, with which I used to watch the window, in which the books lay—and whenever the Sun lay upon them, I would seize it, carry it by the wall, & bask, & read—. My Father found out the effect, which these books had produced—and burnt them.—So I became a *dreamer*.[22]

Mature works by both authors demonstrate that their fascination with *Arabian Nights* was not only juvenile. Coleridge and Gibbon also blend this Orientalism with classical subjects. Biographer G.M. Young finds in the parts of *The Decline and Fall* that treat of Asia 'a child's visions of grave and bearded Sultans who only smiled on the day of battle, the sword of Alp Arslan, the mace of Mahmoud', and other exotic images gleaned from *Arabian Nights*. He notes too the significance of Homer being read alongside, or in 'combination' with *Arabian Nights*.[23] It was perhaps inevitable that Gibbon's favourite book from childhood would colour his own portrayal of Asia, since consultation of this text as a 'picture of human manners' was widely considered permissible in his lifetime by Anglophone readers. Coleridge's acquaintance Richard Hole was amongst those to express the conventional opinion that *Arabian Nights* was a source of practical information: 'it is generally allowed to delineate justly the manners of the Eastern nations'.[24] While Coleridge's early love for Orientalism may have drawn him to Asian subjects, as in

[22] *Collected Letters of Samuel Taylor Coleridge,* ed. Earl Leslie Griggs, 6 vols (Oxford: Oxford University Press, 1956–71), 1:347.

[23] G. M. Young, *Gibbon* (Edinburgh: Peter Davies Limited, 1932), 7.

[24] Richard Hole, *Remarks on the Arabian Nights' Entertainments* (London: Cadell & Davies, 1797), 16.

'Kubla Khan', *Arabian Nights* exerts further influence than on choices of imagery and subject. Tim Fulford argues that interactions between humanity and the supernatural in Coleridge's narrative poems mimic their relations in *Arabian Nights*.[25] For example, to explain the imaginative horrors that await the impulsive sailor who shoots an albatross in 'The Rime of the Ancyent Marinere' (1798), Coleridge refers one perplexed reader to 'The Merchant and the Genie'. In *Table Talk*, Coleridge summarizes this *Arabian Nights* analogue 'of the merchant sitting down to eat dates by the side of a well and throwing the shells aside, and the Genii starting up and saying he must kill the merchant, because a date shell had put out the eye of the Genii's son' (14.1:273). As in this tale, the universe of the 'Ancyent Marinere' is one in which human actions seem to provoke disproportionate responses because everyday actions are revealed to affect invisible spirits. Therefore the familiar laws of cause and effect are suspended. In addition to this Orientalist correspondence between seen and unseen worlds, the Mariner's subjection to capricious divinities is a kind of scenario that Coleridge encountered in Greek and Roman culture. Thus Orientalist and classical ideas mingled freely in Coleridge's imagination.

Like Gibbon's time at Oxford, Coleridge's residence at Cambridge ended prematurely. Coleridge too deviated from the Anglican faith at university. Flirtation with Unitarianism led Coleridge and Southey to dedicate their collaborative drama *The Fall of Robespierre* (1794) to William Frend, who was tried and expelled from Jesus College during Coleridge's studies for offences against the University's statute *de concionibus*. Later Southey considered his own apostasy a 'wrong bias', which he attributed to having had his 'religious principles shaken by Gibbon'.[26] The young poets' devotion to Unitarianism was brief. As the 1790s progressed, Coleridge became deeply interested in inspired prophecy and Pantheism, the latter of which permeates his canonical poetry in and of the few years surrounding *Lyrical Ballads* (1798). He found cognate material in his reading on Asian culture, which was unusually

---

[25] Tim Fulford, 'Coleridge and the Oriental Tale', in *The Arabian Nights in Historical Context: Between East and West*, ed. Saree Makdisi and Felicity Nussbaum (Oxford: Oxford University Press, 2008), 216–17.

[26] *Collected Letters of Robert Southey*, 5:3131, https://www.rc.umd.edu/editions/southey_letters/Part_Five/HTML/letterEEd.26.3131.html (accessed 5 July 2019).

eclectic. In 1793 Coleridge borrowed Awnsham and John Churchill's *Collection of Voyages and Travels* (1704) from the library at Jesus College. The first volume includes a translation of Domingo Fernández Navarrete's *An Account of the Empire of China* (1676). The Daoist cosmology Navarrete outlines is analogous to the Pantheism that interested Coleridge, specifically in the Chinese hypothesis of *taiji*, 'the Universal Substance, which fills and governs the Universe': 'All Spirits or Gods of the Chineses [sic] are reduced to one only, which is the first Principle, call'd *Li*, or *Tai Kie*; which being the *Materia Prima*, or the Air, according to the Learned Sect, is a lively Image of the *European Jupiter*.'[27] As European scholarship on China was dominated by Jesuit Sinology, it is significant that Coleridge had read Navarrete's work too. While the Jesuit fathers distorted Chinese culture casually in order to suggest its compatibility with Christianity, the Dominican friar took Chinese philosophy seriously. Thus Coleridge engaged profoundly with similar Chinese ideas some years before Pantheism became salient in his works.

Gradually Coleridge became a sincere conservative and Trinitarian. Throughout life he was self-conscious about how others perceived his religion and politics, acutely aware that his unorthodoxies were public knowledge in verse and journalism. One reason for Coleridge to disavow Gibbon's influence was that, under the broadest derogatory applications of the term 'deist', Coleridge might be tarred with the same brush as the historian for his former attachment to Pantheism: the Bishop of Llandaff names Spinoza a deist in his response to *The Decline and Fall*.[28] Aptly, this charge had Orientalist overtones, as 'Mahometean' had become a term for anti-Trinitarians.

A further parallel with Gibbon occurred in Coleridge's intellectually crucial period on the Continent. Gibbon spent his second period of residence in Lausanne (1763–64) primarily reading Latin historical texts. This effort culminated with the fateful visit to the Capitol in October 1764 which, Gibbon claimed, inspired him to compose *The Decline and Fall*. Coleridge's transmission of German thought to Britain began in light of his studies at the University of Göttingen in 1799. The

---

[27] *A Collection of Voyages and Travels: Some Now First Printed from Original Manuscripts*, ed. Awnsham and John Churchill, 4 vols (London: Awnsham and John Churchill, 1704), 1:211–13.

[28] Robert Watson, *An Apology for Christianity* (Cambridge: T. & J. Merrill, 1776), 237–8.

influence of the higher Biblical criticism is palpable in Coleridge's critical and theological works, such as the 1829 commentary on Jacob. That the higher criticism was potentially atheistic in its denial of supernatural occurrence is of further relevance to Coleridge's reception of Gibbon. Evidently Coleridge did not allow an antagonistic religious perspective to dissuade him from absorbing Johann Gottfried Eichhorn's analysis (although Eichhorn reportedly dreaded the loquacious Coleridge's presence in the classroom). Similarly, despite his pronouncements against Gibbon, there is much textual evidence that Coleridge was not repelled from *The Decline and Fall* by its alleged blasphemy. Coleridge uses *The Decline and Fall* as a key source for his historical and political works, but adapts the material to his own philosophical purposes. Gibbon's great history is haunted by the implications that fallen empires hold for British expansion. In his own historical writing, and in 'Kubla Khan', Coleridge amplifies Gibbon's anxiety. Misgivings about imperialism lend the poem a mystical air of prediction, characteristically Sibylline in its emotional power and vagueness as prophecy. More explicitly, Coleridge's historical essays supply what he considers the missing element from *The Decline and Fall* by citing precedents to extrapolate future events. The interpretative principles that inform such conclusions are what Coleridge terms the 'truths of political philosophy' in his 1833 critique of Gibbon.

While he never delivered a lecture 'On the Rise, Progress, and Decline of the Roman Empire' that he planned in 1795, Coleridge's close attention to *The Decline and Fall* informed other works. In March 1798 Coleridge wrote an essay entitled 'Rome' for the *Morning Post*, a month after the declaration of the Roman Republic under the rule of Louis-Alexandre Berthier, one of Napoleon's generals. 'The fate of Rome is now sealed forever', begins Coleridge's elegiac and paragraph-long first sentence, in which he announces that the city is 'doomed to be subservient . . . to the Cis-alpine Republic' (3.1:23–24). Gibbon is the primary source for Coleridge's survey of occasions on which Rome was sacked and plundered. Coleridge borrows Gibbon's phrase to specify that Alaric's conquest of Rome (410 CE) occurred 'in the middle of the night', for instance, and he reproduces a quotation from Paulus Orosius that appears in *The Decline and Fall*. 'This last conquest by Gauls will be fatal and final', Coleridge concludes (3.1:24). France's imperial ambition was a great disappointment to Coleridge, who withdrew his support for the Revolution publicly in a contemporaneous poem entitled 'A Recantation'.

Coleridge returned to Gibbon late in 1802 when he authored a series of articles for the *Morning Post*. In light of Napoleon's election as First Consul for life, and his declaration of a new French Republic, Coleridge wrote a four-part 'Comparison of the Present State of France with that of Rome under Julius and Augustus Caesar'. Coleridge's central point is that history offers lessons for modernity. While it 'cannot be denied' that Napoleon's France resembles Rome in some respects, Coleridge identifies key differences as indicators that French expansion will fail in the near future. He outlines the two empires' likenesses and dissimilarities under the premise that French imperialism is unjustified, because Europe is already sophisticated, whereas Rome was 'an enlightener and civiliser of the world' (3.1:325). Fearful that the French will attempt to force their language onto the rest of Europe, Coleridge cites Pliny on the power of a common tongue to 'unite scattered empires', apparently following a reference in Gibbon's footnotes (3.1:313fn).

While *The Decline and Fall* is a source for Coleridge's facts on Rome, his attention to Napoleon's character is also Gibbonian. In Coleridge's estimation, the First Consul is an amalgamation of the first three Caesars. By turns, Coleridge's Napoleon displays 'the decency and decorous ambition of Augustus', who sought to rule 'for ten years only', the 'bold and contemptuous impetuosity of Julius Caesar', and 'the abrogation of all popular elections' reported of Tiberius (3.1:317–8 and fn). While the politicians of revolutionary France model their Republic on Rome, Coleridge detects further resemblances between their societies. He argues that these shared traits bode ill for France. A 'commercial spirit' impelled the Revolution; comparably the spoils of Asiatic conquests corrupted Rome. That the French Constitution is 'identical' to Rome's is less significant to Coleridge than the two societies' inclination towards luxury, Epicureanism, and demagoguery (3.1:315).

The fatal difference that Coleridge identifies between Napoleonic France and imperial Rome is one that allows him to stake a claim for his own significance. In his second instalment on France and Rome, Coleridge credits a recent French ban on the sale of English newspapers to his previous article (3.1:322fn). Subsequently, in his third essay he elaborates that the press poses the only 'truly formidable' threat to Napoleon's rule (3.1:330). Despite 'the warning experience of Rome that despotism cannot last', Coleridge finds that politicians ignore the ominous implications of historical precedents: 'we may always calculate with more safety upon the folly than on the wisdom of nations' (3.1:324–25).

By the time Coleridge's *Biographia Literaria* (1817) was published, Napoleon had safely been exiled to St Helena. Hence Coleridge congratulates himself that predictions he derived from the comparison of France to Rome in 1802 proved accurate years later: 'I feel myself authorized to affirm, by the effect produced on many intelligent men, that were the dates wanting, it might have been suspected that the essays had been written within the last twelve months' (7.1:218). Less happily, further evidence of Coleridge's reliance on Gibbon for the 1802 articles lies in the contemporaneous 'Dejection: An Ode'. This profoundly personal poem articulates unrequited love and Coleridge's fear that he atrophies as a 'natural Man' because of his excessive intellectualism:

> Till that which suits a part infects the whole,
> And now is almost grown the habit of my Soul.
>
> (90–93)

Ironically, this couplet is indebted to Coleridge's re-reading of Gibbon, who describes Commodus' lapses towards vice in similar language:

Nature had formed him of a weak, rather than a wicked disposition. His simplicity and timidity rendered him the slave of his attendants, who gradually corrupted his mind. His cruelty, which at first obeyed the dictates of others, degenerated into habit, and at length became the ruling passion of the soul.[29]

In summary, despite Coleridge's entirely negative appraisals of Gibbon from 1818 onward, he depended upon *The Decline and Fall* as a historical source. That Coleridge's journalism on France assimilates *The Decline and Fall*, and attempts to improve upon that text by identification of patterns that substantiate a teleological view of history, indicates careful dialogue with Gibbon rather than outright dismissal of his work. The controversy that continued to surround *The Decline and Fall* was pertinent to Coleridge's theological pursuits, although he became increasingly opposed to the portrayal of the early church in Gibbon's history. Both authors were impressed by *Arabian Nights* at formative

---

[29] Edward Gibbon, *The History of the Decline and Fall of the Roman Empire*, ed. David Womersley, 3 vols, rev. (London: Penguin, 1995–2005), 1:110. Hereafter cited parenthetically.

stages. Religious belief constitutes an important difference in the authors' perspectives, and so too does the hierophance which, for Coleridge and Blake, and later the Shelleys, was a counter-Enlightenment turn. Deficiencies in Gibbon's historical vision—particularly his failure to predict the French Revolution—led Coleridge to reconsider the course of human affairs documented in *The Decline and Fall* in a mystical light. Coleridge was receptive to Gibbon's treatment of Asia, and hence 'Kubla Khan', like Coleridge's historical journalism, develops Gibbon's trepidations about imperialism into prophecy.

The Vision in a Dream, the Plenipotentiary, and the Sober Historian

In response to Britain's unsuccessful Chinese embassies, Coleridge attempts to provide a compensatory vision in 'Kubla Khan'. He sources this in Marco Polo's meeting with Kublai Khan, which had become the paradigm for diplomatic encounters between East and West. However, the speaker-poet of 'Kubla Khan' is unable to sustain his dream of Xanadu. The crisis of the poem follows the point at which Kublai hears 'ancestral voices prophesying war'. Fantasy yields to a sense of foreboding that has particular relevance to Britain's relations with China in Coleridge's lifetime.

While publication of *The Decline and Fall* predates Britain's embassies to China, the central antagonism of Coleridge's poem occurs in Gibbon's work. The historian wishes to idealize the Khans, but he concedes reluctantly that the tribesmen were cruel and ruthless. Furthermore, the Khans changed over time, abandoning their former principles. As he examines the factors responsible for the Khans' degeneration, Gibbon intimates scepticism about empire per se. At the heart of such considerations is a sense that both *libertas* and *imperium* are necessary to empire in different ways, but that no government has found the balance that would enable empire to survive in the long term.[30] For example, individual freedom stimulates economic demands which, in turn, encourage the acquisition of empire. On the other hand, retention of new territories

---

[30] See J. G. A. Pocock, *Barbarism and Religion*, 6 vols (Cambridge: Cambridge University Press, 1999–2015), 4:12.

entails depriving its peoples of liberty. The Roman failure to sustain *libertas* and *imperium* in correct proportion invites reflection on whether lasting empire is at all possible. His articulation of these doubts, which recur as *The Decline and Fall* chronicles a number of lost civilizations, reflect Gibbon's negative view of British expansion from the mid-eighteenth century onward. Both Gibbon and Coleridge are deprived of their ideal visions of the Khans, the virile warriors who became idle emperors. The ephemerality of these glimpses, due to the transience of the Khans' success, bodes ill for the course of Britain's affairs in Asia. Yet such correspondences with Gibbon and Macartney are not evidence that Coleridge's 'Kubla Khan' should be interpreted strictly as a historicist piece. On the contrary, the likeness is partly attributable to qualities of the visionary poet which are evident in works by the historian and the ambassador. Gibbon and Macartney indulge these imaginative tendencies because, as Coleridge says, 'truths' are superior to 'mere . . . events'.

In 'Kubla Khan', Coleridge substitutes the Mongol rulers' pleasure-dome for the Manchu emperor's Summer Palace, and attempts to replace British humiliation in China with a celebrated version of diplomatic encounter. Yet the historical fact of the Khans' slide into despotism thwarts Coleridge's determination to overwrite the recent ambassadorial narratives with a favourable precedent. Ultimately Coleridge's poem, like Britain's embassies to the Qing court, is frustrated in its bid to redirect history.

This impulse to atone for history manifests as a poem in which art might improve upon reality. 'Kubla Khan' begins with the Khan ordering nature: 'twice five miles of fertile ground | With walls and towers were girdled round' (6–7). The effort to constrain and shape nature, to put a girdle around its abundance, is mimicked by the poet's endeavour to render vision as verse. This connection is heightened by the poem's commitment to the regulatory devices of rhyming couplets and alliteration. The poet imagines he witnesses the construction of Xanadu, like the visiting Marco Polo, or that he is the Khan himself. The speaker places himself close to the action with prepositions, pointing out details for his addressee:

> And here were gardens bright with sinuous rills
> Where blossom'd many an incense-bearing tree;
> And here were forests ancient as the hills,
> Enfolding sunny spots of greenery.
>
> (8–11)

Neologism calls our attention back to the creative force, as Coleridge coins the word 'greenery'. Yet the extent of the Khan's control is in question: that the 'forests' are 'enfolding' the 'greenery' suggests that nature regulates the landscape, and not Kublai Khan. There is also an ominous, secretive quality to the word 'enfolding'. This is a silent contest between man and nature. As in Britain's diplomatic encounters, each party assumes it has the upper hand.

The attempt to construct an ideal version of the diplomatic encounter is thwarted. History bears down on the poem; the verse cannot resist the knowledge that Kublai Khan's dynasty is doomed. Whispered warnings sound through the landscape of wars that were and wars to come:

> Five miles meandering with a mazy motion
> Through wood and dale the sacred river ran,
> Then reached the caverns measureless to man,
> And sank in tumult to a lifeless ocean:
> And 'mid this tumult Kubla heard from far
> Ancestral voices prophesying war!
>
> (25–30)

The transition from 'tumult' to lifelessness is that from war to peace. The 'lifeless' state is a serenity secured by conflict, and perhaps from defeat. Although 'tumult' sinks, it threatens to resurge, as Kublai can hear it: both tumult and peace are perennial. The 'ancestral voices' recall the wars that won Kublai Khan's empire, and foretell the ruin of his successors.

The poem follows the work of empire, to dominate and build. The process yields a fleeting perfection:

> The shadow of the dome of pleasure
> Floated midway on the waves;
> Where was heard the mingled measure
> From the fountain and the caves.
> It was a miracle of rare device,
> A sunny pleasure-dome with caves of ice!
>
> (31–36)

The Khan's dome in itself is not the marvel; the poem calls attention to the elements that have 'mingled'. The 'miracle of rare device' is the combination of nature and artifice in the image of the pleasure-dome reflected in the water, and framed by the caves of ice. Again, Kublai

Khan's power is dubious: nature, his supposed subject, appears to shape his creation. At the outset this situation was reversed; the Khan restructured his environment. For nature to present the ideal vision of the Khan's work appears at first a kind of collaboration between ruler and subject. But the brevity with which the speaker glimpses this beauty intimates revolt, a continuous jostle for dominance.

Just as the Yuan dynasty is foretold to collapse, the poet's vision of Xanadu vanishes. The speaker is desperate to recover this vision through song, or a poem inspired by the Abyssinian maid's song. He wishes to advance Kublai Khan's fusion of nature and artifice by dispensing with reality entirely, to 'build that dome in air' of words and ideas. He fails. Like the British ambassadors, the poet returns from his experience of Asia empty-handed. He faces a crowd that wishes to close its eyes, 'with holy dread' (52). In 1829 Coleridge would recall that blindness was a punishment for failure among Greek heroes. Here the people avert their gaze from the transgressor to deny his reality, in preference of fantasy: be it of the Khan's lasting splendour, or British supremacy, or simply of ideals, in utter rejection of occurrence.

Coleridge revisited 'Kubla Khan' in 1816, and attempted to shape it decisively. So doing, he followed a resumption of political interest in China. This arose after an interval in which the Franco-British wars dominated national attention. Coleridge neither continued his text nor made significant alterations, but introduced a narrative of the interrupted creative process as a framing device. It is perhaps the most famous account of composition in English literature:

In the summer of the year 1797, the Author, then in ill health, had retired to a lonely farm-house between Porlock and Linton, on the Exmoor confines of Somerset and Devonshire. In consequence of a slight indisposition, an anodyne had been prescribed, from the effects of which he fell asleep in his chair at the moment that he was reading the following sentence, or words of the same substance, in 'Purchas's Pilgrimage:' 'Here the Khan Kubla commanded a palace to be built, and a stately garden thereunto. And thus ten miles of fertile ground were inclosed with a wall.' The author continued for about three hours in a profound sleep, at least of the external senses, during which time he has the most vivid confidence, that he could not have composed less than from two to three hundred lines; if that indeed can be called composition in which all the images rose up before him as *things*, with a parallel production of the correspondent expressions, without any sensation or consciousness of effort. On awaking he appeared to himself to have a distinct recollection of the whole, and taking his pen, ink, and paper, instantly and eagerly wrote down the lines that are here preserved. At this moment he was unfortunately called out by a person on business from Porlock, and detained by him above an hour, and on his return to his room, found to his no small surprise and mortification, that though he still retained some vague and dim recollection of the general purpose of the vision, yet, with the exception of some eight or ten scattered lines and images, all the rest had passed away like the images on the surface of a stream into which a stone has been cast, but, alas! without the after restoration of the latter.   (16.1.1:511–12)

Coleridge compares his lost composition to 'images on a stream'. Thus he articulates the overall likeness of his poem to the Khan's palace in an echo of the lines that describe the palace reflected on the water. Yet Coleridge's explanatory Preface only reiterates his original failure to complete the poem. This act of repetition parallels the unsuccessful Amherst Embassy of the same year, which critics supposed would reprise Macartney's frustration rather than advancing British interests in China. The Embassy left Portsmouth in February 1816 and arrived at the Qing court in August. 'Kubla Khan' was published in May of that year. Coleridge's poem was brought before a public whose remarkable lack of interest in Amherst's endeavour intimated an expectation of failure. At its outset there was almost no mention of the Amherst Embassy in British newspapers. The announcement of the Embassy's departure in *The Morning Post* makes no reference to Amherst's political and com-mercial goals which were, as in the Macartney Embassy, to achieve free trade and to place a permanent British ambassador in Beijing. The only ambition the article attributes to the delegation is safe and pleasant passage:

The Embassy hope to obtain permission to return from Pekin through Canton through the Chinese territory, which will give them an opportunity of passing the great wall of China and Tartary, and of viewing the internal appearance of 1,500 miles of that vast, and almost unknown country.[31]

More ominously, Amherst set off for Beijing—literally—under a cloud. 1816 was the Year Without a Summer. The gloom resulted from the eruption of Mount Tambora in 1815, after which a cloud of volcanic ash lingered in the air. Contemporary scientists were unaware that a volcano caused the Year Without a Summer. In the absence of a scientific

---

[31] *The Morning Post*, 13 February, 1816.

explanation for the phenomenon, the darkness was popularly perceived as a punishment from God, and possibly the advent of another Biblical flood. Prophecy was in the air when Coleridge returned to 'Kubla Khan', and the consensus on Amherst's expedition was indifference born of pessimism. If the Embassy was not to be destroyed by an Old Testament God, provoked by the course of human affairs, the diplomatic attempt would most likely replicate Macartney's failure, with the delegates told abruptly to leave China. A sense of repetition pervaded the Amherst Embassy. Amherst even brought his son. The account of third commissioner Henry Ellis is haunted by Macartney, whom he names some fifty times. The earlier ambassador plays an unseen Virgil to Amherst's Dante: Ellis reports an insistent deference to precedent in the 1816 Embassy's dealings with Qing officials. It is odd to rely on an unsuccessful model and expect different results. Yet there was reprisal in a different key as the Amherst delegation placed much more importance on the expected etiquette, and began to magnify the extent to which ceremony had determined their predecessors' fortunes. Ellis portrays his party's interactions with the Qing as fixated upon the kowtow, and retrospectively he reads the Macartney Embassy likewise. Amherst informed the mandarins of 'his intention to approach the Imperial presence with the same demonstration of veneration as he would his Britannic Majesty; that such had been the conduct of Lord Macartney.'[32] This meant that he would refuse to kowtow. As it turned out, he never had the chance. Amherst excused himself from meeting the Emperor due to illness, and was not offered another opportunity.[33] The Embassy was urged to leave China. They did so with nothing to relate other than theories that the mandarins had hoped to trick them into kowtowing, and abandoned diplomacy when this ploy had failed.[34]

Coleridge captures public negativity towards Britain's embassies to China in his poem's sense of foreboding, and more directly in the final

---

[32] Henry Ellis, *Journal of the Proceedings of the Late Embassy to China* (London: John Murray, 1817), 93.

[33] Ellis, *Journal of the Proceedings*, 179.

[34] Ellis, *Journal of the Proceedings*, 183. Old China Hands did not quite share the public's contempt for the Amherst Embassy. For example, John F. Davis claims that trading conditions improved for Britons in China in the decade following 1816, even in the absence of new agreements. See *The Chinese: A General Description of the Empire of China and its Inhabitants*, 3 vols, rev. (London, Charles Knight & Co., 1844), 1:81.

image of the traveller from Paradise judged by a crowd: 'Beware! Beware! His flashing eyes, his floating hair!' (49–50). In the Preface's account of inspiration and interruption, Coleridge also mimics the sudden termination of Macartney's adventure—likewise Amherst's—as he was informed of his expulsion from China. If a caller did arrive when Coleridge was poised to commit the full version of 'Kubla Khan' to paper, it was most probably William Wordsworth. But there is no reason to assume that the explanation Coleridge offers is true. The arrangement of visitor, failure, and lost dream of Xanadu forms a convenient travesty of the China embassies. Moreover, the narrative of Coleridge displaced to Exmoor and subsequently 'called out' from his temporary refuge by another wanderer, and the strange, homeless state in which the resultant poetic fragment leaves its speaker-poet, recalls the overview of inter-related migrations (*Völkerwanderung*) in which Gibbon introduces the Khans.

The effect of the Khans' campaigns on the Roman world illustrates one of two important ideas that Gibbon transposes onto history from mechanical philosophy. That the Mongols displaced other peoples, who impacted upon others in sequence, with the effect that invaders were eventually driven into Roman territory, evokes Newton's model of the universe. Newton theorizes that existence consists only of matter, in which bodies push other bodies directly, and all forces occur between particles. This principle might be juxtaposed with Gibbon's suggestion, in the 'General Observations' that conclude chapter 38, that peace would last in eighteenth-century Europe because of the 'balance of power' between nations, a figure of speech that originates in physics (3:511). The French Revolution had disproved Gibbon's hypothesis, a failure which, to Coleridge, invites reinterpretation of the Khans' history mystically rather than scientifically.

Gibbon says that 'Chinese annals . . . may be usefully applied to reveal the secret and remote causes of the fall of the Roman empire' (2:141). He accounts of the Mongols, their lifestyle and governance, and their rise to eminence under Genghis Khan in the historically wide chapter 26. Gibbon reiterates the significance of the Mongols for their effect on Gothic migration in chapter 30, which concentrates on the incursions to Italy under Alaric and Radagaisus (406–08 CE). In chapter 64 he offers a detailed account of the Mongols' military campaigns, the prowess of their chieftains under the adopted name of 'Khan', and the fate of their

Chinese dynasty, the Yuan. The relevance of 'Chinese annals' to the Roman world is twofold. Gibbon traces the long history of nomads invading the Roman Empire to a series of interactions between Chinese dynasties and steppes peoples, including the Huns and other groups that formed from the remains of the Mongol empire. Repeatedly the nomads were driven westwards in consequence of their engagements with China. In turn, the movement of these Asian tribes drove Gothic and German peoples into Roman territories:

> The invasion of the Huns precipitated on the provinces of the West the Gothic nation, which advanced, in less than forty years, from the Danube to the Atlantic, and opened a way, by the success of their arms, to the inroads of so many hostile tribes, more savage than themselves. The original principle of motion was concealed in the remote countries of the North; and the curious observation of the pastoral life of the Scythians, or Tartars, will illustrate the latent cause of these destructive emigrations. (1:1024–25)

Secondly, Gibbon's primary source for his treatment of the Khans, Joseph de Guignes's assimilation of Jesuit Sinology in the three volume *General History of Huns, Turks, Moghols, and Other Western Tartars* (1757), also provided a model for *The Decline and Fall*, which adopts a comparable historical scope. De Guignes influences Gibbon's tendency to mirror and echo passages elsewhere in *The Decline and Fall* in a way that invites us to compare certain civilizations and personalities. Gibbon's portrayal of the Mongolian pastoral life often echoes his favourable account of the Arabs, while his negative evaluations of the Khans have commonalities with various of his comments on Roman degeneration. In chapter 1 he sets up the 'moderate system' of Augustus and his early followers as a paradigm by which all governments and states in *The Decline and Fall* can be evaluated. Under Augustus 'it became the duty, as well as interest, of every Roman general, to guard the frontiers intrusted to his care, without aspiring to conquests which might have proved no less fatal to himself than to the vanquished barbarians' (1:32–33). Similarly 'the various modes of worship, which prevailed in the Roman world' in the age of the Antonines were regarded by all with 'toleration [that] produced not only mutual indulgence, but even religious concord' (1:56). As elsewhere in *The Decline and Fall*, Gibbon presents imperial expansion and religious conversion as detrimental forces in his treatment of the Khans.

Coleridge's 'Kubla Khan' follows the nuances of Gibbon's narrative, and particular phrases in the poem are indebted to the historian. Ultimately Gibbon judges the Khans negatively, but there is palpable regret in his account of the Yuan dynasty. Like Coleridge, he wishes to deviate from history in order to preserve a vision, but he is unable to do so. Accordingly, his reflection on the fall of the Khans leads Gibbon to anticipate Coleridge's Preface to 'Kubla Khan' with an utterly Coleridgean formulation. Amidst the layers of re-enactment that surrounded the history of Kublai Khan as it was retold around the time of Britain's embassies to China, it is as though Coleridge was bound to imitate Gibbon's creative crisis when he adopted the same subject.

What Gibbon terms the 'pastoral manners' of the Mongols, as those people existed prior to their international conquests, are attractive to the historian. His view of this lifestyle accords with texts by Hume, Robertson, and Rousseau that celebrate primitivism. Gibbon's admiration for the nomadic existence is such that he directs us to many of the same details to introduce the Arabs in chapter 50. He finds the Mongols resourceful in their difficult existence on a barren homeland: 'the pastoral manners of the Scythians seem to unite the different advantages of simplicity and refinement' (1:1028). The Arabs overcome similar challenges on an inhospitable landscape: 'they rose . . . to the more secure and plentiful condition of the pastoral life' (3:154). 'Ever on horseback' (3:159), the Arabs share another trait with the Mongols, who 'were supposed by strangers to perform the ordinary duties of civil life, to eat, to drink, and even to sleep, without dismounting from their steeds' (1:1029). Gibbon attributes the 'perpetual independence' of the Arabs to their ferocity, in a passage that corroborates G. M. Young's citation of *Arabian Nights* as an influence on the Orientalism in *The Decline and Fall*:

The nation is free, because each of her sons disdains a base submission to the will of a master . . . . His speech is low, weighty, and concise; he is seldom provoked to laughter; his only gesture is that of stroking his beard, the venerable symbol of manhood; and the sense of his own importance teaches him to accost his equals without levity, and his superiors without awe. (3:158–61)

Similarly, Gibbon is adamant that 'the power of a despot has never been acknowledged in the deserts of Scythia'. There is a system, Gibbon explains, that prevented despotism among the Khans: 'The immediate jurisdiction of the Khan is confined within the limits of his own tribe;

and the exercise of his royal prerogative has been moderated by the institution of an ancient council' (1:1032). This is a significant detail as modern, historicist criticism of Coleridge's poem, following Beer, invariably interprets 'Kubla Khan' with reference to Montesquieu's portrait of the Oriental despot.

Both the Mongols and the Arabs disappoint Gibbon's ideal. To continue the history he must abandon the paradigm, much as Coleridge's speaker loses his paradise in the knowledge that war must follow. There are ominous undertones as Gibbon describes 'the great eruption of the Moguls and Tartars; whose rapid conquests may be compared with the primitive convulsions of nature, which have agitated and altered the surface of the globe' (3:791). Coleridge represents this subterranean threat as the 'savage place' of the chasm within Kublai Khan's domain (14), and the torrent that bursts to the surface of the realm with unexpected force:

> from this chasm, with ceaseless turmoil seething,
> As if this earth in fast thick pants were breathing,
> A mighty fountain momently was forced:
> Amid whose swift half-intermitted Burst
> Huge fragments vaulted like rebounding hail.
>
> (17–20)

Those aspects of the Khans that Gibbon celebrates are at the same time the seeds of Kublai Khan's subjugation of China, and therefore the eventual ruin of his own dynasty. Gibbon observes that within the Mongolians' resilient character lay their capacity for cruelty. The sense of fraternity within the Mongolian tribe united it in order to 'spread terror and devastation'. While Gibbon wishes to linger on the 'pastoral manners' of the Mongolians, the duty to convey truth compels him to narrate their violent course. Realizing that he cannot sustain a celebration of primitivism, and that he must set aside the idyll of hunters in the wilderness in order to provide a truthful account of 'devastation', Gibbon writes, 'the sober historian is forcibly awakened from a pleasant vision' (1:1025). Scholarly duty calls on Gibbon like his own Person from Porlock.

Gibbon concedes that the Mongols' brutality was crucial to their efficiency as conquerors. Genghis Khan has traitors boiled alive and drives enemies to cannibalism in the account of his rise in chapter 64.

Gibbon implies that the collapse of the Khans' Yuan Dynasty results from their failure to maintain vigour and independence. Weak, luxuriant, and lazy, in Gibbon's depiction the Khans resemble the ineffectual rulers of the Roman Empire in its descent. Gibbon's chief complaint, which Coleridge seizes upon, is that Kublai Khan *changed*. Why did Kublai Khan decree that a pleasure dome be built? Because he came from a nomadic tribe whose chieftains, until that point, had lived in tents. Having conquered China, Kublai Khan built a palace at Shangdu. It was at this moment, to Gibbon, that Kubla Khan fell. Shangdu became a city of more than 100,000 inhabitants during the Yuan dynasty. Gradually the Mongolians became house-dwellers. Gibbon remarks that 'a change of manners is implied in the remove . . . from a tent to a house' (3:805).

In Gibbon's broad vision of barbarism—which encompasses all peoples who did not speak Greek or Latin—the Khans went from being a good kind of barbarian (fierce and free) to a bad kind of barbarian.[35] The Khans' civilizing process entailed weakness. Gibbon expresses approval for aspects of this new identity: he notes that Kublai Khan nurtured education and justice, for example. But the changes were corrosive overall. Gibbon writes that Genghis established 'a system of pure theism and perfect toleration' (3:793). Yet Kublai Khan 'declined from the pure and simple religion of his great ancestor' to adopt Tibetan Buddhism, towards which practice Gibbon displays the commonplace opinion that it is idolatrous. Worse still, in Gibbon's view, 'his successors polluted the palace with a crowd of eunuchs, physicians, and astrologers' (3:806). In short, the Khans' palace became a typical Chinese court. Much as he read in Voltaire and de Guignes, Gibbon presents Chinese culture as stunted, with potential to restrict and counteract the development of its converts. The Mongolian rulers consumed the same Chinese luxuries that Gibbon considers to have corrupted the Romans. These included goods that occasioned British diplomacy to China in Gibbon's lifetime. Gibbon alludes contemptuously to the Roman emperor Justinian's love of silk, an unmanly material which 'might gratify vanity, or provoke desire'. In a parallel of the late eighteenth-century trade deficit, caused primarily by Britain's thirst for Chinese tea, Gibbon observes that the Eastern Roman Empire was 'drained' by demand for Chinese silk, a

---

[35] Gibbon's classically centred definition of barbarism is comparable to the Qing officials' derivation of terms for Europeans, which I discuss in Chapter 6.

commodity monopolized by Persian traders (2:580–83). Like the Roman Empire, the Khans' dynasty was contaminated by foreign cultures, and weakened militarily by territorial overexpansion. That the Khans' adoption of Confucian precepts failed to prevent moral decline recalls the account of Commodus' accession in chapter 3. The laws that were honoured by Marcus Aurelius and several immediate predecessors were obsolete under a corrupt ruler: 'the laws might serve to display the virtues, but could never correct the vices, of the emperor' (1:103–4).

An image of an enclosed hunt epitomizes the Khans' atrophy to Gibbon: 'instead of the boundless forest the inclosure of a park afforded the more indolent pleasures of the chace' (3:805). He writes that the hunters 'draw a circle' around their quarry to set up a lackadaisical pursuit in a confined domain. From 1681 the Qing imitated this Yuan Dynasty hunt in a ritualized form. Observers such as the Macartney delegates noticed that much of Qing military procedure was for show (Figure 2.1).

The Qing emperors held the ceremonial pursuit annually to commemorate their ancestors. The confined hunt has a counterpart in Coleridge's final verse-paragraph. The speaker reports an elaborate act of demarcation. By this intricacy, Coleridge accentuates an attention to ceremony that dominated accounts of British diplomacy in China:

Figure 2.1 *Imperial Horsemanship*, Giuseppe Castiglione (1688–1766).
Photo: The Palace Museum/Image copyright © The Palace Museum.

> all should cry, Beware! Beware!
> His flashing eyes, his floating hair!
> Weave a circle round him thrice,
> And close your eyes with holy dread:
> For he on honey-dew hath fed,
> And drank the milk of Paradise.
>
> (49–54)

The circle drawn around the speaker, who is here made to share in Kublai Khan's guilt, is an image of the hunter turned prey. The gesture connotes revolt against one who has made himself a target by conquest. The speaker-poet and/or Khan and is now susceptible to attack, having gorged on luxuries.

Taken as a set of precedents, the story of the Khans was versatile. Juxtaposed with the collapse of other empires, the Mongols' history illustrates Gibbon's unease over British imperialism. Coleridge transmutes Gibbon's apprehensions into a work simultaneously more forceful and more mysterious than *The Decline and Fall*. Macartney positions his allusion to Kublai Khan's summer retreat not to ruminate on the folly of empire, but in perception of China's military susceptibility. The pleasure dome is a figure for Gibbon's disillusionment with the Khans; influenced by Gibbon it is a figure for Macartney's frustration in China. Macartney's behaviour as British ambassador is cognate with the intellectual environment in which he encountered Gibbon, and with *The Decline and Fall* more directly. Hevia writes that Macartney approached the issue of the kowtow with an Enlightenment disdain for ceremony. This perspective was likely to have been reinforced at the Turk's Head Club.[36] The ambassador became so obsessed with the kowtow that he failed to understand that his delegation was evaluated over the six-month duration of its presence in China. The British were not judged solely on their participation in court ritual. Given Macartney's fixation with the ceremony, it is noteworthy that Gibbon considers the kowtow a humiliating display of servility. The historian contrasts the last Jin emperor, who prostrated himself before his conqueror Genghis Khan in 1234, with the Song ruler who declined to perform the obeisance for the victorious Kublai in 1279:

---

[36] Hevia, *Cherishing Men from Afar*, 74.

The [Jin] emperor, a defenceless youth, surrendered his person and sceptre; and before he was sent in exile into Tartary he struck nine times the ground with his forehead, to adore in prayer or thanksgiving the mercy of the great khan. Yet the war (it was now styled a rebellion) was still maintained in the southern provinces from Hamcheu to Canton; and the obstinate remnant of independence and hostility was transported from the land to the sea. But when the fleet of the *Song* was surrounded and oppressed by a superior armament, their last champion leaped into the waves with his infant emperor in his arms. 'It is more glorious,' he cried, 'to die a prince, than to live a slave.' An hundred thousand Chinese imitated his example; and the whole empire, from Tonkin to the great wall, submitted to the dominion of Cublai. (3:799–800)

Gibbon's opinion of the kotow in unambiguous in this juxtaposition of disgrace and heroism.

Coleridge's 'Kubla Khan' is a poem of the imagination rather than a direct treatment of historical events. Circumstances of Coleridge's life-time made the history of the Mongolian tribe topical in such a way that the different accounts of the Khans floated about in what Lowes called Coleridge's 'subliminal reservoir'. The poem drifts gradually away from the facts communicated by Purchas to Coleridge's own prophecy on empire, as relevant to Britain in 1793 or 1816—or Napoleonic France— as it was to the thirteenth-century Mongols. The adaptability of Kublai Khan's tale appeals to Coleridge: the universal truths the poet perceives in the Mongols' history, borne out by its resemblances to later events, and its exemplification of imperial expansion in a way that is comparable to poesis. Gibbon's proto-Coleridgean complaint that he has been 'for-cibly awakened from a pleasant vision' indicates that the qualities of visionary poetry are amongst the kaleidoscopic attributes of *The Decline and Fall*. Coleridge was among the readers who faulted Gibbon for failing to encapsulate the decline and fall of the Roman Empire in a summative sentence, or an adequate conclusive chapter. For Coleridge to lament the absence of conclusions from Gibbon's narrative is ironic because the historian's resistance to reality in favour of ideals is an impulse that Coleridge shared. In his treatment of the Khans, Gibbon is more interested in the unfulfilled potential of great civilization than its errors. Ultimately, however, he does his duty as a historian.

The downward trend of British opinion on China in the nineteenth century coincided with the emerging idea that Britain was Rome's successor. Coleridge and Gibbon show that such re-enactment was complicated. Errors might be replicated with accomplishments.

A comparable rise might lead to a similar fall. It would also be disingenuous, and politically impracticable, to abstract a paradigm of Roman achievement from the controversies of its imperial history. The Victorian crisis of national identity that I discuss in Chapter 7 involved debate on these issues, and so demonstrated that Coleridge's and Gibbon's fears were well-founded. Gibbon's legacy is evident later in this book where barbarism and civilization are debated, and where authors take interest in marginal figures from antiquity, of whom they probably first learned in *The Decline and Fall*.

Gradually the intimations of a British attack on China came to fruition. The defensive weakness Macartney noted in 1793 was followed, in Thomas Staunton's account of the Amherst Embassy, by the beginning of a justificatory war-rhetoric which would escalate over the next several decades:

Almost every public building we have seen in our route, has exhibited to us more or less evidence of the poverty of the government. I suspect that there can be little doubt that the prosperity of this empire has been on the decline under the government of the present emperor.[37]

Staunton was right: the Chinese economy had worsened under the Jiaqing Emperor (r. 1796–1820), who struggled to curb corruption at court and rebellions elsewhere, and who had survived two assassination attempts. Hence on his return to China as Amherst's second commissioner, Staunton portrays the Qing as inadequate rulers. The examples of Chinese history indicated that change was inevitable, and British diplomats felt such progress would not come about by negotiation. The little boy who charmed the Qianlong Emperor grew into a Tory MP who, in 1840, would urge the First Opium War.

---

[37] George Thomas Staunton, *Notes of Proceedings and Occurrences during the British Embassy to Pekin in 1816* (Havant: Skelton, 1824), 157.

3

The White Snake, Apollonius of Tyana, and John Keats's *Lamia*

A young man strolls through the countryside alone. Suddenly, he encounters a beautiful woman. It's love at first sight. He accompanies her home, where they live in splendour for a time. Yet their bliss is doomed. A sage confronts the couple. He tells the youth that his paramour is an enchantress, and that their life of luxury is unreal. As his lover writhes under scrutiny, the youth denounces the wise man. The maiden begs the visitor for mercy, but the philosopher insists on her falsity, relentless in his accusations even though the woman clearly loves the young man. When the sage reveals that the woman's true form is that of a serpent, his words overpower the enchantress's magic. The lovers are horrified as the illusory fineries the sorceress has conjured disintegrate.

The similarities are striking: to a reader of English literature, the preceding paragraph encapsulates John Keats's narrative poem *Lamia* (1820); to a classicist, it indicates the origin of Keats's plot with the Sophist Philostratus, via the English philosopher Robert Burton (1577–1640); to a person acquainted with Chinese folklore, it summarizes a common iteration of the White Snake legend. The many versions of this Chinese tale include a 2019 television series and a film—*The Sorcerer and the White Snake* (2011)—in which Jet Li portrays a Buddhist monk who not only perceives the Ultimate Reality of the disguised enchantress, but battles her serpent form using Zen martial-arts.

There are several plausible points of contact between *Lamia* and the Chinese White Snake legend; some speculative, others more certain. I think that Keats's classical source-material and the Chinese legend ultimately have the same, Asian origin. The similarities between

China from the Ruins of Athens and Rome: Classics, Sinology, and Romanticism, 1793–1938.
Chris Murray, Oxford University Press (2020). © Chris Murray.
DOI: 10.1093/oso/9780198767015.001.0001

Philostratus' story and the Chinese tale may have been strengthened by mutual influences between Europe and China from the seventeenth to the nineteenth century. Additionally, Keats uses Philostratus' lamia tale as a vehicle for Orientalist concerns: his classical characters behave in the manner of nineteenth-century Orientalists, which enhances the Asian flavour of his poem. *Lamia* adopts a common Romantic motif in which an exotic Graeco-Roman antiquity is invoked to comment on Asia. Contemporary debates on the accumulation of Orientalist knowledge also offered allegories for Keats's reflections over his right to appropriate classical themes. It is possible too that Keats heard reports of Chinese plays based on the White Snake legend, and that these influenced his adaptation of Philostratus. Keats's *Lamia* is remarkable because so many forms of cultural exchange converge in a relatively short text. To consider all of these connections demonstrates that classics enacted multiple roles in British conceptions of China during the early nineteenth-century and this, I argue conclusively, compels us to reconsider the scope of British cosmopolitanism. I might adduce the complexity of this exchange of ideas by my inability to form a neat transition from the previous chapter. Keats met and read Coleridge, and each loved the ancient world in his way, but the younger poet's response to Asia is utterly dissimilar to the elder's. One could say that Keats saw a better vehicle for his thought on Asia in *Christabel* (1816) than in the more explicitly relevant 'Kubla Khan'.

Keats composed *Lamia* in 1819, the *annus mirabilis* in which he produced his odes 'To a Nightingale', 'On a Grecian Urn', and 'To Autumn', the ballad 'La Belle Dame sans Merci', and *Hyperion: A Fragment*. These and other works were published the following year in *Lamia, Isabella, The Eve of St. Agnes, and Other Poems*, the final collection of Keats's poetry issued during his lifetime. *Lamia* articulates a preoccupation with the ancient world—usually mythical, never historical, and twice as ekphrastic response to works of art—that is a central concern in some dozen of Keats's poems, most expansively in his epic love-narrative *Endymion* (1817). Classmate Charles Cowden Clarke recalls Keats's discovery of formative influences in their school library:

The books . . . that were his constantly recurrent sources of attraction were Tooke's 'Pantheon,' Lemprière's 'Classical Dictionary,' which he appeared to learn, and Spence's 'Polymetis.' This was the store whence he acquired his intimacy with the Greek mythology; here was he 'suckled in that creed outworn;' for his amount of classical attainment extended no farther than the 'Æneid;' with which epic, indeed, he was so fascinated that before leaving school he had voluntarily translated in writing a considerable portion.[1]

Graeco-Roman antiquity was both a repository of ideals and a source of personal torment for Keats. Self-consciously Greekless, Keats often expresses anxieties concerning his entitlement to broach classical themes in his poems and, by extension, his qualification to pursue fame as a poet. This neurosis is a natural response to the elitist aura around the ancient world, which was such that Clarke could write decades later, regardless of his friend's various works on classical themes, that Keats's 'classical attainment extended no further than the "Æneid"'. This is a classicist's definition of attainment, based on mastery of languages: Clarke claims that Keats completed his translation of the *Aeneid*, but no part of the text survives. Nothing else counts, Clarke suggests.

In light of his ruminations on the legitimate arrogation of classical culture, Keats is remarkably reticent in his opinion on the Elgin Marbles controversy, although his poems express his aesthetic reactions to the Parthenon Sculptures themselves. He experienced conflicting influences on the Marbles debate. 'Curst be the hour,' Byron wrote of the Marbles, 'when from their isle they roved'; an oft-cited reaction to the dispute that is undoubtedly negative, but which ambiguates about agency with the verb 'they roved' (*Childe Harold's Pilgrimage*, 2.15.7). The artist Benjamin Robert Haydon, Keats's close friend, supported British possession of the relics. Thomas McFarland suggests that conflicting cultural and personal pressures made Keats reluctant to share his sentiments on the Elgin controversy.[2] Aside from his stance on the dispute of ownership, it is credible that Keats was emboldened in his poetic vocation by a cultural moment in which, however contentiously, the ancient world was made accessible to the British public.

Keats's antiquity is primarily that of Homer and Ovid. In a sonnet, 'On First Looking into Chapman's Homer' (1817), he celebrates his introduction to ancient Greek epic via the translations of George Chapman (1559–1634). Through the intimations of kinship in assonantal

---

[1] Charles Cowden Clarke, *Recollections of Writers* (London: Sampson Low, Marston, Searle, and Rivington, 1878), 123–4.

[2] Thomas McFarland, *The Masks of Keats: The Endeavour of a Poet* (New York: Oxford University Press, 2000), 77–86.

groupings—'I' with the 'wide expanse' of Greek epic; 'I breathe the . . . serene' of Homer's 'demesne'—the poet realizes his desired communion with Homer's world:

> Oft of one wide expanse had I been told
> That deep-browed Homer ruled as his demesne;
> Yet did I never breathe its pure serene
> Till I heard Chapman speak out loud and bold.
>
> (5–8)

In another sonnet, 'To Homer' (1818), Homer's blindness allegorizes both Keats's own fear of poetic inadequacy and the possibility of overcoming such hindrance. The speaker-poet portrays himself,

> Standing aloof in giant ignorance,
> Of thee I hear and the Cyclades.
>
> (1–2)

The wary tone, fearful of error, invites elision of the comma, so that ignorance per se is approximate to ignorance of Homer. In his triumph over blindness to chronicle the vicissitudes of heaven, earth, and the underworld, Homer may prove an exemplar for the younger poet. Yet the speaker lacks conviction that the likeness he establishes is substantial enough to ensure that he will emulate his model:

> So wast thou blind;—but then the veil was rent,
> For Jove uncurtain'd heaven to let thee live,
> And Neptune made for thee a spumy tent,
>
> . . .
>
> There is a triple sight in blindness keen;
> Such seeing hadst thou, as it once befell
> To Dian, Queen of Earth, and Heaven, and Hell.
>
> (5–12)

Comparably, in the sonnet 'Mother of Hermes! And still youthful Maia' (1818), the poet deviates from the invocation of the muse in his source material, the *Homeric Hymn to Hermes*, by begging permission of his subject shyly: 'May I sing to thee . . . ?' (2). However, Keats can also portray his unsure relation to antiquity ironically. In a sonnet 'On Seeing the Elgin Marbles' (1817), he concedes that unworthiness of one's subject is a hackneyed authorial position. Hence the ancient world stimulates inner conflict, emotions that 'Bring round the heart an undescribable feud' (10). While the poetic voice of *Lamia* is more assured than that of the early sonnets, it expresses similar concerns although sophisticated, as I shall argue, by the representative power of Orientalist tropes.

Thematically, Keats's *Lamia* is Ovidian. The serpent's physical transformation into a beautiful woman introduces a broader exploration of instability and impermanence, in which love mutates into cruelty, possession is short-lived, and an ostentatious banquet disappears. The poem's heroic couplets bear the particular influence of *Metamorphoses* as translated by Dryden, Addison, and Pope (1717). To the end of his poem, Keats appends his primary source, an episode from Philostratus' hagiographic *Life of Apollonius of Tyana* (c. 220 CE), as paraphrased in one paragraph by Robert Burton in *The Anatomy of Melancholy* (1621). Keats precedes the tale with a bargain between Hermes and Lamia, and concludes with the death of the hero, named simply Lycius in Keats's version. His plot is otherwise faithful to Burton's synopsis of the episode:

Philostratus, in his fourth booke *de Vîtâ Apollonii*, hath a memorable instance in this kinde, which I may not omit, of one *Menippus Lycius* a young man 25 yeares of age, that going betwixt *Cenchreas* and *Corinth*, met such a phantasme in the habit of a faire gentlewoman, which taking him by the hand, carried him home to her house, in the suburbs of *Corinth*, and told him she was a *Phœnician* by birth, and if hee would tarry with her, *he should heare her sing and play, and drink such wine as never any dranke, and no man should molest him; but she being faire and lovely, would live and dye with him, that was faire and lovely to behold.* The young man a Philosopher, otherwise staid and discreet, able to moderate his passions, though not this of love, tarried with her a while to his great content, and at last married her, to whose wedding amongst other guests, came *Apollonius*; who by some probable conjectures, found her out to be a serpent, a *Lamia*, and that all her furniture, was like *Tantalus* gold described by *Homer*, no substance but meere illusions. When she saw her selfe descried, she wept, and desired *Apollonius* to be silent, but he would not be moved, and thereupon, she, Plate, House, and all that was in it, vanished in an instant: *many thousands tooke notice of this fact, for it was done in the midst of Greece.*[3]

Burton provides this précis from Philostratus in the Third Partition of his *Anatomy*, which is devoted to Love-Melancholy. He catalogues literary evidence to advance an argument that 'Love is a plague, a torture,

---

[3] Robert Burton, *The Anatomy of Melancholy*, ed. Nicolas K. Kiessling et al., Oxford Scholarly Editions, 6 vols (Oxford: Oxford University Press, 1994), 3:45–6.

an hell . . . . The *Spanish* Inquisition is not comparable to it.'[4] As such, Burton's *Anatomy* is an important source for several of Keats's 1819 works. 'La Belle Dame sans Merci' and *The Eve of St. Agnes*, like *Lamia*, communicate considerable ambivalence towards women and romantic love. Additionally, Keats's letters of 1819 wrestle with a fear of emotional attachment: 'Ask yourself', he puts it to his great love Fanny Brawne, 'whether you are not very cruel to have so entrammelled me, so destroyed my freedom.'[5] Given the recurrence of Love-Melancholy in the narrative poems, and the anguish over love expressed in his correspondence, it would be logical to assess Keats's decision to read Burton either as a poet's search for material, or an attempt to steel himself against the temptations of sexuality using philosophy. Either hypothesis suggests that Keats simply chanced upon Burton's account of Apollonius and found it suitable for a poem, a conclusion that he does not discourage by reproducing Burton's paragraph without comment. However, as I shall argue, Keats had certainly read of Apollonius elsewhere. The Sage of Tyana was the subject of minor controversy in Keats's lifetime in religious debates that had Orientalist undertones. That Apollonius had Orientalist associations to a nineteenth-century audience—Tyana is in modern Turkey, and the philosopher is said to have visited India—is one point of contact between the White Snake legend and Keats's *Lamia*.

Chinese iterations of the White Snake legend centre on West Lake in Hangzhou, the serpent's home. Xu Xuan is the victim of the serpent-enchantress masquerading as a beautiful lady; his saviour is the Buddhist monk Fahai (Figure 3.1).

Much as the repentant Menippus follows Apollonius in Philostratus' account, Xu Xuan renounces the world and devotes himself to Buddhism after his encounter with the serpent. Fahai imprisons the enchantress beneath the pagoda at West Lake. The White Snake legend appears to have entered China around the twelfth century, by which time Buddhism had been formally practised there for centuries. Neither Buddhism nor the White Snake tale would have occurred to the Chinese as having a foreign flavour. Gradually the story was popularized by operatic adaptations and plays. The folklorist Feng Menglong provides the earliest

---

[4] Burton, *Anatomy of Melancholy*, 3:148.
[5] *The Letters of John Keats*, ed. Hyder Edward Rollins, 2 vols (Cambridge, MA: Harvard University Press, 1958), 2:123.

Figure 3.1 In Chinese iterations of the White Snake legend, Xu Xuan is the victim of the enchantress. Woodblock print from Shandong, China, *c.* 1870–1940.

Photo: National Heritage Board, Singapore.

extant record of the Chinese White Snake tale in his anthology, *Stories to Caution the World* (1624), although versions are likely to have been staged as early as the sixteenth century.

In the eighteenth century, at least three different plays based on the White Snake legend were staged under the title *Thunder Peak Pagoda* (*Leifengta*). This increased attention exemplifies a Qing anxiety about witchcraft. Huang Tubi's 1738 script is probably the version that was staged when the Qianlong Emperor demanded a performance of the White Snake play on a visit to Yangzhou in 1765. A sentimental version of Huang's text was written by the actor Chen Jianyin in collaboration with his daughter. Here, the reformed serpent settles down with her erstwhile victim. The two have a child, who becomes a distinguished bureaucrat. Contemporaneously, Feng Chengpei authored a more literary drama on the legend (1772). Chen's mawkish version became the most popular, and was probably the *Thunder Peak Pagoda* play that was performed at court for the empress dowager's eightieth birthday in 1771.

From Chen's text arose no fewer than four different versions as 'banner-men tales', a recent, Manchu form (*zidishu*, 子弟書). These were written in verse, published with musical notation for a young audience, and disseminated by such booksellers as the illustrious 'One Hundred Copies' Zhang Baiben.[6] A novel based on the White Snake legend was published in 1806, and translated into French as *Blanche et Bleue* by Stanislas Julien (1834). From high theatre to acrobatic opera and children's literature, the tale had become ubiquitous in China by the early nineteenth century. In this chapter, primarily I discuss the Chinese legend by reference to Feng Menglong's text, 'Madam White is Kept Forever under Thunder Peak Tower', which provides the basis for many subsequent adaptations of the tale.[7]

The commonalities between Keats's *Lamia* and the Chinese White Snake legend, as outlined in my first paragraph, are too numerous to be considered accidental. Nuances of Keats's poem that are absent from Philostratus' text coincide with Feng Menglong's version. Like Lamia, Madam White claims that she has no family. As in Keats's poem, Madam White's home is hidden in plain sight; although it stands opposite Prince Xiu's mansion, 'Xu Xuan asked for directions . . . but no one knew where it was' (479). Retreating from the world like Keats's lovers, 'the two spent all their time together in delirious pleasure' in Feng's tale (486). The denouement of Madam White, in which she reveals her past, accords with the love for Lycius that Lamia expresses to Hermes, and with Keats's sympathetic treatment of the enchantress throughout his poem:

'Abbot, I am a python. In a raging storm of wind and rain one day, I went to West Lake to find shelter. . . . And then, something unanticipated happened. I met Xu Xuan. Unable to control my desires, I violated the heavenly rules, but I never took a life. Please have mercy on me, Abbot!'   (503)

As in Keats's *Lamia*, Feng's sage must resolve the dilemma that although the serpent is piteous in her love for her husband, she harms him all the while.

---

[6] Wilt L. Idema, *The White Snake and Her Son* (Indianapolis: Hackett Publishing Company, 2009), xxiii–iv.

[7] Feng Menglong, *Stories to Caution the World: A Ming Dynasty Collection*, trans. Shuhui Yang and Yunqin Yang, 3 vols (Seattle and London: Washington University Press, 2000–09), 2:474–505. Hereafter cited parenthetically. Quotations are from this translation except, where stated, Nai-tung Ting's version is used.

Academia Scientiarum Fennica's folklore classification-system posits the archetypal ogre-tale as the original narrative in the family-type to which it assigns the lamia legends. *Academia*'s Type 411—attributed to Indian oral tradition—is the sub-type *The King and the Lamia: The Snake Wife*, in which 'a king sees, falls in love with, and marries a lovely girl who is actually a snake-woman'.[8] In light of this stenographic description, the number of parallels in the White Snake and Keats's adaptation from Philostratus appears even more remarkable. Hence I do not think it would not be credible to hypothesize that the two tales evolved separately from this ancient source, and to ascribe the proximity of their plots to mere chance. I suggest that the texts manifest a long accretion of exchange between East and West.

Certainly the resemblances of Keats's poem to the Chinese tale haunted pioneering Hangzhou native Nai-tung Ting (1915–89), who in 1966 produced a substantial research article on lamia tales of the world.[9] In particular, Ting is fascinated by the magical power of a sage's words to control supernatural beings, common to Keats's and the Chinese versions, and cites the analogous legend of a demon that refuses to be cast out until correct Latin is used.[10] While the White Snake originates in West Lake, as Ting notes, Keats's Lamia awaits Lycius by a pool in Cenchreas (*Lamia* 1.182). An admonishment that Ting translates from the conclusive speech in Feng's text is downright Keatsian. The monk Fahai states the moral of the episode:

> Let me advise you not to love beauty
> Or beauty will certainly turn your head.[11]

The reformed Xu Xuan is now dedicated to philosophy in the manner of Menippus, the disciple in Philostratus' account. He answers Fahai with a chiastic formulation evocative of 'Beauty is truth, truth beauty', the aphoristic culmination of 'Ode on a Grecian Urn' (49):

> Just as beauty reverts to the beauty-less,
> So can the formless assume forms.

[8] Antti Aarne, *The Types of the Folktale: A Classification and Bibliography*, trans. Stith Thompson, rev. (Helsinki: Suomalainen Tiedeakatemia, 1964), 138–9.

[9] Nai-tung Ting, 'The Holy Man and the Snake-Woman. A Study of a Lamia Story in Asian and European Literature', *Fabula* 8, no. 1 (January 1966):145–91.

[10] Nai-tung Ting, 'The Holy Man and the Snake-Woman', 159fn.

[11] Nai-tung Ting, 'The Holy Man and the Snake-Woman', 174.

> Beauty is vanity and vanity beauty—
> The vainness of beauty must needs be told.[12]

Ting—virtually become one of Burton's melancholians, unhinged by his own abstruse research, and frustrated for want of a single, clear connection between Keats and Chinese myth—finds the extent of similarity between *Lamia* and the White Snake tale uncanny. Yet I think that the resemblance can be attributed to a combination of several factors related to Keats, Burton's source in Philostratus, and the likely foreign origin of the Chinese myth (of which term more below). First I wish to examine the Orientalist aspects of Keats's *Lamia*, which draw it nearer to the Asian atmosphere of the White Snake legend than Burton's summary of Philostratus' account.

Orientalist Keats: Visions of Asia in *Lamia*

Keats produced little work overtly concerned with Asia in the manner of 'Kubla Khan' or Thomas Moore's *Lalla Rookh* (1817), but he had considerable interest in the continent. At two different times Keats contemplated a career as ship's surgeon with the East India Company. Moreover, Orientalism bubbles beneath the surface of Keats's oeuvre. His attraction to an enigmatic Orient accords with his desire for literature to offer mystical experience, in which the poet exerts a shadowy presence—palpable yet inscrutable—and the reader does not seek to extract didactic reward from a text. In the most famous epistolary statement of his aesthetics, Keats theorizes such wilful obscurity as '*Negative Capability*, that is when man is capable of being in uncertainties, Mysteries, doubts, without any irritable reaching after fact & reason'.[13] Elsewhere he identifies one source of this 'intense pleasure of not knowing' in the music and evocative power of unfamiliar, Asian place-names he encounters in *Paradise Lost*, and the tantalizingly fragmentary state of the canon from which *Arabian Nights* arose:

---

[12] Nai-tung Ting, 'The Holy Man and the Snake-Woman', 174.
[13] *Letters of John Keats*, 1:193.

A sense of independence, of power from the fancy's creating a world of its own by the sense of probabilities—We have read the Arabian Nights and hear there are thousands of those sort of Romances lost—we imagine after them.[14]

In *Endymion*, the eponym encounters an Indian maid, later revealed to be Selene (named Cynthia in Keats's account). The maid recounts her procession behind Bacchus in an Orientalist pastiche of 'the tiger and the leopard', and 'Asian elephants' (4.241–42):

> 'I saw Osirian Egypt kneel adown
>   Before the vine-wreath crown!
> I saw parch'd Abyssinia rouse and sing
>   To the silver cymbals' ring!
> I saw the whelming vintage hotly pierce
>   Old Tartary the fierce!
> The kings of Inde their jewel-sceptres vail,
> And from their treasures scatter pearled hail;
> Great Brahma from his mystic heaven groans,
>   And all his priesthood moans;
> Before young Bacchus' eye-wink turning pale.'
>
> (4.257–67)

The maid tells Endymion that she left the group because she became 'sick-hearted, weary'; the excess of detail in her account suggests that it was not the journey alone that exhausted the maid, but the sensory stimulation of a resplendent Orient (4.269). Scholars such as William Jones and Thomas Maurice theorized that the cult of Bacchus originated in Asia. Keats would also have encountered this theory in John Lemprière's *Bibliotheca Classica* (1788). Hence, in the god's wake as he returns from conquest of India, Keats's Indian maid emerges from an Orientalist pageant into a Greek myth. As Egypt 'kneels' and Tartary is 'pierced', Graeco-Roman culture threatens to efface Asian civilizations. This procession foresees high imperialism later in the nineteenth century, whose rhetoricians—including de Quincey, as I argue in Chapter 6—often invoke Britain's classical heritage to argue for its cultural superiority to India and China. 'Tartary' reminds us of Britain's failed embassies to Qing China, and 'Abyssinia' of 'Kubla Khan'. When the Qing Emperors rejected the two offers of trade with Britain, despite

---

[14] Beth Lau ed., *Keats's Paradise Lost* (Gainesville: University Press of Florida, 1998), 87. Here Keats annotates *Paradise Lost* 1.701–30.

the array of goods presented to them, British political rhetoric shifted away from self-definitions that referred to its modern produce, which had clearly been snubbed on the international stage. Instead there was a shift towards claims of the ancient heritage which was presumed to underlie British civilization. Humorously, Keats pursues the logic of Britain conceived as antiquity's inheritor so that high culture itself invades Asia in a Bacchanal procession, a *komos* of conquest.

While *Lamia* is set in a mythical Greek past, one of its central themes is the methodology by which knowledge of Asia was obtained and disseminated in Keats's lifetime, with particular emphasis on the acquisition of artefacts. The poem corresponds to emerging theories of how Asia might be known. In his *Lectures on the Philosophy of World History* (1821–31), Hegel hypothesizes that spatial distance corresponds to temporal remoteness: he juxtaposes a backward, 'Far Eastern principle' with a primitive, historical Europe. In turn, Hegel argues that cultures are gradually more advanced as plotted from east to west, illustrated by their religious practices. He sees 'the Christian, Western European world' as the pinnacle of 'the spirit's recognition of itself and its own profundity' in comparison with the 'Oriental World', whose people remain 'in the position of children'.[15] By extrapolation of this logic, a Hegelian might identify the state of China with a specific time and place in the Hellenistic world. These lectures post-date *Lamia*, although Keats may have encountered their roots in Coleridge's assimilation of Hegel's earlier works. Elsewhere Keats encountered more nuanced attitudes to Asia. At the outset of Byron's poem *The Giaour* (1813), the narrator contemplates a site of ancient Greek heroism that has become an outpost of the Ottoman Empire. It appears that the valour of that lost age is required to challenge Asian tyranny, incarnated in the avenging Giaour. Yet in an instance of what Homi K. Bhabha terms 'cultural hybridity', it becomes apparent that the eponym and his Ottoman opponent have much in common.[16]

Keats's classicism looks eastward to juxtapose two kinds of Orientalist in *Lamia*: one the explorer of distant lands, who returns with impressive accounts and quaint souvenirs; the other, superior in Keats's estimation, a poetic visionary who is strictly a mental traveller. This figure enacts a

[15] G. W. F. Hegel, *Lectures on the Philosophy of World History*, trans. H. B. Nisbet (Cambridge: Cambridge University Press, 1975), 128–30.
[16] Homi K. Bhabha, *The Location of Culture* (New York: Routledge, 1994), 4.

kind of cultural hybridity, later informing Yeats's endorsement of such fusions, which I explore in Chapter 8. In *Lamia*, Keats redoubles the sense of the exotic. The poem's opening 'upon a time' refers us not to the historical setting of Philostratus' *Life of Apollonius*, but to a mythical antiquity of nymphs and satyrs, dryads and fauns, in which Keats re-imagines the episode (2.1). From a locale that, to the reader, is already a faraway realm, the characters are perpetually in quest of otherness. In the initial description of Lamia in serpent's form, the poem foregrounds its prismatic absorption and scatter of materials. Sensory overload occurs, akin to the Indian maid's account in *Endymion*. The creature is por-trayed in a kaleidoscopic blur of exotic images:

> She was a gordian shape of dazzling hue,
> Vermilion-spotted, golden, green, and blue;
> Striped like a zebra, freckled like a pard,
> Eyed like a peacock, and all crimson barr'd;
> And full of silver moons, that, as she breathed,
> Dissolv'd, or brighter shone, or interwreathed
> Their lustres with the gloomier tapestries—
> So rainbow-sided, touch'd with miseries,
> She seem'd, at once, some penanced lady elf,
> Some demon's mistress, or the demon's self.
> Upon her crest she wore a wannish fire
> Sprinkled with stars, like Ariadne's tiar:
> Her head was serpent, but ah, bitter-sweet!
> She had a woman's mouth with all its pearls complete.

(2.47–60)

It is an impossible accumulation of features, many of which individu-ally seem incompatible with others: Lamia is 'spotted', 'striped', 'freckled', 'barred'; 'demon', 'zebra', 'peacock', 'pard'. As a whole, the passage disorients us continuously; its protean language frustrates our attempts to focus on its subject, with the effect that Lamia remains eternally unfamiliar. Locally, unusual pairings put the details in tension: 'tapestries' rhymed with 'miseries'; the oxymoronically 'wannish fire' on Lamia's crest. Certain details correspond to Keats's flirtation with one Jane Cox, whose 'rich eastern look' and 'Beauty of a Leopardess' the poet records in correspondence.[17] In *Lamia* the personal significance of such details mingles with diverse cultural allusions, each of which can have

---

[17] *Letters of John Keats*, 1:395.

multiple referents. 'Gordian' refers us to Alexander the Great, to the short-lived Roman emperor Marcus Antonius Gordianus (Gordian III, 225–44 CE), and Milton's serpent (*Paradise Lost*, 4.348). 'Vermilion', with its wormish etymology, was most commonly applied in the form 'vermilion', in Keats's lifetime, nominatively to cinnabar, the pigment imported from China that colours the red of lacquered temples.[18] Within its meticulous construction of Lamia, the poem intimates that she might yet disappear—'full of silver moons, that, as she breathed, | Dissolv'd'— and thus foreshadows the dissolution of the marriage feast.

The poem centres on manoeuvres and gradations of otherness; departures, travellers, strangers, and the unworldly. Hermes 'empty left | His golden throne' to visit the mortal realm (2.7–8). 'Whither fled Lamia?'; she has 'escaped from so sore ills'; her song is 'too sweet for earthly lyres' (1.171, 1.183, 1.299).[19] Before he meets Lamia, Lycius longs for fulfilment from an exogenous source: 'wearied of their Corinth talk | Over the solitary hills he fared' (1.232–33). In her first exchange with Lycius, Lamia implores not to be left, and then threatens to leave (1.245, 1.276–86).

In *Lamia*, Keats makes recurrent use of the *curioso*, one who seeks objects of fascination overseas. The *curioso* is salient in travel narratives of the Romantic period, from the wild adventures alleged in James Bruce's *Travels to Discover the Source of the Nile* (1790) to Reginald Heber's sober records of a British India that was increasingly familiar to readers at home (1828). Generally, travel writers had gained a reputation as untrustworthy, yet this might increase their allure to a poet. In a sentiment that befits Keats's attraction to the *'Negative Capability'* of lost *Arabian Nights* tales, Nigel Leask notes that 'writers . . . would appreciate precisely the *inutility* of the curious travel account as a model for the autonomous imagination'.[20] Percy Bysshe Shelley's 'Ozymandias' (1818) is a further influence on Keats's use of the *curioso* and the interactions between the exotic and the familiar in 'Lamia'. Shelley composed the

[18]   See for example William Anderson, *The London Commercial Dictionary, and Sea-Port Gazetteer* (London: E. Wilson, 1819), 807.

[19]   The latter exoticism borrows from the speech in which Romeo declares Juliet 'a rich jewel in an Ethiop's ear | Beauty too rich for use, for earth too dear' (*Romeo and Juliet*, 1.5.59–60).

[20]   Nigel Leask, *Curiosity and the Aesthetics of Travel Writing, 1770–1840* (Oxford: Oxford University Press, 2002), 60.

poem following the British Museum's acquisition of a bust of Rameses II in 1817, the latest development in a craze for Egyptology that had commenced with Napoleon's conquest of Egypt in 1798. In 'Ozymandias' our uncertainty originates in the pesky preposition of the first line— 'I met a traveller *from* an antique land'—which dissembles whether this adventurer has returned home from a great tour, is a spirit of antiquity that transcends time and space to address the poet, or is now a foreign visitor who views the speaker-poet as an exotic curiosity (my emphasis). The word 'antique', moreover, could refer at the time either to a culture of the distant past, or a contemporary one considered primitive (*OED*). In *Lamia* too the ancient is confounded with the Asian, as we meet characters of classical myth who behave as though they are nineteenth-century *curiosi*, and who in turn become curiosities to others.

The first such *curioso* we encounter is Hermes, in the prologue that Keats attaches to the tale. The god is tantalized by the imagined beauty of a nymph 'to whom', he has heard reports, 'all hoofed Satyrs knelt' (1.14). The poem replicates this enticement in the reader by refusing to offer physical descriptions of the nymph or, subsequently, the anthropomorphic Lamia with more than the conventional vagaries of 'beautiful' and 'fair' (1.185, 1.200). It is the *idea* of the beautiful nymph, 'unknown to any muse', that compels Hermes to violate Jupiter's decree, which forbids the gods to leave Olympus:

> Ah, what a world of love was at her feet!
> So Hermes thought, and a celestial heat
> Burnt from his winged heels to either ear.
>
> (1.19–22)

Yet the curiosity Hermes finds first is not the nymph, but the serpent Lamia, who explains that the god's intended lover is concealed by magic. Lamia proposes an exchange in which she will grant Hermes access to the invisible nymph if he will empower Lamia to claim a treasure previously discovered, the Corinthian Lycius, whom she has admired in dream journeys. Hermes agrees to the plan. Transformed, Lamia flies to the hills by Corinth to contrive a meeting with Lycius, while Hermes claims the nymph.

As lovers, Lycius and Lamia enjoy the prospect of mutual indulgence in the exotic by their foreignness to each other. For fear that Lycius is intimidated by her immortality, Lamia offers to reduce their difference by pretence that she is a maid who has been 'long in Cornith' (1.311). However, Lycius' domestication of Lamia as 'a real woman' entails self-deception (1.332). He is unwilling to relinquish the fantasy of an exotic lover entirely, 'pointing to Corinth' to demonstrate its distance from where they stand, a needless gesture if he believed Lamia a local (1.342). An 'eastern . . . wind' guides Lycius to his fateful first meeting with the enchantress, and the narrative associates her with 'Persian mutes' who appear in Corinth simultaneously; further adumbration of her captivating foreignness (1.223, 1.390).

Roles are not fixed in Keats's dynamic of traveller and curiosity, nor does Keats adhere to the gendered Orientalist relationship of masculine gaze and feminine object that Said theorizes.[21] Lamia is introduced as a subject of fascination, both to Hermes and to the reader. Yet thereafter she quests for, and thereby objectifies, Lycius. In turn, Lycius is the desired prize not only of Lamia, but Apollonius who, in the source material to which Keats refers us, is not a resident of Corinth, but an itinerant philosopher in search of sages and disciples.

In the penultimate verse paragraph of Part I, Lamia and Lycius encounter Apollonius on their journey to Lamia's home. Although the philosopher does not speak, his gaze unsettles the lovers, foreshadowing their end, but more immediately casting doubt on the possibility of possession in their imminent consummation:

> 'I'm wearied,' said fair Lamia: 'tell me who
> Is that old man? I cannot bring to mind
> His features:—Lycius! wherefore did you blind
> Yourself from his quick eyes?' Lycius replied,
> ''Tis Apollonius sage, my trusty guide
> And good instructor; but to-night he seems
> The ghost of folly haunting my sweet dreams.'
>
> (1.371–77)

How can a 'sage' represent 'folly'? Lycius has inverted the situation, so that Lamia appears real, while Apollonius is insubstantial, a 'ghost' whose intangible philosophy has been dispelled by the sensuous lures of a love affair.

---

[21] Edward W. Said, *Orientalism: Western Perceptions of the Orient*, rev. (London: Penguin Classics, 2003), 188.

In Part II a curiosity is retrieved, contained, and displayed as though in a museum. 'Love' here corresponds to Lamia and Lycius' mutual capture of the other:

> Love in a hut, with water and a crust,
> Is—Love, forgive us!—cinders, ashes, dust;
> Love in a palace is perhaps at last
> More grievous torment than a hermit's fast:—
> That is a doubtful tale from faery land,
> Hard for the non-elect to understand.
>
> (2.1–6)

The narrative is unsure whether Love should be personified or objectified. Sought and retained as a prize, the item, Love, is set up for ekphrastic contemplation, placed before us in anticipation of Wallace Stevens's 'Anecdote of a Jar' (1919). The wish to exhibit his treasure impels Lycius to death. He proposes marriage to Lamia as an opportunity for ostentatious procession. Lamia's value to Lycius consists considerably of the satisfaction he can derive from public verification that he owns her. This wish for recognition suppresses his awareness of imperilment, which Lycius reveals by his vision that the Corinthians will respond to Lamia not with envy, but as an object of 'alarm':

> 'What mortal hath a prize, that other men
> May be confounded and abash'd withal,
> But lets it sometimes pace abroad majestical,
> And triumph, as in thee I should rejoice
> Amid the hoarse alarm of Corinth's voice.'
>
> (2.57–59)

Reluctantly Lamia agrees to marriage, on condition that Apollonius is not invited. However, the philosopher attends the feast unrequested. Hence the objectified lovers are opposed by the person whom Lamia declared previously to be inscrutable or irreducible to image. Apollonius, who lacks 'features' in the bride's recollection, attends a marriage feast that appears luxurious, but lacks substance. To dispel this illusion is the 'knotty problem' before the philosopher, a phrase that also returns us to the Miltonic, serpentine associations of 'Gordian' earlier in the poem:

> One, who look'd thereon with eye severe,
> And with calm-planted steps walk'd in austere;
> 'Twas Apollonius: something too he laugh'd,

As though some knotty problem, that had daft
His patient thought, had now begun to thaw,
And solve and melt:—'twas just as he foresaw.

He met within the murmurous vestibule
His young disciple. ''Tis no common rule,
Lycius,' said he, 'for uninvited guest
To force himself upon you, and infest
With an unbidden presence the bright throng
Of younger friends; yet must I do this wrong,
And you forgive me.' Lycius blush'd, and led
The old man through the inner doors broad-spread;
With reconciling words and courteous mien
Turning into sweet milk the sophist's spleen.

(2.157–72)

Lamia has arranged a lavish banquet, but in the philosopher's presence, her deceptions are evidently the low trickery of smoke and mirrors:

fifty wreaths of smoke
From fifty censers their light voyage took
To the high roof, still mimick'd as they rose
Along the mirror'd walls by twin-clouds odorous.

(2.179–82)

Exhibition proves fatal to Lamia and Lycius. When Apollonius gazes upon Lamia, he fulfils the wish Lycius expressed when he insisted on marriage, that his prize should receive notice. Yet the philosopher's stare pains the enchantress:

The bald-head philosopher
Had fix'd his eye, without a twinkle or stir
Full on the alarmed beauty of the bride,
Brow-beating her fair form, and troubling her sweet pride.

(2.245–48)

A hush falls over the banquet. One of the close parallels with the White Snake tale occurs where Keats's Lamia appears a 'sweet', sympathetic character and Apollonius a cruel one, whereas in Philostratus' account the philosopher is unequivocally the disciple's saviour from a monster. Keats's Lycius remonstrates with Apollonius as Lamia suffers:

'Begone, foul dream!' he cried, gazing again
In the bride's face, where now no azure vein
Wander'd on fair-spaced temples; no soft bloom

Misted the cheek; no passion to illume
The deep-recessed vision:—all was blight;
Lamia, no longer fair, there sat a deadly white.

(2.271–76)

Words dispel Lamia's illusions. For Apollonius to identify her true
nature aloud, with the word 'serpent', banishes her. Each plays *curioso* to
the other as curiosity; Lycius and Lamia are so enmeshed that one cannot
survive the loss of the counterpart. Lycius' identity too is brought forth
and destroyed, as he has sought to establish himself publicly as the owner
of a treasure, but it transpires not to be genuine:

'Fool!' said the sophist, in an under-tone
Gruff with contempt; which a death-nighing moan
From Lycius answer'd, as heart-struck and lost,
He sank supine beside the aching ghost.
'Fool! Fool!' repeated he, while his eyes still
Relented not, nor mov'd; 'from every ill
Of life have I preserv'd thee to this day,
And shall I see thee made a serpent's prey?'
Then Lamia breath'd death breath; the sophist's eye,
Like a sharp spear, went through her utterly,
Keen, cruel, perceant, stinging: she, as well
As her weak hand could any meaning tell,
Motion'd him to be silent; vainly so,
He look'd and look'd again a level—No!
'A Serpent!' echoed he; no sooner said,
Than with a frightful scream she vanished:
And Lycius' arms were empty of delight,
As were his limbs of life, from that same night.

(2.277–308)

The arrangement of an objectified Love continues the allegory for the
accumulation of Orientalist knowledge in Keats's lifetime; the stage at
which the adventurer returns home with material evidence of remote
cultures. In an influential study, Marjorie Levinson detects an anxiety
over processes of commodification in Keats's work, specifically the
means by which a poet must exchange imaginative power for worldly
wealth.[22] *Lamia* offers evidence in support of this theory: Orientalist

---

[22] Marjorie Levinson, *Keats's Life of Allegory* (Oxford and New York: Basil Blackwell,
1988), 262.

practises provide allegories for Keats's role as a poet. Specifically, Keats is preoccupied with the means by which an author must exchange imaginative power for worldly wealth, in the form of commercial success. Undoubtedly Keats craves renown and income—'What a thing to be in the Mouth of Fame', he declares in a letter—but this should not be overemphasized.[23] Michael O'Neill states, correctly I think, that to Keats 'the imaginative [is] more than an illusory superstructure reared on a monetary basis'. He refers to a Shelleyan turn of phrase in Keats's letters: 'mental pursuit . . . takes . . . worth from the ardour of the pursuer—being in itself is nothing'.[24]

The passionate Hermes is of greater interest to Keats than his consummation, which is transient. Keats permits his *curiosi* to travel and marvel, but attempts to retain and exhibit their discoveries are doomed: Lamia returns to her serpentine form; Apollonius loses his disciple; dead Lycius resembles a curiosity himself—an Egyptian mummy—in the conclusive triplet:

> On the high couch he lay!—his friends came round
> Supported him—no pulse, or breath they found,
> And, in its marriage robe, the heavy body wound.

(2.309–11)

Throughout Keats has used couplets, but now extends the couplet in the Drydenesque flourish of a triplet, breaking form emphatically at the point at which objectification has proved fatal.

The change of poetic form in which we view Lycius' death duplicates the shift in context that occurs when a curiosity is displayed. In its new setting, the object both loses its original import and gains new significance. For example, the subject of Keats's 'Ode on a Grecian Urn' is a commonplace item of a past culture, become a museum piece that is compelled to speak across history. In the 'bold lover' depicted on the urn—who 'never canst . . . kiss' his intended—is a version of Hermes' ardent pursuit that has been prolonged impossibly: '*still* unravish'd', remarks the viewer of the urn (17, 1, my emphasis). Had Keats written

---

[23] *Letters of John Keats*, 1:139.

[24] Michael O'Neill, '*Lamia*: Things Real—Things Semireal—and No Things', in *The Challenge of Keats: Bicentenary Essays 1795–1995*, ed. Allan C. Christensen (Amsterdam: Rodopi, 2000), 128.

an ode on viewing Tipu's Tiger in India House, to which he alludes in 'The Jealousies' (1819), I think he would likewise have found the toy tiger mauling a British soldier inscrutable because of its detachment from an environment of Asian animals and tyrannical invaders. The curiosity is not coy, but the voice that reaches the poet is in part the ventriloquism of a display facility, proud that it has cheated time and space. 'Ode on a Grecian Urn' intimates sympathy for the curiosity's coerced performance as exotic objet d'art. The poem formulates the process that leads to this misprisonment as an unnatural lineage in which the urn is a 'foster-child' (2).

As Lamia's illusions disintegrate and pass into mythical history, the attempt to represent the Orient through artefacts is destined for failure. Orientalist exploration is therefore subject to the instability that fascinates Keats. Lamia's dream of Lycius should have sufficed her. She has been both poetic visionary and, subsequently, literal explorer, greedy to prolong the ephemeral bliss enjoyed in her imagination. But the vision in a dream is Lamia's allocation of happiness with Lycius. She fails to recognize the superiority of that faculty. The gods too comprehend the supremacy of imagination over objectification of the other, or commodification of experience. For this reason Jove issued the edict that prohibits Hermes from leaving Olympus. It is unnecessary to make such a journey, for 'real are the dreams of gods' (1.127). As such, the poem's precursory tale of Hermes and the nymph warns the reader that Lamia's wish can only be fulfilled in the godly or poetic faculty of imagination. Keats anticipates and refutes Hegel's argument by removing the tale from its historic context. By this gesture, Asia becomes unknowable.

Fixated with material possession, the thwarted *curiosi* in *Lamia* recall the unhappy British Embassies to China in 1793 and 1816. The delegates brought gifts of clocks and cloths and jewellery to the court of the Qing Emperor. However, material evidence of British culture did not capture the interest of the Celestial court. Ultimately Keats left Asia to the explorers, abandoning the idea of a career as a ship's surgeon with the East India Company, but as a poet he staked a claim to the imagined world of the Orient. Hence, one dimension of *Lamia*'s resemblance to the Chinese White Snake legend is its kindred Asian spirit, the Orientalist strains that Keats detects in Burton's version of the tale and brings to the fore. Further correspondence between the English poem and the Chinese folktale is due to their common origin in Indian lore, a relationship which is more substantial than *Academia Scientiarum Fennica*'s *The King and the Lamia* archetype suggests.

Apollonius' Lamia Tale as Folklore and Myth

The extent of the commonalities between Keats's *Lamia* and the Chinese White Snake tale is partly explained by their common source, but I wish to supplement *Academia Scientiarum Fennica*'s classification. I argue that the lamia story associated with Apollonius of Tyana is also the origin of the Chinese story, and that this is a specific iteration of the lamia tale rather than the broad category outlined as Type 411. This does not require us to posit that Philostratus' contentious *Life of Apollonius* is strictly factual. Modern commentators view Philostratus' work variously as credulous hagiography, sincere biography that uses the artistic licence of fictional elements to accentuate genuine aspects of Apollonius' character, and as outright fiction in which even Philostratus' primary source—the loyal disciple Damis—is an invention. However, it is significant that in Philostratus' account, prior to the lamia episode in Corinth, Apollonius visits India. The Hellenistic world had been aware of India since Alexander the Great (356–323 BCE). The twentieth-century excavation of Taxila verified features of the city described in Philostratus' narrative. By Philostratus' time it was not unheard of for Greeks to travel in India, as Apollonius' predecessor Pythagoras is said to have done. By Apollonius' time, an Indian pilgrimage had even become a desirable item on the itinerary of a self-respecting Sophist. Leonid Zhmud writes of Philostratus' foreign adventures that 'we have no reason to believe that they ever happened'. However, as Zhmud demonstrates, such histories were often bestowed on philosophers retrospectively, to account for perceived connections between Greek and Asian thought, and to fill in gaps in biographies with exotic fictions.[25] Keats, conversely, knew of the tradition of Greek and Indian exchange from his reading of Voltaire. Hence in *Endymion* he stages a convergence of the two cultures, with 'Great Brahma . . . before young Bacchus' eye-wink turning pale'.

It is feasible that Greek visitors to India brought back the lamia tale that became associated with Apollonius. Similarly, the Buddhist flavour

---

[25] Leonid Zhmud, *Pythagoras and the Early Pythagoreans*, trans. Kevin Windle and Rosh Ireland (Oxford: Oxford University Press, 1994): 83–91.

of the White Snake story indicates origins in India, the source of Buddhism. This hypothesis, based on the story's philosophical characteristics, corroborates *Academia Scientiarum Fennica*'s geographical location of the archetypal ogre-tale, *The King and the Lamia: The Snake Wife*, in India. The lamia tale with the perceptive sage and enchanted disciple is therefore an *oicotype*, a derivative of *The King and the Lamia: The Snake Wife* that has acquired Buddhist characteristics. The transmission of this *oicotype* can be plotted as a dichotomy from the Indian source: north-east to China, and north-west to Greece and Philostratus, then onward to Burton and eventually Keats. Yet there is a multiplicity of correspondences between these points, mirrors that reflect mirrors, in which classical literature both provides Keats's connection with the Asian material and is the vehicle for expressing his sentiments on contemporary Orientalism. Further exchanges are evident in correspondences between classical aspects of Keats's philosophy and the Buddhism that underlies the *oicotype*; the Asian aspects of a controversy surrounding Apollonius of Tyana in Keats's lifetime; and a coincidental attraction that Keats and Feng Menglong each felt towards the lamia tale, a certain kind of artistic temperament common to the English poet and Chinese folklorist that led to a similar extrapolation of detail in their respective treatments of the story. Zhang Longxi hypothesizes such a resemblance between unconnected authors as 'unexpected affinity', but argues that these likenesses are valuable to scholars because 'certain critical insights are available only from the cross-cultural perspective of East-West studies'.[26]

In the case of *Lamia*, the affinity is clear. Keats's psychological engagement with the ogre tale was so profound that, in effect, he rewrote the same story twice. He was probably unaware that his sources for *Lamia* and 'La Belle Dame sans Merci', in Burton and *Arabian Nights* respectively, were iterations of the same folkloric archetype. In a letter to Fanny Brawne, contemporaneous with the composition of *Lamia* in 1819, Keats summarizes 'an oriental tale of a very beautiful color' that he read in Henry Weber's *Tales of the East* (1812), a select translation of *Arabian Nights*. Coincidentally, elsewhere in Weber's translation Keats read a version of the archetypal ogre-tale, *The King and the Lamia*.

---

[26] Zhang Longxi, *Unexpected Affinities: Reading Across Cultures* (Toronto: University of Toronto Press, 2007), xii.

Although Keats sets his poem in the realm of medieval romance, Weber's text is evidently an influence on Keats's ballad 'La Belle Dame sans Merci', another narrative poem with the theme of Love Melancholy, which Keats first drafted earlier in 1819. In Keats's poem, a knight-at-arms encounters a mysterious beauty who lures him to her 'elfin grot' (29):

> And there she lulled me asleep,
> And there I dream'd—Ah! woe betide!—
> The latest dream I ever dream'd
> On the cold hill's side.
>
> (33–36)

The knight dreams of the Belle Dame's previous conquests, 'pale warriors' with 'starv'd lips', who warn him that he is the latest victim of a vampiric enchantress (38, 41). The knight awakes bereft, abandoned by the Belle Dame, but compelled to haunt the spot, 'Alone and palely loitering' (45). In the *Arabian Nights* tale entitled 'The Story of the Visier that was punished', the antecedent of Keats's knight is a prince:

Whilst he rode up and down, without keeping any road, he met, by the way side, a handsome lady, who wept bitterly . . . The young prince taking compassion on her, asked her to get up behind him, which she willingly accepted.

As they passed by the ruins of a house, the lady signified a desire to alight on some occasion. The prince stopt and suffered her to alight, then he alighted himself, and went near the ruins with his horse in his hand; But you may judge how much he was surprised, when he heard the lady within it say these words, Be glad, my children, I bring you a handsome young man, and very fat; and other voices which answered immediately, Mamma, where is he, that we may eat him presently, for we are very hungry.

The prince heard enough to convince him of his danger; and then he perceived that the lady, who called herself daughter to an Indian king, was a Hogress, wife to one of those savage demons called Hogres, who live in remote places, and make use of a thousand wiles to surprise and devour passengers.[27]

'La Belle Dame' originates in the archetypal ogre-tale; *Lamia* is based on a story, associated with Apollonius, descended from the same Indian source. The folkloric origins of the lamia tale corroborate the impression that Keats was preoccupied with Love-Melancholy in 1819, drawn back unknowingly to revisit the paradigmatic being that encapsulates the

---

[27] *Arabian Nights Entertainments*, 1:60–1.

assortment of compassion, distress, sensuality, bliss, and betrayal that the poet associates with love. From this perspective it is significant that Lycius is distracted from his study of philosophy by a creature whose true form is rather phallic. *Lamia* therefore has significance to Keats comparable to the enticements and phobias that Idema associates with the White Snake: 'As a reflection of men's sexual anxieties she embodies both their insatiable desire and their fear of being dominated.'[28] Comparably, Orhan Pamuk says that *Arabian Nights* 'confirms all the worst male fears and prejudices about the female sex'. As Pamuk recalls how forceful he found these tales, 'when I was in my twenties, and riddled with very male fears about never-to-be-trusted women', he could as well describe Keats.[29]

To analyse the lamia tale as myth rather than folklore yields an alternative comprehension of the story as an expression of Keats's philosophical interests, which have much in common with the Buddhism in Feng Menglong's account. While it is problematic to divide the two genres neatly, I posit that myth demonstrates the veracity of a philosophical or religious belief, while the primary purposes of folklore are entertainment and the preservation of cultural histories or traditions. Crucially, folklore does not promote a system of belief. Myth often portrays remarkable feats, performed by divine or quasi-divine beings, such as the sages Apollonius and Fahai, who demonstrate supernatural vision and even omniscience. This lamia *oicotype*, read as myth, validates the sages' insistence that appearance belies reality, and therefore endorses their pursuit of philosophical truth rather than sensuous pleasures. Thus the myth validates Neopythagorean thought and Buddhism. This myth, I argue, appeals to Keats because of its commonality with philosophical interests he reveals in other works.

Neopythagorean schools adopted Apollonius of Tyana as a paradigmatic sage whose example encouraged a return to Pythagoras' central teachings.[30] It is contentious to assert what Pythagoras' original tenets were with confidence, and particular philosophical principles are also

[28] Idema, *The White Snake and her Son*, xvi.

[29] Orhan Pamuk, 'Love, Death and Storytelling', *New Statesman* 135, no. 4823–25 (2006): 36.

[30] Holger Thesleff, *An Introduction to the Pythagorean Writings of the Hellenistic Period* (Abo: Abo Akademi, 1961), 54 and 106.

elusive in Philostratus' *Life of Apollonius*. The hero's dedication to Pythagorean practice appears to reside in vegetarianism, a five-year vow of silence, abstinence from wine, and belief in metempsychosis. Additionally, Apollonius undertakes hardship in search of great philosophers. Hence he travels to India, a land portrayed by Philostratus as a learned man's utopia whose wise rulers have taken the trouble to learn Greek. To highlight the believed historical connections between Greek and Indian philosophy, Philostratus establishes similarities between Pythagoras and the Brahmans whom Apollonius meets: 'The Indian said, "These must stay here, but you must come as you are, because they themselves invite you." The word "themselves" in itself seemed Pythagorean to Apollonius, and he followed gladly.'[31] The kinship is elaborated in details of their respective philosophies when Apollonius interviews Iarchus, leader of the Brahmans, on metempsychosis: 'He said, "What is your belief about the soul?" "It is what Pythagoras transmitted to you Greeks," said Iarchas, "and we to the Egyptians" (1:261). Apollonius associates the Brahmans with knowledge beyond the perception of the eye, and comments, 'These Brahmans are on the earth and not on the earth' (1:253). He uses a near-chiasmus again describing the wedding feast in Corinth. Here Apollonius informs his disciples that they are in the presence of a lamia:

'Do you all know . . . about Tantalus's gardens, which exist and yet do not exist? . . . That . . . is how to regard this display. It is not material, but the appearance of matter. To prove to you what I mean, this excellent bride is one of the vampires.' (1:375)

Reportedly both Pythagoras and Apollonius visited India, a connection which, if not grounded in historical fact, strengthens the probability that the lamia tale associated with Apollonius is Indian, and suggests that the Tyanan sage's preoccupation with illusion was directly influenced by Asian thought. The mythical interpretation of the lamia tale renders Love-Melancholy a lesser concern than the conflict between sensory impressions and reality represented by the confrontation of sage and enchantress. The distinction between unseen truth and delusive

---

[31] Philostratus, *Apollonius of Tyana*, ed. and trans. Christopher P. Jones, 2 vols, The Loeb Classical Library (Cambridge, MA: Harvard University Press, 2005), 1:247. Hereafter cited parenthetically. Jones comments that Pythagoreans invoked the Master's authority by the words *autos epha*, 'he himself said' (1:247fn).

appearance underpins both Hinduism and Buddhism. Keats was interested in such concepts but, as I shall argue, for his own reasons. These, in addition to the Love-Melancholy theme, would have attracted him to Philostratus' lamia story.

Deirdre Coleman likens Keats's epistolary reflections on poetic indolence—a receptive state in which Keats says the writer must 'sit like Jove' to encourage creative inspiration—to descriptions of Buddhist and Hindu meditation practices by the British Orientalists.[32] For example, in Charles Wilkins's translation of the Hindu epic *Bhagavad Gita* (1785), 'rest is called the means for him who hath attained devotion'. Consequently, the devotee 'beholdeth the soul', a vision of a microcosm within that is only perceptible in the correct state of tranquillity.[33] Such revelation appeals to Keats as enabling a 'voyage of conception' in which the poet could record his insights. Characteristically, Keats mixes the classical with the Oriental, as it is Jove, rather than Buddha or a Brahman, who sits. However, the metaphor that Keats selects for the visionary experience of meditation is a journey to China: 'When Man has arrived at a certain ripeness in intellect any one grand and spiritual passage serves him as a starting point towards the "two and thirty pallaces" . . . . What delicious diligent Indolence!'[34] Historians such as Charles Middleton claimed that China contained thirty-two palaces.[35] This meditating Jove, a fusion of Graeco-Roman antiquity with not only Indian but also Chinese culture, represents the capacity for imaginative flight to achieve discovery beyond the possibilities of spatial exploration. Keats represents this scope in the letter as an exaggerated exoticness, for which emphasis he needs to include China. Thus the letter anticipates *Lamia*, in which Jove orders the gods not to travel, but the gods have the power of *poesis* to materialize fantasy: 'real are the dreams of gods'.

[32] Deirdre Coleman, '"Voyage of Conception": John Keats and India', in *India and Europe in the Global Eighteenth Century*, ed. Simon Davies, Daniel Sanjiv Roberts, and Gabriel Sánchez Espinosa (Oxford: Oxford University Press, 2014), 97.

[33] Charles Wilkins trans., *The Bhagvat-geeta, or Dialogues of Kreeshna and Arjoon* (London: C. Nourse, 1785), 62–4.

[34] *Letters of John Keats*, 1:121.

[35] Charles Middleton, *A New and Complete System of Geography*, 2 vols (London: J. Cooke, 1778–79), 1:28.

Ting cites Feng's use of poetic chiasmus among the remarkable coin-cidences of this version of the White Snake story with Keats's poetry, and quotes 'Beauty is truth, truth beauty' from 'Grecian Urn'. One example of chiasmus occurs in penitent disciple Xu Xuan's poem, which concludes Feng's account:

> The phenomenal world is elusive,
> The formless, in fact, is not lacking in form.
> The Form is the Void, the Void is the Form;
> Yet the two should be clearly set apart.
>
> (505)

Feng offers this formulation because chiasmus is integral to the lamia tale, for example in the oppositional pairing of enchantress and sage. Keats's *Lamia* also has an overall chiastic structure, which commences with the early 'real are the dreams of gods', in which thought becomes reality, and concludes with the disintegration of luxuries. In Zen Bud-dhist texts, chiasmus is often used to indicate the proximity of the phenomenal world to the imaginary: under the hypothesis that material existence is illusory, physical and imaginary objects are considered equally unreal. For example, the sixth-century master Fu Shan-hui's reflects on the impossibility of separating mind from reality, which he terms 'Buddha': 'Apart from mind is not Buddha; apart from Buddha is not mind.'[36] Hence the philosophical speeches in Feng's version of the White Snake tale are faithful to a tradition in which meditative chiasmus is common. Apollonius of Tyana does not advance such a theory of the material world explicitly, but merely says that the lamia and her banquet are insubstantial. Therefore Keats's reflections on material reality approach the philosophy of the Chinese story more closely than Philos-tratus does. If Keats is a poet of the Buddha's party without knowing it, I think that his attraction to such a myth has different motivations from the philosophical principles that inform the Chinese version. It is the possibility of *poesis*, rather than philosopher's lesson on the deceptive nature of phenomena, that appeals to Keats. His *Lamia* is the myth of an artist who creates irresistible forms. Lamia attempts the godly act of materializing thought. If Lamia is therefore an immortal or a quasi-

---

[36] Thomas Cleary trans., *Classics of Buddhism and Zen*, 5 vols (Boston: Shambhala, 2005), 2:9.

divinity, Apollonius can be interpreted as a religious sceptic, who dismisses the miraculous. In this light, Keats's Apollonius is consistent with commentary on Philostratus during the Romantic period, in which the Sage of Tyana was considered a threat to Christianity, a subversive character who had suspicious, Asian associations.

Transmissions of Apollonius

In a book that the schoolboy valued so highly that he 'appeared to learn' it by heart, John Lemprière's evaluation of Philostratus' *Life of Apollonius* is likely to have made the Tyanan sage an enticing subject for the young Keats. Lemprière finds that Philostratus' work is 'written with elegance', but complains that 'the improbable accounts, the fabulous stories, and exaggerated details which it gives, render it disgusting'.[37] John Potter's *Archaeologia Graeca* (1697–98) is a further source for *Lamia*. While Keats consulted this work for details of a Greek wedding-banquet, Potter's book also contains an anecdote in which Apollonius reveals his ability to communicate with birds, as a sparrow invites the philosopher and his party to a feast.[38] The conceit of looking into Greek myth via Homer—and in turn, into Homer through Chapman's translation—in Keats's sonnet 'On First Looking into Chapman's Homer' may be indebted to a phrase in the *Life of Apollonius*, which had been translated into English by Edward Berwick in 1809. When Apollonius informs his disciples that the lamia's banquet is unreal, he asks whether they have heard of the gardens of Tantalus: 'We have seen, said they, in Homer'.[39] Whether or not Keats had read Philostratus in full, many writers alluded to the sage in English-language texts. In fact, such a wealth of material on Apollonius of Tyana was available to Keats that his unannotated reproduction of Burton's paragraph at the end of *Lamia* constitutes a coy understatement of the poem's literary analogues as apparent to an informed reader of the period. Amongst these, Apollonius was a person

---

[37] John Lemprière, *Bibliotheca Classica; or, A Classical Dictionary* (Reading: T. Cadell, 1788), PH Q3.

[38] John Potter, *Archaeologia Graeca, or the Antiquities of Greece: A New Edition*, ed. G. Dunbar, 2 vols (London: Stirling & Slade, 1818), 1:381.

[39] Philostratus, *The Life of Apollonius*, trans. Edward Berwick (London: T. Payne, 1809), 219.

of interest to Orientalists in several contexts. Most prominently, the Sage of Tyana was cited by commentators who questioned the veracity of Christianity. Some used Apollonius to contest Christian theology, and several did so to champion non-Christian Asia instead.

Apollonius was fiercely debated in Keats's lifetime. The reception of Philostratus' work in the eighteenth and nineteenth centuries is remarkable in the context of the craze for pseudo-epigraphy in fiction of the period. It was a cliché for Gothic novels to announce themselves as ancient manuscripts retrieved from Continental libraries, and to pose as histories or confessions rather than fictions. Yet Philostratus' *Life of Apollonius* was nearly always interpreted as a sincere hagiography during the same era.

Even when contemplated apart from his Asian connections, the Sage of Tyana was perceived as a threat to Christianity. Debate on Apollonius focussed on parallels between his feats and those of Christ. In the course of his adventures, Apollonius casts out spirits, heals the sick, raises the dead, and finally ascends bodily to heaven. Readers were either delighted or discomforted by these similarities, depending on their theological perspective. Berwick is evidently displeased by Philostratus' report that the lamia 'begged not to be tormented', a phrase that closely matches Christ's encounter with a spirit as documented in Luke (8.28).[40] Most controversially, Apollonius appeared to be more successful than Christ. Tried by Emperor Domitian himself, Apollonius talks his way out of execution, unlike his counterpart. He makes specific prophecies concerning the deaths of Vitellius, Galba, and Otho (2.21). At least one commentator claims that Damis, Apollonius' scholarly companion and Philostratus' professed primary source, is a more reliable witness than the New Testament fishermen.[41]

In Lucian's second-century satire, a probable source for Philostratus that was translated into English in 1796 as *The Private History of Peregrinus Proteus*, the eponym meets the now-elderly Menippus Lycius, who explains that the lamia was an avaricious woman, a vampire merely in an 'allegorical' sense. Lucian describes Apollonius' miracles rationally, as an oblique means to discount Christianity:

[40] Philostratus, *The Life of Apollonius*, 219fn.
[41] Debated for example in Eusebius, *Against Hierocles*.

What enables this extraordinary man to perform the most of his miracles, said Menippus, was the majestic height and beauty of his figure, and the magic of his eloquence, which by the importance he had acquired, and the tone of his voice, possessed a captivating force.[42]

Hence, Menippus Lycius reports Apollonius' initial detection of the youth's danger, in gradual alterations to his complexion, as scientific rather than supernatural. In *Lover of Truth* (c. 311–13 CE), Sossianus Hiercoles, like Lucian, doubts the fabulous reports of Apollonius, but the main motive of his sceptical assessments is to undermine any belief in the supernatural, primarily the views of Christians.[43]

Implicitly, later authors who celebrated Apollonius' miracles equated him with Christ. Many Anglican scholars therefore felt compelled to respond to Apollonius of Tyana. I infer that the same elitist associations of classical culture that intimidated Keats also originated Anglican scholars' uneasy reception of Apollonius. Graeco-Roman culture was embedded in prestigious education, and classical scholarship was intimately connected with the Church of England. Yet Philostratus' credentials were too strong to dismiss his work as inconsequential. The *Life of Apollonius* was commissioned by Julia Domna, wife of the Emperor Septimius Severus (145–211 CE). Moreover, the parallels with the life of Christ entailed that Apollonius could not be discounted as primitive in the manner that later scholars patronized Graeco-Roman polytheism. Hence, to Anglican scholars, resolving the problem of Apollonius of Tyana may have seemed an inexorable duty. Frequently, theologians dismissed Philostratus' account as blasphemy simply because its events resembled the life of Christ. Christian apologist Thomas Stackhouse cites Apollonius' 'zeal . . . for the pagan idolatry' as evidence 'that his miracles were false', but alludes to the Tyanan's 'idolatry' as a generality rather than providing examples.[44] In his 1754 analysis of miracles, John Douglas rubbishes Apollonius' 'Legerdemain Tricks'. To account for the reported miracles of Apollonius, Douglas suggests that Philostratus'

---

[42] Lucian, *The Private History of Peregrinus Proteus*, trans. William Tooke, 2 vols (London, J. Johnson, 1796), 1:134.

[43] Hierocles' text survives only as fragments reproduced in Christian apologist Eusebius of Caesarea's roughly contemporaneous response, *Against Hierocles*.

[44] Thomas Stackhouse, *A Defence of the Christian Religion from Several Objections of Modern Antiscripturists*, 2nd ed. (London: Edward Symon, 1733), 239.

book plagiarizes the Bible.[45] An assessment of Berwick's translation in the *Eclectic Review* terms Philostratus' work 'silly and absurd', likening Apollonius and Damis to Samuel Johnson and James Boswell.[46] Nathaniel Lardner suggests in *Testimonies of Antient Heathens* (1764–67) that Apollonius' defenders merely feel threatened by Christianity—an appraisal in which the self-irony appears to be entirely unintentional—but believes that this was not Philostratus' intention for the *Life*.[47] Lardner makes the common-sense observation that Philostratus was never a highly regarded author, hence his works should not be afforded excessive respect. With this logic, however, Lardner is in a minority among scholars. In *A Series of Important Facts* (1820), Joseph Jones claims that Philostratus' sole purpose could only be to set up a rival to Christ, and discounts reports of Apollonius' virtue as elements of this deception. Jones calls Apollonius 'an impostor'.[48] Yet such commentators did much to keep the name of Apollonius alive. To condemn Philostratus' work as 'silly' belied the fact that scholars identified it as a 'knotty problem'.

While the extent of critics' attention to the *Life of Apollonius* contradicted the commonplace declarations of its insignificance, the weakness of scholars' argumentation frequently appears capable of, inadvertently, stimulating interest in the text, and even legitimating it. Ralph Cudworth claims that Apollonius was 'assisted by the Powers of the Kingdom of Darkness' in a career of necromancy and black magic, by which the Adversary aimed to make Christ appear a lesser light.[49] Lardner says that ancient scholars did not pay significant attention to Philostratus' work, and reasons thence that the Sophist should not concern modern readers. However, he feels obliged to qualify his dismissal of Apollonius, which results in rather weak distinctions between Christ and the Tyanan. 'Our Lord never travelled abroad', Lardner ventures.[50] Subsequently, he suggests that the girl resurrected by Apollonius was not actually dead; a

[45] John Douglas, *The Criterion or, Miracles Examined with a view to Expose the Pretensions of Pagans and Papists* (London: A. Millar, 1754), 56 and 62.

[46] *The Eclectic Review* 13, no. 1 (1811): 217.

[47] *Works of Nathaniel Lardner*, 10 vols (London: T. Bensley, 1815), 4:261–2.

[48] Joseph Jones, *A Series of Important Facts, Demonstrating the Truth of Christian Religion* (London: Rowland Hunter, 1820), 160.

[49] Ralph Cudworth, *The True Intellectual System of the Universe: The First Part* (London: Richard Royston, 1678), 265.

[50] *Works of Nathaniel Lardner*, 4:263.

difficult claim to substantiate with textual evidence, as Philostratus recounts the 'unfathomable' miracle as transpiring when Apollonius interrupted the funeral procession to inspect the bier (2:419). Lardner too praises with faint damnation when he concedes that Apollonius was 'called a god by many', but argues that 'every good man is honoured with it [being "called a god"]'.[51]

Apollonius' Asian associations constituted another aspect of the Tyanan sage that aggravated Christians, was useful to opponents of Christianity, and was of interest in its own right to Orientalists. In *The Decline and Fall*, Gibbon juxtaposes Apollonius and Christ in a footnote phrased mischievously to accentuate the possibility of muddling the two:

Apollonius of Tyana was born around the same time as Jesus Christ. His life (that of the former) is related in so fabulous a manner by his disciples, that we are at a loss to discover whether he was a sage, an impostor, or a fanatic.   (1:315fn)

Unlike Christ's career, the life of Apollonius was not 'related . . . by his disciples', but primarily documented by Philostratus, based on the account of *one* disciple. The confusion Gibbon sows here appears deliberate.

Gibbon's scepticism towards Christian miracles contrasts with his allusions to a civilized Asia under Islam. Other of Philostratus' readers were indifferent to religious debate, or even Apollonius himself, but valued Philostratus' accounts of Asian culture in their own right. John Dove, for example, finds Apollonius 'conceited' and 'insolent', but describes the Brahmans as 'excellent' in his 1756 exploration of inspiration theories.[52] Apollonius is known in Arabian literature as Balinus, Master of Talismans, who authored various texts on Hermeticism. Keats may not have known of this further Asian connection, but another of his schoolboy favourites, Spence's *Polymetis* (1747), alludes to the seven talismanic rings worn by Apollonius in accordance with the planets.[53] Thus when he sought reading matter on Hermetic traditions, Keats may unwittingly have encountered Apollonius again in the guise of Balinas.

Ironically, given most contemporaneous theology scholars' failure to consider that Philostratus' text might not be intended as sincere hagiography, the work that did most to disseminate the story of Apollonius

---

[51] *Works of Nathaniel Lardner*, 4:256.
[52] John Dove, *An Essay on Inspiration* (London: E. Withers, 1756), 114.
[53] Joseph Spence, *Polymetis*, 2nd ed. (London: R. and J. Dodsley, 1755), 181.

amongst a popular audience during the Romantic period was a Gothic pseudo-epigraphy. This book casts the Sage of Tyana emphatically as an Oriental character. In Friedrich Schiller's novel *The Ghost-Seer* (1787–89), a Prince is haunted by a mysterious being known as the Armenian. Keats alludes to the work in an 1819 letter.[54] The 1800 English translation of the novel amplifies its Oriental threat by retitling the work *The Armenian; or, the Ghost-Seer*. It, like the 1795 translation by Daniel Boileau, includes a synopsis of Philostratus' *Life*. The instance of foreknowledge with which the Armenian reveals his powers recalls Philostratus' account of Domitian's death, as described from afar by Apollonius. Hence, Schiller's well-read characters suspect that their visitor is Apollonius of Tyana. In one episode the Armenian, like Apollonius, uses his supernatural powers to reveal deception at a wedding-banquet. The bridegroom, like Keats's lamia, writhes in torment.

It is also relevant that Schiller had first published Goethe's *Bride of Corinth* (1797) in the magazine *Die Horen*. Goethe's primary source was Phlegon of Tralles, but Philostratus' lamia episode is likely to have been a model too. Schiller's *Ghost-Seer* influences two works by Coleridge that, in turn, were well known in the Romantic period. The plot of Coleridge's successful drama *Remorse* (1813) is indebted to the aforementioned episode in which Schiller's Armenian spoils the wedding of a man who has murdered his brother and love-rival. Moreover, Schiller's elaboration of the Armenian as an eternal wanderer, a supernatural being impelled by recurrent, physical pain to find the persons he must educate, is a source for Coleridge's 'Ancyent Marinere', who likewise ruins wedding celebrations with his oracular pronouncements. As Coleridge had also read Philostratus' *Life of Apollonius*, his Mariner therefore blends at least two versions of the Tyanan sage. Comparably, while *Lamia* is ostensibly a version of Philostratus' account, Keats's unsympathetic Apollonius— before whom 'all charms fly'—manifests the sinister qualities of Schiller's version, the Armenian (2.229). Evidently, authors recognized Apollonius as a vehicle for reflections on Orientalism before Keats commenced *Lamia*.

Further to its established Orientalisms, it is possible that Keats's *Lamia* also reflects direct exchanges between Philostratus' text and the Chinese legend. European visitors who took interest in Chinese popular-culture were likely to encounter versions of the White Snake legend during

---

[54] *Letters of John Keats*, 2:194.

the eighteenth century, particularly in theatre and opera. But had the Chinese heard about Apollonius of Tyana? Surprisingly, they had. Jesuit missionaries established a number of Greek and Latin libraries in China, including a collection of some 5,000 volumes in Beijing, the Pei Thang Jesuit Library. In 1619, Nicolas Trigault and Johann Terrentius, procurators for the library, brought a consignment that included a parallel Greek and Latin text of *Philostratus of Lemnos: Extant Works* (1608), which also includes Eusebius' *Against Hierocles*.[55] For Philostratus' book to reach Beijing necessitated a complex and costly process of justification, purchase, and delivery to China. Books for the library were requested by the expatriate missionaries and sourced in Europe by the procurators, who then transported the volumes to China personally.[56] Hence, books that appeared in China's Western libraries did not arrive on whim, but on specific instructions: Philostratus was in demand by at least one Jesuit classicist, who took great trouble to obtain *The Life of Apollonius*. While very few Chinese learned Western languages, locals (and the few religious-converts in particular) visited the Jesuit libraries as curiosities, whose curators discussed the contents of the books and displayed the fine binding. Thus *The Life of Apollonius* was deliberated by Beijing literati in the five years prior to the first publication of the White Snake legend in Feng's folklore anthology, and Philostratus' text was housed in the same city in which 'One Hundred Copies' Zhang sold children's versions of the Chinese story.[57] It is possible in turn, although speculative, that Keats heard reports of the *Thunder Peak Pagoda* plays. The East India Company factory at Canton contained a library that had amassed some 200 Chinese play scripts by the early nineteenth-century, including multiple versions of *Thunder Peak Pagoda*. If an anecdotal account of the *Thunder Peak Pagoda* plays reached Keats from a visiting Company employee, undoubtedly the information would have intensified his apprehension that Apollonius was a suitable vehicle for reflections on Orientalism and classicism.

---

[55] Listed in a reproduction of the library's records, *Catalogue de la Bibliotheque du Pe-t'ang* (Paris, Société d'Édition Les Belles Lettres, 1969).

[56] Noël Golvers offers a detailed account of these transactions in *Logistics of Book Acquisition and Circulation*, vol. 1 of *Libraries of Western Learning for China* (Leuven, Ferdinand Verbiest Institute KUL, 2012), 199–214.

[57] The Pei Thang Jesuit Library was entrusted to the care of Lazarist missionaries from 1785.

In *Lamia* the poetic visionary is one kind of Orientalist, the *curioso* is another. While the dazzling description of the snake encapsulates the poem's eclectic Orientalism, Apollonius represents the transmission of the tale itself between cultures: the circulation of Apollonius' lamia tale between Europe and Asia mirrors the Sage of Tyana's own reported travels. Keats's and Feng's versions are similar because they are ultimately the same *oicotype*, versions of which were subject to later exchanges of influence, retold by authors with comparable philosophies. While the archetypal ogre-tale encapsulates universal themes, *Lamia* and the White Snake tale express more complex relationships between the authors and their sources. The Buddhist principles of the Indian *oicotype*, eventually popular in China, were refracted by the Neopythagorean sophist Philostratus, and correspond with Keats's sentiments on the poetic imagination. The presence of Philostratus' text in a Jesuit library—a curiosity to Chinese visitors—illustrates that cultural influence is rarely unilateral. The praise for Chinese civilization that Keats encountered in Voltaire, via Leibniz and the Jesuits, had a counterpart in the effect Jesuit classicists had on Chinese culture. To investigate the details that *Lamia* shares with White Snake texts that follow Feng leads us to such scholarly matters as the Deist Controversy, but also to Chinese popular culture, as in the bannermen tales.

The greater point is that the web of relations behind British views of China advances our comprehension of nineteenth-century cosmopolitanism. That subject is treated in a more familiar way in the following chapter, where Charles Lamb documents East India Company imports and covets *chinoiserie*. Yet it should be evident from the present chapter that British cosmopolitanism was temporally broad as well as spatially so. The set of ideas that Anglophone authors and readers brought to bear on China originated in diverse periods. Graeco-Roman antiquity could be invoked as a fluid concept rather than a static paradigm, and one's reading about Ovid's universe was not shut off in a separate mental-compartment from one's thinking about contemporary China. These and other settings were in constant imaginative relation.

The accumulation of exchanges between East and West befits Keats, repeatedly between worlds as the apothecary who abandoned his profession, the poet who felt underqualified, and the invalid who recognized his journey to Rome as departure for the afterlife. Strange, then, for this poet who hovers between realms to formulate a classicism that would be a key ingredient in treatments of Chinese subjects after his death.

4

Charles Lamb, Roast Pork, and Willow Crockery

Keats's classicism informs Charles Lamb's writings on Chinese culture, which situate Asian ideas within both the gradual course of human progress and the caprices of contemporary fashion. Lamb (1775–1834) was obsessed with the past, in both personal and historical senses. Published under the pseudonym Elia, Lamb's most celebrated essays are distinguished by their elegiac tone. William Hazlitt writes that 'Mr Lamb has the very soul of an antiquarian, as this implies a reflecting humanity; the film of the past hovers forever before him.'[1] Accordingly, 'A Dissertation upon Roast Pig' (1822) and 'Old China' (1823) typify a corpus that reflects upon personal vicissitudes, altered landscapes, and changes in popular taste. Lamb is also interested in the tendency for personal and social developments to intersect and illuminate each other. These essays, on gastronomy and Chinese aesthetics respectively, have unexpected classical sources. They are also very influential works which have shaped imaginative discourse on China. 'Roast Pig' was frequently anthologized for school children in the nineteenth and twentieth centuries. 'Old China', as this chapter explores, instigates a tradition of comic prose about *chinoiserie* which contains the dominant interpretation of Willow imagery as narrative. In a different way from Keats's *Lamia*, Lamb's essays tell us much about nineteenth-century British cosmopolitanism. Lamb writes explicitly on consumerism and popular *chinoiserie*, addresses the notion that the Chinese aesthetic was a gendered interest, and captures changing public-opinion on China.

[1] William Hazlitt, *The Spirit of the Age, or, Contemporary Portraits*, 2nd ed. (London: Henry Colburn, 1825), 397.

China from the Ruins of Athens and Rome: Classics, Sinology, and Romanticism, 1793–1938.
Chris Murray, Oxford University Press (2020). © Chris Murray.
DOI: 10.1093/oso/9780198767015.001.0001

As in the Elia essays generally, classical culture performs two functions in 'Roast Pig' and 'Old China'. First, Lamb invokes the ancient world to contemplate the passage of time, even when his primary subject has little overt relevance to Graeco-Roman antiquity. Secondly—and barely disguising himself under the assumed persona of Elia—Lamb associates classical learning with unfulfilled promise, and a happier period in his life. While professional duty with the East India Company compelled him to contemplate Britain's affairs in China, Lamb retained his dedication to literature and the ancient world throughout his life.

The Deputy Grecian at East India House

Lamb was another of British Romanticism's frustrated classicists. Born in the Temple, he attended the charity school Christ's Hospital, and left at the rank of Deputy Grecian in 1789. 'But what is a Deputy Grecian?' Leigh Hunt poses in his autobiography:

When I entered the school, I was shown three gigantic boys, . . . who, I was told, were going to the University. These were the Grecians. They are the three head boys of the Grammar School, and are understood to have their destiny fixed for the Church. The next class to these, like a College of Cardinals to those three Popes (for every Grecian was in our eyes infallible), were the Deputy Grecians. The former were supposed to have completed their Greek studies, and were deep in Sophocles and Euripides. The latter were thought equally competent to tell you anything respecting Homer and Demosthenes. These two classes, and the head boys of the Navigation School, held a certain rank, over the whole place, both in school and out.[2]

In addition to loving classics, Lamb was deeply religious. Advancement to the Grecian form, University study, and a career in the clergy may have suited him. Yet 'this choice rests entirely . . . with the Head Master', records former classics master William Trollope in his *History* of the school.[3] Critics have surmised that, as with Hunt, Lamb's stammer may have impeded his acceptance as Grecian, which would have required oratorical performance. The sense of an abandoned vocation haunted him. In an 1831 letter to George Dyer, Lamb compares his recipient's

[2] Leigh Hunt, *Lord Byron and Some of His Contemporaries*, 2nd ed. (London: Henry Colburn, 1828), 2:144–5.
[3] William Trollope, *A History of the Royal Foundation of Christ's Hospital* (London: William Pickering, 1834), 182.

handwriting to the 'conjuring characters' of Samuel Parr, a clergyman schoolmaster and accomplished Latinist, and the 'Missal hand' of Richard Porson, Regius Professor of Greek at Cambridge. Next, Lamb considers his own script, painfully unsuited to his occupation:

Mine is a sort of deputy Grecian's hand, a little better, and more of a worldly hand than a Grecian's, but still remote from the mercantile. I don't know how it is, but I keep my rank in fancy since my school-days. I can never forget I was a deputy Grecian! And writing to you, or to Coleridge, besides affection, I feel a reverential deference as to Grecians still—I keep my soaring way above the Great Erasmians, yet far beneath the other: Alas! what am I now? what is a Leadenhall clerk, or India pensioner, to a deputy Grecian? How art thou fallen, O Lucifer![4]

The course of Lamb's life was determined by poverty and personal tragedy. His friends Wordsworth and Coleridge secured annuities that, although modest, enabled them to pursue careers as professional authors. Lamb had no such luck, and was less certain of his literary vocation. He found employment as a clerk, and from 1792 held a position at East India House. In 1796 Lamb's sister, Mary, killed their mother with a kitchen knife. Diagnosed with 'lunacy', Mary was institutionalized until 1799, and again sporadically until the end of her life.[5] Lamb remained unmarried and, having assumed custody for Mary as an alternative to her permanent detention in asylums, felt bound to continue with the East India Company as family breadwinner. 'The Superannuated Man' (1825), written on Lamb's retirement, recalls his employment in terms such as 'tedious', 'melancholy', and 'irksome confinement'.[6] He felt like 'a prisoner in the old Bastile [sic]' as city life passed him by outside the walls of the counting-house (2:195). 'Oxford in the Vacation' (1820) foreshadows, in gentle humour, the unfulfilled aspirations of Thomas Hardy's *Jude the Obscure* (1895). The unhappy Elia catalogues the 'indigos, cottons, raw silks, piece-goods' that occupy his days as ledger entries (2:7). Such work, he continues, 'sends you home with . . . increased appetite to your books' (2:8). On holidays, Elia reports that he and a friend (based on George Dyer) visit Oxford and

[4] *The Letters of Charles and Mary Lamb*, ed. E. V. Lucas, 3 vols (London: Methuen, 1935), 3:305–6. Hereafter cited parenthetically.

[5] For an account of the siblings' relationship see Sarah Burton, *A Double Life: A Biography of Charles and Mary Lamb* (London: Penguin Books, 2003).

[6] *The Works of Charles and Mary Lamb*, ed. E. V. Lucas, 7 vols (London: Methuen & Co., 1903), 2:193–4. Hereafter cited parenthetically.

fantasize that they are scholars: 'I can here play the gentleman, enact the student . . . . In graver moments, I proceed Master of Arts.' Elia elaborates that he even dresses the part: 'I go about in black, which favours the notion' (2:9).

Lamb's disappointment at his station was reasonable. Deputy Grecians underwent an excellent classical-education, which Trollope explains qualified them 'for the medical or legal professions, or for scholastic pursuits'. Academically, Lamb had distinguished himself from 'that great mass of children' who proceeded only to the level of Christ's Hospital's Little and Great Erasmus forms. It was these less-accomplished students, according to Trollope, who were 'destined for some trade or mercantile occupation'. [7] Hence, Lamb was a misfit, who saw a metaphor for alienation in his script: too 'worldly' for the visionary scrawl of a Grecian such as fellow old-boy Coleridge, yet also 'remote' from the neat, 'mercantile' characters of his professional colleagues. While the tedium of clerkship frustrated him in its own right, Lamb also perceived a strong connection between professional activity and identity. It is less obvious why no opportunity for significant advancement was available to a man of Lamb's talents. It may simply be that the nature of his duties offered little chance to distinguish himself. His work became more lucrative in time, but remained a source of dissatisfaction.

Compelled to drudgery and bachelordom, Lamb began to idealize his childhood. His most famous poem, 'The Old Familiar Faces' (1798), has received critical attention for its raw emotion and biographical significance. It articulates desolation in stages. The first stanza of the published text laments the loss of loved ones. The second tercet reports the nightly cessation of revelry, at which the speaker returns to solitude. In the third tercet a definitive moment of exclusion occurs, which precludes the possibility of the speaker forming new attachments:

> I have had playmates, I have had companions,
> In my days of childhood, in my joyful school-days,
> All, all are gone, the old familiar faces.

> I have been laughing, I have been carousing,
> Drinking late, sitting late, with my bosom cronies,
> All, all are gone, the old familiar faces.

---

[7] Trollope, *Christ's Hospital*, 184.

> I loved a Love once, fairest among women:
> Closed are her doors on me, I must not see her—
> All, all are gone, the old familiar faces.
>
> (1–9)

A cancelled verse that Lamb included in the original, epistolary version clarifies that this is an autobiographical poem in which Lamb yearns for the happiness that preceded the death of his mother:

> I had a mother, but she died, and left me,
> Died prematurely in a day of horrors—
> All, all are gone, the old familiar faces.
>
> (1:120)

The sense of irretrievable loss that Lamb formulated in this poem of his early twenties persisted. Simultaneously, he knew that his obsessive regret hindered his experience of the present. It was not until his regular contributions as an essayist for *The London Magazine* (1820–25) that Lamb found his most suitable creative-outlet. Lamb's Elia essays articulate an undiminished fondness for the past, yet the nostalgia is measured and self-aware. This voice, sadder and wiser, is closer to the calm retrospect of Thomas Gray's lines 'On a Distant Prospect of Eton College' (1742) than the intense 'Old Familiar Faces'.

The ancient world occasions a dream within a dream to the nostalgic Elia. In essays based on Lamb's childhood visits to Gilston, a stately home in Hertfordshire under the care of his grandmother, he recalls that the classical décor transported him to greater happiness still. In 'Blakesmoor, in H—shire' (1824), Elia remembers his excitement on seeing 'Ovid on the walls, in colours vivider than his descriptions'. The tapestries that portrayed scenes from *Metamorphoses*, such as 'Actæon in mid sprout, with the unappeasable prudery of Diana', established the boy's commonality with the house's departed owners (2:155). Since they evidently loved Roman myth, the boy understood the 'feeling of gentility' and began to imagine himself owner of the house, much like the Elia who plays 'Master of Arts' on visits to Oxford (2:156). Elia documents his realization that the busts have a dual nature, signifying both their subjects' death and the eternal life of art, which he cannot replicate. The 'coldness of death, yet freshness of immortality' echoes the oxymoronic forces at play in Keats's 'Ode on a Grecian Urn' (2:157).

In 'Dream-Children; a Reverie' (1822), Elia depicts himself once more 'gazing upon the old busts of the Twelve Caesars . . . till the old marble heads would seem to live again, or I be turned to marble with them' (2:102). He reiterates the wish to share the same existence as the Caesars, to overcome their difference either by the emperors' return to life, or by young Elia becoming a work of art. The essay disarms the reader when the apparent framing-device becomes its main focus. 'Children love to listen to stories about their elders, when *they* were children', the piece begins. 'It was in this spirit that my little ones crept about me the other evening' (2:100). The loss that Elia recounts initially is not the death of Grandmother Field, but of his brother. Furthermore, at the climax of the essay, the children reveal themselves to be figments: 'both the children gradually grew fainter to my view, receding, and still receding'. Elia emerges from his reverie, awoken from the credible vision that he had children of his own, but recalled to the death of his brother. The piece concludes, 'John L. (or James Elia) was gone for ever' (2:103). In a typical blurring of personae, Elia's imaginary son has been named after Lamb's late brother. Reconsidered in light of the essay's conclusion, Elia's encounter with the Caesars' busts is cognate with the insurmountable otherness of the Dream-Children, who never were, and never will be.

Lamb's most substantial work of classical reception looked back to his schooldays. A Deputy Grecian's Monday mornings were devoted to learning Homer by heart. The master, James Boyer, set Greek translation exercises on Wednesday and Friday evenings, which might also include Homer (Trollope, 183). In 1808, William Godwin published Lamb's *The Adventures of Ulysses*, a text for children which was intended to capitalize on the success of Charles and Mary's collaborative *Tales from Shake-speare* (1807). Lamb introduces *Adventures* as a didactic work:

The picture which it exhibits is that of a brave man struggling with adversity; by a wise use of events, and with an inimitable presence of mind under difficulties, forcing out a way for himself through the severest trials to which human life can be exposed. (3:207)

Lamb's primary model is George Chapman's translation. He announces that 'the moral and the colouring are comparatively modern' in his own text, and that he has omitted much of Homer's dialogue to create an all-action story for children (3:207). However, Godwin balked at the gratuitous violence of Lamb's treatment, which he suspected was unsuitable for the readership of the Juvenile Library. Polyphemus, discovering the intruders in his cave, 'dashed their brains out against the earth, and . . . tore in pieces their limbs, and devoured them, yet warm and trembling, making a lion's meal of them, lapping the blood' (3:211). Ulysses' vengeance upon the Cyclops is no less detailed:

[The men] bored the sharp end of the huge stake, which they had heated red-hot, right into the eye of the drunken cannibal . . . till the scalded blood gushed out, and the eye-ball smoked, and the strings of the eye cracked, as the burning rafter broke in it, and the eye hissed, as hot iron hisses when it is plunged into water.

(3:212)

The 'moral colouring' to which Lamb adverts manifests in summary judgments of the characters, for the edification of young readers. As Eurylochus and his men reluctantly leave their company to explore Circe's island, Lamb describes their tears as 'wet badges of weak humanity' (3:216). The winds that toy with the shipwrecked Ulysses are guilty of 'horrid tennis' (3:236).

Combinations of classicism with Orientalism stared Lamb in the face. The Revenue Committee room at East India House was dominated by an unsubtle allegory named *The East Offering its Riches to Britannia* (1778, see Figure 4.1). This immense, oval work of oil on canvas was mounted on the ceiling. No visitor to the room could entertain misconceptions of the Company's self-image. Hermes stands at the right of the canvas. With his caduceus he ushers Asian figures towards Britannia, who is seated and surrounded by cherubim. The deified Britain inspects a string of pearls from a platter of jewellery, offered by a kneeling and bare-breasted Indian woman. Next in line, a Chinese woman prostrates herself, cowering behind her gift of a large, blue-and-white Ming vase. A lion of intense expression, at Britannia's feet, hints at the potential for his mistress to unleash might. Understandably, an elephant and a camel keep their distance at the opposite end of the canvas. In the background an Indiaman sets off, St George's flag aflutter from its stern. In the immediate foreground, water gushes from a pipe that props up the august Old Father Thames. This localized Poseidon indicates the destination of the Asian luxuries. It was difficult to avoid this imagery in East India House. The artist, Roma Spiridone, sourced his symbolism in a marble bas-relief in the Directors' Court Room, John Michael Rysbrack's *Britannia Receiving the Riches of the East* (1730). Spiridone's painting is

Figure 4.1 At East India House, Lamb saw Orientalism and classicism fused in *The East Offering its Riches to Britannia*.
© The British Library Board.

now, strikingly, displayed in the Commonwealth Relations Office on Downing Street. Conversely, if the tapestry Elia describes at Blakesmoor was real, it may have emulated a Gobelins tapestry (*c.* 1690) that portrays Vertumnus and Pomona (*Metamorphoses* 14.623–771), bordered with Chinese motifs.[8]

The Adventures of Ulysses bears faint traces of Lamb's professional identity. His situation of war on 'the fruitful plains of Asia' depicts Troy as an East India Company procurer might, mindful of the region's commodities (3:208). Henry Crabb Robinson reports Lamb's 'droll history of a clerk in the India House suspected of living on human flesh', a bureaucrat cannibal possibly inspired by the Cyclops' diet and, by association, no more cultured a colleague than that troglodyte.[9] More

    [8] Edith A. Standen, 'Ovid's "Metamorphoses": A Gobelins Tapestry Series', *Metropolitan Museum Journal*, 23 (1988): 177fn73.

    [9] Quoted in Edmund Blunden, *Charles Lamb and His Contemporaries* (London: Hogarth Press, 1934), 66.

substantial conflations of Asian and classical ideas occur in Lamb's essays on aspects of Chinese culture.

'Roast Pig' Recipes from Greece to China

Elia claims that his source for 'A Dissertation upon Roast Pig' is 'a Chinese manuscript, which my friend M. was obliging enough to read and explain to me'. The document, Elia says, refers to an ancient period in Chinese history, details of which are verified by 'their great Confucius in the second chapter of his Mundane Mutations'. Although doubtless Lamb delighted in the absurd-sounding 'Mundane Mutations', he may allude to the Book of Changes (*Yi Jing*), to which the Jesuits referred as *Liber Mutationum*. A set of commentaries on *Yi Jing* was traditionally, but falsely, attributed to Confucius. Jesuit scholar Jean-Baptiste Régis (1663–1738) had executed the first European translation of *Yi Jing*, but his *I-king, Antiquissimus Sinarum Liber* would not be published until a German edition appeared in 1834. Leibniz's interest in the text arose from a manuscript of the hexagrams with commentary, sent to him by Régis's colleague, Joachim Bouvet. Lamb's pseudo-epigraphy replicates the exchange between Leibniz and the missionary, in which textual knowledge is acquired indirectly.

Elia tells us that at the primitive time of these events, 'mankind . . . ate their meat raw, clawing or biting it from the living animal, just as they do in Abyssinia to this day' (2:120). Like the allusion to the spurious Confucian text, the reference to Abyssinia lends a parodic, scholarly authority to Elia's account. In his contentious memoirs, James Bruce claims to have bitten the flesh from a live animal during residence in Abyssinia. Lamb refers to this as a 'suspected narrative' in correspondence (3:247). The essay on 'Roast Pig' recounts the discovery of cookery, as described in the supposed Chinese manuscript, deciphered for Elia by his scholarly friend.

The culinary breakthrough at the heart of the essay occurs 'accidentally':

The swine-herd, Ho-ti, having gone out into the woods one morning, as his manner was, to collect mast for his hogs, left his cottage in the care of his eldest son Bo-bo, a great lubberly boy, who being fond of playing with fire, as younkers of his age commonly are, let some sparks escape into a bundle of straw, which kindling quickly, spread the conflagration over every part of their poor mansion, till it was reduced to ashes. Together with the cottage (a sorry antediluvian make-shift of a building, you may think it), what was of much more importance, a fine litter of new-farrowed pigs, no less than nine in number, perished.   (2:120–21)

The fatal revelation happens when Bo-bo, wondering at the source of an aroma unfamiliar yet irresistible, touches one of the recently deceased pigs:

He burnt his fingers, and to cool them he applied them in his booby fashion to his mouth . . . . For the first time in his life (in the world's life indeed, for before him no man had known it) he tasted—*crackling!* . . . Surrendering himself up to the new-born pleasure, he fell to tearing up whole handfuls of the scorched skin with the flesh next it, and was cramming it down his throat in his beastly fashion, when his sire entered.   (2:121)

Furious at the loss of his swine, Ho-ti is disgusted to learn that his son has eaten their burnt flesh, and amazed by Bo-bo's 'barbarous ejacula-tions' that he should sample the meat himself. The situation leaves Ho-ti 'wavering whether he should not put his son to death for an unnatural young monster.' Elia explains that Bo-bo is saved by good fortune. As he deliberates over his son's punishment, with evidence in hand, Ho-ti too burns his fingers on a pig's smouldering carcass, attempts the 'booby' solution of sucking his blisters, and concludes likewise that the meat is delicious (2:122). Elia reports that father and son sit down together to devour the entire litter of piglets.

The discovery related, Elia explains how cookery was disseminated: 'It was observed that Ho-ti's cottage was burnt down more frequently than ever. . . . At length they were watched, the terrible mystery discovered' (2:122). Elia relates a trial scene of curiously European format. Ho-ti and Bo-bo are sent before a judge and jury on an unspecified charge related to their diet:

They all handled it, and burning their fingers, as Bo-bo and his father had done before them, and nature prompting to each of them the same remedy . . . they brought in a simultaneous verdict of Not Guilty.   (2:122–23)

The last historical occurrence that M's Chinese manuscript documents is a further, decisive advancement in gastronomy: 'A sage arose, like our Locke, who made a discovery, that the flesh of swine, or indeed of any other animal, might be cooked . . . without the necessity of consuming a whole house to dress it' (2:123).

Lamb's readers tend to assume that his source, the Sinologist 'M.', was Thomas Manning (1772–1840), and with good reason: in a letter, Lamb claims that 'the idea of the discovery of roasting pigs' was 'borrowed from my friend Manning' (2:373). A polymath and adventurer, Manning travelled to Canton in 1808 in the hope that he could proceed to the Chinese interior. When this plan failed, he went to Calcutta in 1811, hoping to access China from this direction. In 1812 Manning reached Tibet, where the Dalai Lama received him. He stayed on as a medical doctor, but left Lhasa under the impression that he was in danger from Qing officials, amidst violence between insurgent Tibetans and the imperial forces. Manning joined the Amehurst embassy to China in 1816 in the capacity of interpreter, but was marginalized for his eccentric character.

Manning shared Lamb's wit. By letter, the two traded puns across continents while Manning was in Asia. He encouraged Lamb to develop his talent as an essayist, and it is credible that Manning would have proposed subjects for particular Elian works. Manning respected both Chinese literature and the status of literature in Chinese culture, as he records in his notebook: 'They have horror of degrading books, writings, & make curious reflexions upon our making privy paper of them.'[10] Yet the real source for Lamb's essay is not a Chinese text translated by Manning, but the Neoplatonist Porphyry of Tyre (234–305 CE), whose treatise *On the Abstinence from Animal Food* contains the story that Elia relates of Ho-ti and Bo-bo.

Three sources are likely to have brought Porphry to Lamb's attention. First, Manning had strong Greek. That the original source is not a Chinese text, therefore, does not discount the possibility that 'M.' alerted Lamb to the story. Lamb may have Sinified the tale as an affectionate acknowledgement of his colleague. Secondly, the anecdote of the priest who burnt his fingers was excerpted in Joseph Ritson's *Essay on Abstinence from Animal Food: As a Moral Duty* (1802). John Lamb was an advocate of animal rights, and may have told his brother about Ritson's work. Third, Porphyry had a champion in London. Although his translation of *On the Abstinence from Animal Food* would not appear in print until the year after Lamb's essay, 'the English Pagan' Thomas Taylor (1758–1835) was a prominent philhellene. Taylor was Assistant

---

[10] Thomas Manning, 'Notes on Chinese Life, Culture and Language' (Royal Asiatic Society Online Collections, 2015), 4. https://royalasiaticcollections.org/notes-on-chinese-life-culture-and-language/(accessed 31 October 2019).

Secretary to the Society for the Encouragement of Art from 1798 to 1805, and produced dozens of translations from Greek philosophy, particularly Neoplatonism, during Lamb's lifetime. His friends included Mary Wollstonecraft, who inspired Taylor to compose the satirical *Vindication of the Rights of Brutes* (1792), and Thomas Lovell Peacock. Like Lamb, Taylor explored the didactic possibilities of the *Odyssey*. His translation of Porphyry's treatise on vegetarianism includes an appendix on 'the Allegory of the Wanderings of Ulysses'. Taylor interprets Odysseus' trials as a battle between body and soul, in which the hero must achieve spiritual perfection. By blinding the Cyclops, Taylor argues, Odysseus overcomes sensuality. The winds of Aeolus represent life's vicissitudes, Circe betokens degradation by sense pleasures, and Odysseus' return to Ithaca in the guise of a peasant signals his rejection of wealth and status.

In Porphyry's account of forbidden meat consumption—which he claims to have derived from Asclepiades—a priest tastes flesh accidentally during a sacrifice, and develops an appetite for it:

When the victim was burnt, a portion of the flesh fell on the earth, which was taken by the priest, who, in so doing, having burnt his fingers, involuntarily moved them to his mouth, as a remedy for the pain which the burning produced. Having, therefore, thus tasted of the roasted flesh, he also desired to eat abundantly of it, and could not refrain from giving some of it to his wife. Pygmalion, however, becoming acquainted with this circumstance, ordered both the priest and his wife to be hurled headlong from a steep rock.[11]

In summary, Lamb has transferred the action to China, with reference to an imaginary Confucian text, made the priest and his wife into a Chinese farmer and his son, and inserted a trial scene in place of wrathful Pygmalion. Unlike the source text, Lamb reports that roast flesh, specifically pork in his version, was celebrated rather than reviled in ancient China.

In the portion of Lamb's 'Roast Pig' essay that follows his Sinified version of Porphyry, Elia becomes rapturously eloquent on the subject of pork: 'Of all the delicacies in the whole *mundus edibilis*, I will maintain it to be the most delicate—*princeps obsoniorum*.' His gratuitous use of Latin creates a scholarly tone which is offset by the carnality Elia communicates in his lust for meat. Elia prefers piglets, 'guiltless as yet

---

[11] *Selected Works of Porphyry*, trans. Thomas Taylor, vol. 2 of *The Thomas Taylor Series*, repr. (Lydney, Gloucestershire: The Prometheus Trust, 1999), 126.

of the sty—with no original speck of the *amor immunditiae*, the hereditary failing of the first parent' (2:123). Overwhelmed by his appetite, Elia laments a childhood incident in which, foolishly, he wasted a cake by giving it to a beggar. The essay becomes a parody of the treatises on vegetarianism by Porphyry and Ritson. Thus it is a 'Dissertation', a scholarly argument, in which the thwarted student demonstrates his academic talent. Elia advocates the consumption of meat on moral grounds. To consume a piglet, he contends, prevents its advancement to the 'grossness and indocility' of 'mature swinehood' (2:124). Possibly responding to Taylor's tongue-in-cheek *Rights of Brutes*, Elia considers himself 'one of those, who freely and ungrudgingly impart a share of the good things of this life', and argues that pork is too good to forego (2:125–26). Furthermore, to be eaten should be considered fulfilment for the piglet, which 'helpeth, as far as his little means extend' in self-sacrifice, as a meal (2:125). We infer that it is just to make the most of the piglet's sacrifice. The dish is 'his second cradle' (2:124).

As 'Roast Pig' nears its conclusion, Elia recalls a moral question that was debated in his schooldays:

Whether, supposing that the flavour of a pig who obtained his death by whipping (*per flagellationem extremam*) superadded a pleasure upon the palate of a man more intense, than any possible suffering we can conceive in the animal, is man justified in using that method of putting the animal to death?

Yet Elia evades the matter: 'I forget the decision' (2:126). The opposite of Taylor's Odysseus, who ascends spiritually, Elia becomes ever more preoccupied with his appetite. The essay loses direction as, parenthetically, he meditates upon crackling. Elia forgets his learning with the thought of food. He has neglected his philosophical argument. Like Ho-ti and Bo-bo, Elia finds pork irresistible. Appetite overpowers all other considerations. The final paragraph reads as though M. has discarded the Chinese manuscript and taken up a recipe book: 'His sauce should be considered. . . . Barbecue your whole hogs to your palate' (2:126).

The Chinese setting connects Lamb's tale of burnt meat to several contemporary issues. Kitson compares Elia's pork obsession to opium addiction.[12] Denise Gigante notes that vegetarianism was advocated by the temperance movement, whose activities would undoubtedly have

---

[12] Kitson, *Forging Romantic China*, 170.

attracted the attention of Lamb, a heavy drinker.[13] In 1813 Lamb wrote a bleak essay, which divulges 'the secrets of my Tartarus', entitled 'Confessions of a Drunkard' (1:136). The piece was published anonymously in *The Philanthropist*, but a version appeared as an Elian essay in 1822. Later, in a kind of retraction, Lamb claimed that Elia had merely 'imagined the experiences of a Great Drinker' (1:432), inspired by Thomas de Quincey's *Confessions of an English Opium-Eater* (1821). 'Roast Pig' rejects temperance implicitly by its celebration of a meat diet. Donald H. Reiman argues that the pig consumed in the latter stages of the essay is Lamb himself, figuratively whipped to death in service of the East India Company. The Asian setting strengthens this hint. Reiman's opinion that Lamb intimates exploitation in the Honourable Company is appropriate to the reflections on civility and barbarism that permeate the essay: Elia wonders whether one gives rise to the other, or can masquerade as its opposite.

Despite an interval of centuries since Bo-bo's time, the behavioural distance that Elia articulates between savagery and modern gastronomy is slight. The advancements that predicate civilization are not the fruits of genius, in Elia's vision, but of chance. To clarify the point, Elia demonstrates that humanity's progress is reversible. He begins the essay as a historian, and takes a philosophical turn, only to become possessed by carnivorous instincts. Ostensibly, 'Roast Pig' derides ancient Chinese culture by travestying its culinary discovery, but Elia's lapse into rapacious hunger communicates a suspicion that humanity remains innately primitive, and that this is common to all races. Elia shares the Chinese love of pork, and their potential to lapse into instinctive barbarism. With the first enjoyment of meat, the pioneering arsonist of antiquity inaugurated a 'golden age' (1:120). The hidden punch-line, for Elia's informed readers, is that the exemplary tale of human savagery is not taken from Chinese history, but is closer to the foundations of British culture in Hellenistic philosophy. The essay appears to invite judgment of the 'booby' Chinese, but the joke is on the reader who fails to realise that the Chinese are really Greeks. To identify Lamb as the whipped pig, and the real hungry barbarians of the piece as the Directors of the

---

[13] Denise Gigante, *Taste: A Literary History* (New Haven: Yale University Press, 2006), 96.

Honourable Company, undermines the notion of Britain improving a backwards Asia.

If Lamb's transposition of a tale sourced in Porphyry to a Chinese setting constitutes humorous reflection on the evolution of society, he continues the line of thought in a letter, in which he speculates on the reception of his quasi-Oriental tale amongst 'tawny Hindoos':

What a supreme felicity to the author (only he is no traveller) on the Ganges or Hydaspes (Indian streams) to meet a smutty Gentoo ready to burst with laughing at the tale of Bo-Bo! for doubtless it hath been translated into all the dialects of the East.   (3:420–21)

In a further essay, Lamb invokes classical paradigms as he reflects on receptions of Chinese aesthetics, and the fads of London consumerism.

Elia's Tea Set and Keats's Urn

Keats's 'Ode on a Grecian Urn' is a major influence on 'Old China', Lamb's ekphrastic essay on porcelain *chinoiserie*. Lamb had met the poet at Benjamin Haydon's Immortal Dinner in 1817. He was delighted by Keats's 1820 volume, and reviewed *Lamia* as being 'of as gorgeous a stuff as ever romance was composed of' (1:202). Thus a further uncommon trait of Lamb is that the older Romantic responds creatively to the younger.

As in 'Roast Pig', classics provides the vehicle that conveys the vision of 'Old China', except here the classical mode is Keatsian. Elia's tea-set follows an aesthetic derived—distantly—from *shan shui* (山水), the Chinese tradition of painting 'mountains [and] water', or landscapes. Lamb does not specify whether the crockery in his essay is a Chinese import or a British artefact, but his attitude to the tea-set suggests that it is commonplace. British-manufactured *chinoiserie* was popular from its first manufacture in the late eighteenth-century. By 1785 the classic Willow pattern had emerged from the workshop of Josiah Spode, and would also be mass produced by the pottery of his rival, Josiah Wedgwood. The name 'Willow' refers to the Sinified images of Willow trees, and a particular arrangement of pictures that became known as the classic Willow pattern. However, some commentators use 'Willow' more generally as a term for any porcelain *chinoiserie*. The imagery on Elia's crockery does not correspond to any traceable work of porcelain from the British manufacturers. The illustrations are more probably inspired by Keats's imaginary Urn.

Some scholars suggest that the primary appeal of the ubiquitous crockery *chinoiserie* was that it enabled its owners to imagine themselves in China. For example, Willow porcelain was an indispensable prop to American housewives, who constructed stories for children about the images on ceramics.[14] To Western owners, Chinese motifs invited such ekphrasis. Many took the stock imagery of *chinoiserie* for an accurate depiction of China. Those who actually travelled to China were often disappointed that the truth did not correspond to the idyllic Cathay portrayed on porcelain. Commodore Matthew Perry (1794–1858) was one such visitor, dismayed that the 'sober realities' of China were unlike 'the sketches of imaginative boyhood . . . and, in short, anything but a picture of quiet content and Arcadian simplicity'.[15] Amongst those porcelain connoisseurs who possessed factual knowledge of China, David Porter writes, 'there was . . . no desire for substance' in place of 'flimsy fantasy'.[16] That porcelain *chinoiserie* facilitated escapist reverie is appropriate to Elia, unhappy in his profession. For modern critics to associate such mental travel with housewives is especially pertinent to an essay in which, as I shall discuss, Lamb explores a popular belief that *chinoiserie* is a gendered interest.

Like Keats's Urn, Elia's crockery has a complex relationship with time, which the essayist treats with playful ambiguity. The cup and saucer, Elia writes, are from 'that world before perspective'; their decoration is a primitive, two-dimensional art (2:248). The language recalls a letter to Manning in which Lamb pretends that his correspondent, like the majority of European visitors, is in Asia to enrich himself: 'I *heard* that you were going to China, with a commission from the Wedgwoods to collect hints for their pottery, and to teach the Chinese *perspective*' (1:265–66). 'Old China', like the letter, posits that Chinese art lacks 'perspective'. The porcelain images of 'men and women [who] float about, uncircumscribed by any element' serves as an apt assessment of

---

[14] John R. Haddad, 'Imagined Journeys to Distant Cathay: Constructing China with Ceramics, 1780–1920', *Winterthur Portfolio* 41, no. 1 (Spring 2007): 53–80.

[15] Francis L. Hawks, *Narrative of the Expedition of an American Squadron to the China Seas and Japan 1852–54* (New York: D. Appleton, 1856), 135.

[16] David Porter, *Ideographia: the Chinese Cipher in Early Modern Europe* (Stanford: Stanford University Press, 2001), 135.

Manning's footloose existence in Asia as well as an observation on art that appears to lack structure. Yet this is not haphazard, uncultivated Chinese artistry comparable to prehistoric craft, but an Orientalist aesthetic of asymmetry that had been adopted in eighteenth-century Britain under the faux-Chinese name *sharawadgi*. The cup is both exotic for its Asian pattern, and familiar because of its ubiquity in Britain, to the extent that the characters depicted are 'old friends'. Comparably, Elia's appreciation of the 'men with women's faces' accords with a Chinese preference for delicately featured males, but also adumbrates his interest in stage comedy, with its play on gender-roles and tradition of cross-dressing (2:248). The imagery painted on the porcelain appears to illustrate a mythical Chinese past, and the 'world before perspective' suggests antiquity, but the plate was probably made in Staffordshire within the previous thirty-five years. Lamb's syntax is unclear in this phrase. He may mean that the cup is itself, before the viewer's 'perspective', a separate and self-contained 'world'.

If the aesthetic of Elia's porcelain purports to be Chinese, the narrative that gradually emerged of the most popular Willow design is Ovidian. Read as narrative, the Willow motifs form a tale of two thwarted lovers who, pitied by the gods, are transformed into doves. The story (of which more below) does not correspond to any discernible Chinese source, and its most pertinent literary analogue is *Metamorphoses*. Christopher Allen observes that visual artists were attracted to Ovidian subject-matter by 'a mood that is at once magical and ironic, a floating, fictional environment in which the mythic imagination is allowed free play', an appraisal that also captures the spirit of Lamb's essay on the tea set.[17]

By allusion to Keats in his essay, Lamb avails himself of a classicism that, like *chinoiserie*, has unsteady cultural foundations. Keats's ode describes an urn that is imaginary rather than real. He may have been in awe of the Elgin Marbles, but Keats has also been described as 'near . . . obsessed' with Wedgwood neoclassicism. Dwight E. Robinson terms 'Maternal Affection', a jasper decoration first produced by Wedgwood from Lady Templetown's design in 1788, an 'almost totally English' derivative from the Portland Vase, a first-century Roman artefact. Connecting imagery in Keats's poetry both to the *bona fide* relic, the

---

[17] Christopher Allen, 'Ovid and Art', in *The Cambridge Companion to Ovid* (Cambridge: Cambridge University Press, 2002), 354.

Portland Vase, and to the neoclassical 'Maternal Affection', Robinson provides a parallel for the non-Chinese principles of *chinoiserie* when he elaborates that the sentimental 'Maternal Affection' is a 'Briton's dream of what classical art *should* have been like'.[18] The domestic scene of a mother caressing her daughter is not an image typical of classical-Greek pottery. With such influences, Keats's 'Ode on a Grecian Urn' is bound neither to the reality of a particular object nor the canon of creative principles derived from a specific time and place. Keats describes an artistic ideal, but his 'Attic shape' may not be of thoroughbred Attic origin (1). Lamb's essay, consequently, is an idea of China informed by an idea of antiquity, as opposed to a description of a Chinese artefact juxtaposed with paradigmatic relics of Greece and Rome.

The unusual connection that 'Old China' makes with Keats, and Elia's elusiveness about his aesthetic commitment to *chinoiserie*, enable him to make useful insights to receptions of Chinese culture in 1820s London. As Elia contemplates the porcelain, his predominant response is that the exotic novelty of the crockery has faded. It, like his choice of Hyson tea, has become 'old-fashioned' (1:248). Hence, ekphrastic reflection on the cup and saucer prompts a personal reverie. Personal trajectory is plotted by consumption: Elia measures the course of his life by the purchases he has made. He gauges his own social status against the changing reception of *chinoiserie* in cosmopolitan London. By ironic ekphrasis, and implicit juxtaposition of commonplace porcelain with the idealized Grecian Urn, Elia alerts us to the capricious nature of consumer fads in comparison with the reverence afforded to timeless art. He delineates an economy in which Chinese goods and aesthetics were imported, and considers fluctuations in their popularity during his lifetime.

Generally, the ekphrastic method of 'Old China' brings to mind Lamb's enjoyment of Keats's 1820 volume. Elia's crockery is more directly indebted to the Grecian Urn in its imagery. Like Keats's Urn, the design on Lamb's plate is imaginary. Such association of commonplace *chinoiserie* with classicism was not outlandish. The two writers would have associated both *chinoiserie* and classical motifs with Wedgwood. Lamb's description of the cup and saucer as 'azure tinted' evokes the unwieldy vase in *The East Offering its Riches to Britannia*, but also

---

[18] Dwight E. Robinson, 'Imprint of Wedgwood in the Longer Poems of Keats', *Keats-Shelley Journal* 16 (Winter 1967): 27.

Wedgwood's range of blue jasperware, for which John Flaxman provided neoclassical designs from 1775. Furthermore, Elia's crockery has more specific relevance to the Grecian Urn. He describes on its surface 'a young and courtly Mandarin, handing tea to a lady from a salver—two miles off' (1:248). This image recalls the frustrated youth of Keats's poem:

> Bold Lover, never, never canst thou kiss,
>   Though winning near the goal—yet, do not grieve;
>   She cannot fade, though thou hast not thy bliss,
>   For ever wilt thou love, and she be fair!
>
> (17–20)

In each text, the viewer implies that enforced stasis is an enviable alternative to the effect of time. Echoing Keats's 'cannot fade', Elia greets the Mandarin and lady as his 'old friends whom distance cannot diminish'. But while Keats consoles the lover with reference to the endurance of passion in the world of the Urn, and the maiden's immortal beauty, Lamb jokes at the separation of the Mandarin from the lady: 'See how distance seems to set off respect!' The Greek lovers' ardour is refigured in a parody of dispassionate Chinese etiquette, the kiss replaced by the act of serving tea. Lamb's humour occurs at the expense of Chinese protocol, but it also requires the reader to consider that the kiss and the tea ceremony might be equivalent gestures in their respective cultures. The tautologous phrase 'courtly Mandarin' intimates stuffy social rules. Although he acts within the parameters of his imagined social-context, the 'young and courtly Mandarin' is neither less 'bold' nor less deeply frustrated than the Grecian lover (2:248). The translation of the unfulfilled romantic gesture from kiss to tea service parallels the transformation of classical influences evident in Wedgwood's sentimental vision of antiquity.

Elia notes a 'rabbit and cow' depicted on his cup, which are 'couchant'—a word with which Keats introduces Lamia—and 'co-extensive' (2:248). Elia's animals are transformed from their ordinary existence in a manner comparable to the cow in Keats's 'Grecian Urn':

> Who are these coming to the sacrifice?
>   To what green altar, O mysterious priest,
>   Lead'st thou that heifer lowing at the skies,
>   And all her silken flanks with garlands drest?
>
> (31–34)

The 'heifer' has become enigmatic in its garlands, and by its involvement in an eerie, ancient sacrifice. Similarly, Elia finds that the images of the cow and oversized rabbit have deeper significance than their familiar referents; they become exotic when 'seen through the lucid atmosphere of fine Cathay'. In a further image, the lady steps 'into a little fairy boat' (2:248). If the animals signify a ceremony any more mysterious than the tea service, whether the woman flees as in the conventional Willow narrative, and if the man and woman are united at the top of the saucer, transformed into birds, we are not to know. Elia ceases analysis of the porcelain itself as more personal reflections arise. He gazes into his cup, realizes that his choice of unmixed Hyson tea is 'old fashioned', and ponders the significance of outdated tastes. The moment of distraction encapsulates consumerism itself as one commodity is ignored for another.

Elia reveals that the 'set of extraordinary old blue china (a recent purchase)' was beyond his means in his youth, when *chinoiserie* was popular. By contrast, he writes that 'of late years . . . we could afford to please the eyes with some trifles of this sort' (2:248). Cousin Bridget, proxy for Mary Lamb in Elia's essays, observes that 'a thing was worth buying then, when we felt the money we paid for it' (2:249). Bridget's final remark to Elia does not distinguish the cup and saucer with the elevated tone of ekphrasis, but halts the imaginative exercise by causing the crockery to appear ridiculous: '"Now do look at that merry little Chinese waiter holding an umbrella, big enough for a bed-tester, over that pretty insipid half Madona-ish chit of a lady in that very blue summer-house"' (2:252). Bridget's language—'waiter', 'Madona', 'umbrella'—strips the crockery of exoticness and mystery. The lady's eternal youth is an 'insipid' state. The bureaucratic origin of the word 'chit' recalls the banal means by which Elia paid for the tea set. That the essay both dignifies and derides the crockery causes us to wonder whether Elia first desired it only because it was popular, and attached himself to a symbol of economic aspiration in youth. The uneven popular opinion of *chinoiserie*, amidst which Elia now finds himself a man of kitsch tastes, is akin to canonical Romantic authors' admiration for Ovid in an age that generally dismissed him as 'as artificial, trivial, and insincere'.[19] This commonality is noteworthy because, as I shall

---

[19] David Hopkins, 'Ovid', in *The Oxford History of Classical Reception in English Literature III: 1660–1790*, ed. David Hopkins and Charles Martindale (Oxford: Oxford University Press, 2012), 197–8.

discuss, Lamb and Ovid are the two authors who definitively shape nineteenth-century literature on Wedgwood *chinoiserie*, despite their works being associated with poor taste in various ways.

Modern critics have seized upon the first sentence of Lamb's essay, which seems to corroborate perceptions that appreciation of porcelain was gendered in the Romantic period: 'I have an almost feminine partiality for old china' (2:247). Beth Kowaleski-Wallace cites Lamb in her study of porcelain. She proposes that crockery symbolizes a certain kind of female consumer who, like a piece of china, was preoccupied with appearance: all surface, like a plate, or hollow inside, as a cup (154).[20] Joanna Baillie's 'Lines to a Tea-Pot' (composed 1790) is a useful analogue for Lamb's essay. This poem addresses a teapot, describing its illustration, and subsequently imagines its journey from China to Britain, and its fortunes as a consumer good. Baillie (1762–1851) portrays the fashionable women who compete for china sets at auction:

> dames of pride
> In morning farthingals, scarce two yards wide,
> With collared lap-dogs snarling in their arms,
> Contend in rival keenness for thy charms.

> (51–54)

Kowaleski-Wallace cites novels such as Frances Burney's *Camilla* (1796) and Susan Ferrier's *Marriage* (1818), in which women with keen interest in their china collections also neglect their families. While men imported china, women domesticated it.

Lamb raises the cliché of the female china aficionada, but manipulates it. His essay is more than evidence that this stereotype existed. Having acknowledged his 'feminine partiality' for porcelain, Elia becomes defensive: 'I had no repugnance then—why should I now have?' (2:248). Gender roles are reversed in the essay, as Elia hints by reference to the 'men with women's faces'. Scenes from Elia and Bridget's life together are set out like images on the porcelain. We see Elia 'thread-bare' in his youth, having spent his money on an old folio of Beaumont and Fletcher for Bridget (2:249). The two walk, not by Chinese streams with 'fairy' boats, but on the banks of the Lea (2:250). The story of transformation is not from human to dove, but from poverty to affluence. Elia and Bridget

---

[20] Beth Kowaleski-Wallace, 'Women, China and Consumer Culture in Eighteenth-Century England', *Eighteenth-Century Studies* 29, no. 2 (1995): 154.

correspond to the couple on the crockery, but it is Bridget who, like the young Mandarin, is unsatisfied. She assumes the masculine role, assessing the crockery sceptically in relation to household finances and her fatigue with other luxuries, such as strawberries. It is Elia, preoccupied with appearances, who is 'too proud to see a play anywhere now but in the pit' (2:250). Since the two can now quite easily afford such 'trifles' as porcelain, Bridget laments that 'we have no reckoning at all at the end of the old year—no flattering promises about the new year doing better for us' (2:251). The two bonded in financial difficulties that compelled them to set their budget carefully, an annual ritual in which they reconciled (masculine) earning with (feminine) expenditure. Unlike the youth on his crockery, Elia has at last possessed what he desired, but to Bridget, the porcelain has become a symbol for age rather than attainment. Unlike the lady on the crockery, she has had her tea, and is disappointed. Bridget envies eternal tantalization, the Keatsian stasis of the figures on Elia's crockery. Perhaps Lamb's autobiographical Elia gazes on the crockery with deeper regret at what might have been. It was Josiah Wedgwood—flush from the proceeds of *chinoiserie* and neoclassicism—who paid Coleridge's annuity from 1798 to 1812.

The background to the change in Elia's fortunes from admirer to owner of porcelain *chinoiserie*, and the shift in public reception of Chinese aesthetics from popularity to disdain, is a broader change in attitudes to China during Lamb's lifetime. While the British public of the 1820s had not tipped towards the hostility to China that characterized mid-nineteenth century attitudes, it had lost what had been considerable respect for the country. It is not only Elia's porcelain that has become 'Old China'. The essay captures the demise of an imaginary, sophisticated Cathay, and new conceptions of a China that the British public disdained.

Material culture dictated British popular opinion on China. Perception of China's industrial achievements influenced the spirit in which most British thinkers considered the country's history and culture. Since *The Travels of Marco Polo*, Western accounts of China fixated upon consumer goods. British travel to China was almost entirely motivated by acquisition, not intellectual enrichment. Porcelain fascinated the visitors so long as they could not replicate it. Alluding to this period, Lamb terms ceramics '*speciosa miracula*' (2:248). The manufacture of china mystified foreigners, amongst whom legends arose of procedures that took centuries. This awe deteriorated slowly during the eighteenth century. When German potters first made their own porcelain in 1710, Europeans realized that their efforts were hindered by lack of the correct materials rather than ignorance of an intricate process. In 1754, beds of the necessary kaolin clay were discovered in Cornwall, and thus British potters were equipped to make their own porcelain. This advancement did not cause an immediate collapse in demand for Chinese crockery. John Bell, a Scot who accompanied a Russian embassy to China in 1763, published a memoir that reinforced the myth of esoteric Chinese craftsmanship, 'still . . . unrivalled by . . . any other nation'.[21] Macartney notes that 'great quantities' of porcelain were still purchased by European merchants in Canton, where artists decorated crockery to Western tastes.[22] Baillie's position is a kind of compromise. The Chinese pottery is simultaneously a site of expertise and of barbarism, with the former European belief in esoteric Asian knowledge replaced by hints of black magic. The craftsman appears a kind of wizard to the near-naked 'urchin group' before him in Baillie's Orientalist tableau. Well might these peasants stand amazed at the 'potter's wheel', a device unknown in China, but which is nonetheless at the centre of Baillie's scene:

> When round the potter's wheel, their chins raising,
> An urchin group in silent wonder gazing,
> Stood and beheld, as, touched with magic skill,
> The whirling clay swift fashioned to his will,—
> Saw mazy motion stopped, and then the toy
> Complete before their eyes, and grinned for joy;
> Clapping their naked sides with blythe halloo,
> And curtailed words of praise, like ting, tung, too!
> The brown-skinned artist, with his unclothed waist
> And girded loins, who, slow and patient, traced,
> Beneath his humble shed, this fair array
> Of pictured forms upon thy surface gay.

(29–40)

The ability to replicate Chinese production gradually brought about a decline in respect for China. As Baillie's poem progresses, the teapot is

---

[21] John Bell, *Travels from St. Petersburg in Russia to Diverse Parts of Asia*, 2 vols (Glasgow: Foulis, 1763), 2:57.
[22] Cranmer-Byng, *Embassy to China*, 42.

auctioned again, but it has become unfashionable. Its appraisers are 'no longer the gay, the young', but 'sober connoisseurs, with wrinkled brow'. Finally the piece is unwanted:

> Like moody statesman in his rural den,
> From power dismissed
> . . .
> Thou rest'st in most ignoble uselessness.
>
> (125–29)

Elia is one of the 'sober connoisseurs'. His interest in porcelain dates him. Yet the fortunes of ceramic *chinoiserie* continued to fluctuate in the nineteenth century. The reception of Lamb's 'Old China' is bound to these trends.

'Talked of in China': Willow Narratives and Later Servings of Lamb

Lamb's essays have exerted a forceful presence in Anglophone culture. The two pieces on China were particularly popular. 'Roast Pig' endured by frequent republication, particularly in school textbooks. 'Old China' is important, less directly, as a source for the narratives that arose on Willow imagery during the nineteenth century.

'Roast Pig' was instantly canonical. In 1826 the essay was included in *The Modern Speaker*, a collection of exemplary works for aspiring rhetoricians. A discussion of roasted piglets in Charles Dickens's *Nicholas Nickleby* (1839) echoes Lamb's macabre details. Mrs Nickleby likens the cooked animals to 'very little babies'.[23] 'Roast Pig' has been reproduced on hundreds of occasions, from periodicals that adopted materials from other publications, to canon-forming anthologies such as *The Golden Treasury* (1883). One volume includes Lamb's piece under the title *Crowned Masterpieces of Eloquence that have Advanced Civilization* (1902). From the mid-nineteenth to the mid-twentieth century, 'Roast Pig' was ubiquitous in English schoolbooks. As recently as 1985 the essay

---

[23] Charles Dickens, *Nicholas Nickleby*, ed. Paul Schlike, Oxford World's Classics (Oxford: Oxford University Press, 2009), 163.

was included in an anthology for students of English as a foreign language.[24]

The obscurity of Lamb's Neoplatonic source has led some commentators to assume that the essay is a direct commentary on China. In 1825, *The Every Day Book* reproduced Lamb's 'Roast Pig' with a significant alteration. Dedicating his anthology to the essayist, editor William Hone provides his own introductory paraphrase in place of Lamb's first paragraph: 'Elia, author of the incomparable volume of "Essays", . . . indulges in a "Dissertation in Roast Pig." He cites a Chinese MS. to establish its origin.'[25] Here Elia appears to have made a closer engagement with Chinese culture than he does in the original text. A 1909 reprint of 'Roast Pig' is preceded by an editorial note which is unsure whether the humour of the essay precludes the possibility of a textual source: 'Whether this story is founded upon historical evidence I am unable to say but according to the author, the whole art of cooking originated in China.'[26] Such puzzlement indicates contradictory aspects to the status the essay has attained. Anthologizing it as an uncontested masterpiece, editors have upheld 'Roast Pig' as a model essay, a tour-de-force of wit and eloquence, despite widespread confusion over its content. In 1922, an American teacher wrote to the National Council of Teachers of English, concerned that, although high-school texts would 'invariably' include 'Roast Pig', nobody seemed to understand the essay.[27]

From the mid-twentieth century, the reception of 'Roast Pig' has been uneven. Some readers have been uncertain how to interpret Lamb's humour. Others overlook the humour entirely in service of their research themes. Present-day values, applied retrospectively to 'Roast Pig', often lead commentators to read the essay as sincere and so to justify its critical neglect, much as is the case with de Quincey's China essays, as I discuss in Chapter 6. Animal-studies scholar Richard W. Bulliett reads 'Roast Pig' as an imaginative expansion of the theory that cooked meat was discovered accidentally. 'Charles Lamb cast this logical supposition in its

---

[24] Charles M. Cobb, *Process and Pattern: Controlled Composition for ESL Students* (Belmont, California: Wadsworth Publishing Company, 1985).
[25] William Hone ed., *The Every Day Book*, or, a *Guide to the Year*, 2 vols (London: William Tegg, 1825), 2:218.
[26] *The Timberman*, 11 (1909): 69.
[27] Clarence S. Dike, 'The Humor of "Roast Pig"', *The English Journal* 11, no. 5 (1922): 288.

classic form,' Bulliett writes. Exasperated, he attacks Lamb for his want of realism: 'The notion that [farmers] would have started deliberately preserving and then kindling fires just to cook meat without first becoming expert at acquiring game defies logic.'[28] A student discussion of 'Roast Pig' at Northwestern University terms the work 'an attack on the Chinese' and 'horribly racist'.[29] A 2010 feature in *The Guardian* makes no reference to sources, but celebrates Lamb's humour: 'the Romantic essayist imagines how the Chinese discovered the joys of roast pork with crackling'.[30] Regardless of whether they know their Porphyry, I suspect that most contemporary readers recognized Lamb's pseudo-epigraphy as absurd, and treated his piece as light entertainment, with no expectation of reliable information on China.

Compared to 'Roast Pig', the cultural impact of 'Old China' has been subtle, but is no less significant. The piece inspired a tradition of writing about Willow crockery. Despite its decline in popularity during Lamb's lifetime, Willow did not disappear from use. It had nostalgic collectors, such as Elia, and genuine demand for the design revived during the Victorian period. The dominant interpretation of Willow imagery as a transformation narrative gained solidity. The earliest surviving prose account of the story appeared in *Bentley's Miscellany* in 1838, under the editorship of Dickens, alongside part of the serialized *Oliver Twist*. The essay, entitled 'A True History of the Celebrated Wedgewood [sic] Hieroglyph, Commonly Called the Willow Pattern', was authored by Mark Lemon (1809–70). Lemon so admired Lamb that twelve incidents in his anecdotal *Jest Book* (1865) concern the essayist. In his farcical treatment of Willow motifs, Lemon both continues Lamb's humorous treatment of porcelain and perpetuates the Ovidian interpretation of its imagery. Lemon depicts the house that appears on Willow sets in the language of an estate agent. The lakeside setting of 'THIS SINGULARLY ELIGIBLE PROPERTY', he writes, is 'a particular desideratum in this land of tea. . . . A bow-window, admirably situated for FISHING, BATHING, OR SUICIDE, overhangs the lake.' In accordance with Lamb's remark that the

---

[28] Richard W. Bulliett, *Hunters, Herders, and Hamburgers* (New York: Columbia University Press, 2005), 56–7.

[29] 'Cosmopolitanism and Composition', http://pidgeonenglish.blogspot.co.uk/2005/05/dissertation-upon-roast-pig.html (accessed 12 March 2016).

[30] 'Ten of the best pigs in literature', *The Guardian*, 21 August 2010. http://www.theguardian.com/books/2010/aug/21/ten-best-pigs-in-literature (accessed 5 July 2019).

figures on *chinoiserie* 'float about, uncircumscribed by any element', to discern the principles of *sharawadgi* from the estate is a Sphinx' riddle to Lemon: 'The arrangement of the grounds has "TASK'D THE INGENUITY OF MAN" (*Sophocles*).'[31] He remarks on the 'PRUSSIAN-BLUE complexion' of the estate, and the willow tree that 'has given it celebrity as undying as that of the STAFFORDSHIRE POTTERIES'. Whereas Lamb's Keatsian ekphrasis gently mocks his subject by association with classical ideals, Lemon ridicules Willow crockery with his inflated treatment. He resigns his account of the house with a declaration of ineffability, in which he quotes Benjamin Jowett's commentary on Plato's allegory of the chariot: 'the force of language can no farther go' (63).

Further to Lamb's witty *ekphrasis*, Peter Perring Thoms's *Chinese Courtship in Verse* (1824) is likely to have inspired aspects of Lemon's Willow narrative. Thoms translates a *muyu* (木鱼), a popular Cantonese form that intersperses prose with verse and musical accompaniment. Lemon's treatment of the Willow love story with the language of estate agents recalls the unlikely pairing of subjects signalled by Thoms's subtitle: *to which is added an Appendix, treating of the Revenue of China*. This translator also identifies the absence of Graeco-Roman supernaturalism as a deficiency. In *Chinese Courtship*, true love is swayed by the relative banalities of study and a Tartar rebellion. Lemon takes a hint from Thoms's introduction that a Chinese love-story could benefit from classical ingredients: 'Though the Chinese are fond of poetry, they have no Epic poems; and while they are wanting of those beauties which distinguish the works of the Roman and Grecian Poets, they have nothing that resemble the extravagance of their Gods and Goddesses.'[32]

Initially the story Lemon transposes onto Willow porcelain is that of Hero and Leander. He imagines the former owner of the house as 'Chou-chu, vender of areca-nuts and betel'. The merchant's daughter, Si-so, 'had . . . some very preposterous ideas', from Chou-chu's perspective, on 'who was most likely to suit her for a husband'. Consequently, unbeknown to her father, Si-so 'might have been nightly seen watching, like another Hero, the progress of a celestial Leander (in a boat). . . .

---

[31] *Bentley's Miscellany* 3 (1838): 62. Hereafter cited parenthetically.
[32] Peter Perring Thoms trans., 花箋: *Chinese Courtship in Verse; to which is added an Appendix, treating of the Revenue of China* (London: Parbury, Allen, and Kingsbury, 1824), iii.

Ting-a-ting (Si-so's Leander) was one of the sweetest minstrels in Fou-loo' (63). The formal behaviour of the characters on Lamb's crockery, in comparison with the lovers on Keats's Urn, is echoed in Lemon's departure from the lusty words of Hero and Leander in *Heroides* (18–19). In this naïve tale, Ting-a-ting does not bed Si-so, but keeps a respectful distance and serenades her from the garden. The two enjoy a 'delightful interchange of soul', which we understand is without physical contact (64).

When the lovers' nocturnal exchanges are betrayed by a series of noises—a wayward, airborne bouquet; Ting-a-ting falling on his sitar—Chou-chu decides to act. He finds a potential husband for Si-so, in the belief that an arranged marriage will curtail the advances of the unsuitable Ting-a-ting. At the climax of Lemon's tale, a distraught Ting-a-ting arrives at the wedding uninvited:

> Si-so . . . rushed towards her lover, who . . . 'buried a dagger in his own heart.' Amazement for a while blinded the spectators, and when they did recover their perceptive faculties, the bodies of Si-so and Ting-a-ting had disappeared; but perched upon the sill of the window were two doves of extraordinary dimensions.   (65)

Lemon switches from *Heroides* to *Metamorphoses* to save the lovers. While many characters in *Metamorphoses* become birds (such as Philomela, Cycnus, Nyctimene, Picus, and Cornix), Lemon's tale recalls particularly the aggrieved lover Aesacus, transformed to a bird in the act of suicide (11.749–95). However, Lemon provides an Orientalist provenance for the transformation of Si-so and Ting-a-ting. The lovers are converts to 'the doctrine of metempsychosis' preached by 'the great philosopher Fum'. While 'metempsychosis' implies transmigration of the soul, it is clear that Lemon means that physical transformation befalls the Fumites: 'anticipating death, they insisted on being something else' (61). It is an imperfect process that leaves us with two unaccountably large doves. Nonetheless Lemon concludes that 'Fumism had proved the divinity of its origin' (65).

Versions of the Willow narrative that followed Lemon's essay are inconsistent in their reception of the tale as serious or ridiculous, as a recent fabrication or a Chinese legend of distant origin. In 1849 an American journal, *The Family Friend*, included a synopsis of the Willow story. 'Who is there', the author wonders, 'since the earliest dawn of intelligent perception, who has not inquisitively contemplated the mysterious figures on the willow-pattern plate?'[33] The piece recounts the same episodes as Lemon's essay, with additional details. The most obvious departure from Lemon is that the *Family Friend* account assumes a scholarly tone, as though it summarizes an established, literary work. A subsequent issue of *The Family Friend* features a puzzle that accentuates Ovidian aspects of the Willow narrative. It is a maze puzzle, with labyrinthine walls laid over the image of a Willow plate (Figure 4.2). The reader's goal is to trace a path to the house at the centre of the maze. The puzzle is accompanied by couplets, delivered in the persona of the

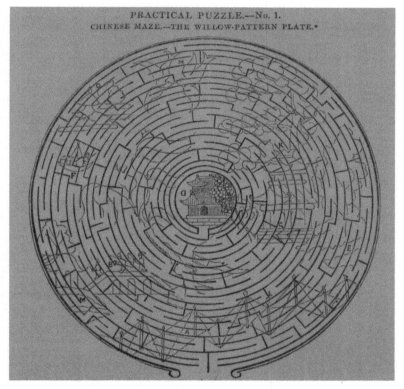

Figure 4.2 A puzzle in *The Family Friend* accentuates the Ovidian aspects of the Willow narrative.

Photo courtesy of the Matheson Library.

[33] *The Family Friend*, 1 (1849), 124.

maiden. As in the journal's prose account of Willow imagery, the maiden is here named Koong-see. The maiden awaits in the house, and her verse encourages us to reach her. Each couplet is marked with a letter that corresponds to a segment of the maze, and therefore to a part of the underlying plate and its derivative episode in the Willow story. The reader, who undertakes the maze, becomes Leander to Koong-See's Hero.[34] The verse elaborates on the similarities between Leander's Hellespont swim and the challenge of the maze. Ovid's Hero longs for her lover, but knows that to encourage Leander endangers him in treacherous waters. 'Koong-see's Whispers' encourages a journey in defiance of parental disapproval; comparably we infer from Hero and Leander's secrecy that they are very young lovers. The reader of *Heroides* knows that Leander's efforts will prove fatal. Like Hero's letter to Leander, Koong-see's verse juxtaposes risk and reward rationally, but is troubled by a sense of imminent catastrophe:

> B   Beware of rivals—mischief hovers near;
>   Or, worse mischance, parental frowns appear.
>
> . . .
>
> E   The ground is rough, and difficult the road;
>   But, faint not, thou shalt reach thy love's abode!
>
> F   Against thy course runs the opposing tide,
>   And waves of trouble cast thy hopes aside.
>
> G   A modest competence thy lot will be;
>   But richer joys than wealth are stored for thee.
>
> H   Take heed! take heed! a strange transforming doom
>   May fix thy love, but never let it bloom.[35]

The heroic couplet-form recalls Christopher Marlowe's humorous *Hero and Leander* (1598). While Kong-see urges her suitor to 'kindle up a flame' (A), Leander's 'secret flame' is detected by his irate father in Marlowe's treatment:

---

[34] Byron had made Leander's Hellespont a motif for challenge in *Don Juan* (1819, 2.837–40) and 'Written after Swimming from Sestos to Abydos' (1810).

[35] *The Family Friend*, 2 (1850): 34. The puzzle was reprinted in various books including *Family Pastime* (1852), *The Magician's Own Book* (1857), and *The Book of 500 Curious Puzzles* (1859).

> The light of hidden fire itself discovers,
> And love that is concealed betrays poor lovers.

(617–19)

Koong-see promises 'richer joys than wealth', an offer of love in language that echoes the 'rich jewels' of Hero's body as described by Marlowe (724). A further analogue for 'Koong-see's Whispers' exists in Tennyson's 'Hero to Leander' (1830), which—rather than Marlowe's irony—captures the emotion of *Heroides* and Leigh Hunt's *Hero and Leander* (1819):

> Oh! kiss me, kiss me, once again,
>> Lest thy kiss should be the last.
>> Oh kiss me ere we part;
>> Grow closer to my heart.
> My heart is warmer surely than the bosom of the main

(5–9).

Closer to Tennyson than Marlowe, *The Family Friend*'s sentimental presentation of the Willow tale is likely to have influenced a nineteenth-century nursery rhyme: 'A kindly power, by pity stirred, | Changed each into a beautiful bird'.[36]

The Mandarin's Daughter! (1851), a farce produced at Punch's Theatre, retains the names that *The Family Friend* account assigns to characters in the Willow story, but revives Lemon's disrespectful humour, and is dubious about the notion that the story was originally Asian. The entertainment begins with an address from magician Chim-Pan-See, who announces that he was enticed to visit London by reports of the Great Exhibition. 'But conceive my surprise', he says, to find a familiar story displayed on Willow crockery:

> On plate, cup, and saucer, dish, basin, tureen,
> A picture, which is but a full illustration
> Of an olden love story, well known in my nation.[37]

When Chim-Pan-See surmised that the British public had cultivated respect for Chinese legend, he was quickly undeceived:

---

[36] Anthologized, for example, in Ada Walker Camehl ed., *The Blue-China Book* (New York: E.P. Dutton, 1916), 287.

[37] W.P. Hale, *The Mandarin's Daughter!* (London: Thomas Hailes Lacy, 1851), 4.

> For when I told the story, they said 'You be blowed,
> That's the old willow pattern of Copeland and Spode!'[38]

Hence, Chim-Pan-See proposes to correct misconceptions on the Willow narrative. He introduces the characters depicted on the plate, who emerge onstage to perform the tale of forbidden love and elopement. Yet in assuming characters, the actors do not take the personae of Chinese legend. There are metadramatic references to contemporary Britain, and slang is used throughout. The actors, like the Willow tale, don Orientalist garb, but have British identity. Lovers Koong-See and Chang marry rather than metamorphose at the conclusion, and announce their intention to honeymoon in London.[39]

Apparently the sentimentality of the Willow story proved the basis of its longevity. Basil Hood's comic operetta *The Willow Pattern* (1901) portrays China as a carefree, Orientalist playground, while insisting that the aesthetic and the tale itself are ancient and Chinese:

> A thousand years ago I fancy was the date
> When the pretty willow pattern first was put upon a plate.[40]

Hood accentuates the Ovidian aspects of his source in Lemon by making the divine, transformative power tangible and anthropomorphic:

> The God of Lovers chang'd them
> Into turtle-doves for safety.[41]

A further song clarifies the point in the guise of the deity:

> Nid-Nod I'm a Chinese God
> With disposition sunny![42]

Closest of all accounts to the Willow tale's literary source in Ovid, by its humane gods and the culminative device of transformation, Hood's operetta simultaneously makes the most unabashed claims to Chinese origins. His work is oblivious to the satirical tradition that derides the origins of the Willow narrative. With the mutual accentuation of its classical elements and its *chinoiserie* aesthetic, the Willow narrative had stabilized as a sentimental tale fit for romantic comedy.

---

[38] Hale, *The Mandarin's Daughter!*, 4.   [39] Hale, *The Mandarin's Daughter!*, 25.
[40] Basil Hood, *The Willow Pattern* (London: Chappell, 1901), 64.
[41] Hood, *The Willow Pattern*, 70.   [42] Hood, *The Willow Pattern*, 74.

Ovid was unfashionable for much of the period covered by this book, but other names that have arisen so far in this study of China have never been canonical. It is remarkable that Keats and Lamb, who felt excluded from classics, were drawn to peripheral figures from the ancient world. We might speculate that one appeal of the marginal text to the marginalized reader is that the material has not such a tradition of arrogation by scholars: there's less interpretative baggage and, with that, a certain freedom for imaginative usage. More crucial to our understanding of how classics informs Anglophone visions of China is to register that the authors making these relations did not always rely on the established, timeless paradigms or canonical works. This China reflects the liveliness of nineteenth-century classical debate, representing such areas of contemporary inquiry as Rome's transition from Empire to church, and late antiquity in general. In the next chapter, by contrast, Tennyson's adherence to the ultra-canonical Homer and Virgil has much to do with the popular and personal opinion of his own canonicity. Invoking these predecessors in contemplations of China, he speaks to Britain's affairs with a Virgilian sense of duty to account of expansion overseas.

The decline of Lamb's popularity to modern readers accords with a general loss of interest in the familiar essay as a genre. The trend parallels the changes in British attitudes to *chinoiserie* that Lamb communicates, and the alteration in perceptions of the Chinese: once regarded with awe as advanced beings, later derided as backwards. But aspects of China, like Greek and Roman antiquity, had been ingested and assimilated by Britain. For all their synthesis of classical sources and Orientalism, Lamb's essays—like Willow crockery—endure as British culture. The most remarkable evidence for this claim is perhaps that 'Roast Pig' was reprinted in a Taiwanese university textbook in 1939.[43] As Lamb foretold, his work spread to distant corners of Asia. That a Chinese community would anthologize his work to teach English confirms that 'Roast Pig', despite its Neoplatonic source and Orientalist vision of China, is a work of English wit above all.

To the extent that the Elia essays portray Lamb himself, a therapeutic aspect is detectable in the works on China. Lamb's instinctive reaction to

---

[43] Fook-Tan Ching ed., *Freshman Readings in English* (Taipei: Taiwan Commercial Press, 1939).

foreigners is xenophobic. He confesses these sentiments in an 1815 letter. Here Lamb responds to Southey's Orientalist poetry:

I do not willingly admit of strange beliefs or out-of-the-way creeds or places. . . . I can just endure Moors, because of their connection as foes with Christians; but Abyssinians, Ethiops, Esquimaux, Dervises, and all that tribe, I hate. I believe I fear them in some manner.   (2:164)

Unlike de Quincey (whose reluctance to analyse his blistering rage towards Asia I assess in Chapter 6), Lamb perceives that beneath his own disdain lies 'fear'. When he imagines a Keatsian lover in ceramics, and shares a love of pork with Chinese peasants, he establishes common ground, and so gestures towards recovery. In a letter that echoes his conjecture that 'Roast Pig' might be enjoyed by a Hindu readership, Lamb urges Manning to remember him to a Factory Employee at Canton. It is though, like his transcultural tale, Lamb himself could be reimagined in Asia: 'I should like to have my name talked of in China' (2:8).

5

'Better Fifty Years of Europe than a Cycle of Cathay'

British Progress, the Opium Trade, and Tennyson's Retrospection

Alfred Tennyson (1809–92) associates the undiscovered country of the future with literal exploration of exotic realms in 'Locksley Hall' (1842). In a famous passage, the railway exemplifies British pre-eminence:

> Not in vain the distance beckons. Forward, forward let us range,
> Let the great world spin for ever down the ringing grooves of change.
>
> (181–82)

This dizzying contraption is a triumph in itself, but can also bear its inventors to further achievement. Metaphorically, Britain surges into a 'younger day' by railway. The 'great world' follows, a wheel impelled by a British engine. In the age of conquest, 'Britain' even has the potential to become metonymical for the 'great world'. 'Let', the imperative that commands passivity, assures us that Providence has laid out the grooves to the future. Tennyson may also intend, more plainly, an allusion to railway construction in India. This endeavour commenced in 1832, three years before Tennyson began to compose 'Locksley Hall'. Railway was both a representative of scientific achievement and a mechanism of imperial control. The former might justify the latter in pro-imperial rhetoric.

Tennyson's subsequent lines indicate the role allocated to China in the Victorian zeitgeist. The poem invites the obvious juxtaposition of Britain with China, but also of India, as beneficiary of British industry, with China as subject of a different empire, the Qing:

China from the Ruins of Athens and Rome: Classics, Sinology, and Romanticism, 1793–1938.
Chris Murray, Oxford University Press (2020). © Chris Murray.
DOI: 10.1093/oso/9780198767015.001.0001

Through the shadow of the globe we sweep into the younger day:
Better fifty years of Europe than a cycle of Cathay.

(183–84)

To many readers these lines constitute 'the *locus classicus* for students of Tennyson the apostle of progress'.[1] Because the speaker describes a disappointment in love that bears some resemblance to Tennyson's experience, readers have tended to assume that the character's sentiments are the poet's. Historical and critical studies reproduce these lines, without attention to their context, as evidence of the arrogance behind British imperialism and even as 'a term of contempt' for China.[2] As the word was archaic long before the nineteenth century, Tennyson's adoption of 'Cathay' for 'China' accentuates disparity: a stagnant China acts as foil to a progressive Britain. 'Cathay' was rare and self-consciously literary; Tennyson's usage recalls Byron's situation of 'Ceylon, Inde, or far Cathay' in distant time as well as space in *Don Juan* (1824, 9.66). In the relevant part of 'Locksley Hall', the tone blends superciliousness and jubilance. The narrator makes an implicit case for empire. Yet it would be erroneous to interpret Tennyson's words as a ringing endorsement, so to speak, of British imperialism, or even as an untroubled celebration of progress. Classical presences in 'Locksley Hall' are among the elements that compromise the vision of British supremacy so that it becomes doubtful, and perhaps even ironic.

Amongst other reasons, it is fallacious to read 'Locksley Hall' as an articulation of Tennyson's thoughts because the words are delivered by a wild and juvenile speaker. There is no reason to assume that the dramatic monologue expresses the poet's own sentiments. The sheer incongruity of such a character using the term 'Cathay' signals that we should hesitate before suspending disbelief. We readers should not be swept up in his enthusiasm in the way that he is by the excitement of his times. The affinity the youth intimates between his own agitation and the buzz of progress does not flatter Victorian Britain. The character is aware that Britain enjoys a significant historical-moment. Heartbroken, the youth hopes to find redemption. He appeals to the spirit of the age, with

---

[1] F. J. Sypher, 'Politics in the Poetry of Tennyson' *Victorian Poetry* 14, no. 2 (1976): 108.
[2] See for example Barry Ahearn, '*Cathay*: What Sort of Translation?', in *Ezra Pound and China*, ed. Zhaoming Qian (Ann Arbor: University of Michigan Press, 2003), 44fn.

optimism that the energy he perceives in commerce, empire, and science might similarly impel him to higher achievement. Britain is not only a 'younger' power than China, but is more efficient if we infer allusion to a traditional Chinese cycle of sixty years, twice as productive if we read 'cycle' as *siècle*, or infinitely so if the 'cycles' carry China back to where it started. The hyperbole of the 'better fifty years' declaration is instructive. That such a man personifies Britain's 'younger day' communicates Tennyson's scepticism towards the dominant narrative of national greatness. British progress might have the transience and short-sightedness of adolescence, denoted by the cavalier verb 'sweep'. The youth's self-absorption has a parallel too in the potential for imperialism to harm other cultures. Articulated by such a character, the confidence that 'change' will progress along predictable 'grooves' is naïve. Similarly, 'Not in vain the distance beckons' is a typical, contradictory Tennysonian formulation. The phrase stirs the addressee to action while planting a suspicion of possible failure. As such the poem recalls the shadow of self-doubt that falls over the conclusion to 'Ulysses' (1842). In that poem too overseas exploration entails uncertainty, represented by a negative formulation of strength: 'To strive, to seek, to find, and not to yield' (70).

In 'Locksley Hall', the poet's concerns about British treatment of China are encoded in an irony that would have been obvious to informed contemporaries. Casting Cathay as a rhetorical counterpoint to Britain's advancement was problematic because the two civilizations had become intertwined. Conditions in nineteenth-century China were determined by British interference in forms that varied from legitimate trade to opium smuggling and punitive warfare. This chapter examines Tennyson's anxieties concerning Victorian pre-eminence. In his poems he questions whether the accomplishments of science and empire necessarily benefit the individual. He intimates kinship between those disadvantaged in the age of British ascendancy, from the speaker of 'Locksley Hall' to—broadly conceived—the Chinese victims of the opium trade. This drug, shipped to Britain and to China, is emblematic of empire's capacity to cause damage both domestically and overseas. The sale of opium would sustain British expansion, but halt the development of those addicted.

Tennyson destabilizes the message of progress in 'Locksley Hall' with his verse form. The quick tempo befits the theme of onward rush, yet Tennyson's source is ancient and possibly Asian. The poem occurs in couplets of fifteen-syllable lines, of which each half-line contains four trochees (a stressed followed by an unstressed syllable). Thus Tennyson recalls the trochaic tetrameter catalectic in fifteen-syllable lines that Aeschylus introduces in *Agamemnon* (458 BCE) at the time of the eponym's death, and uses again at the end of the play (1344, 1346–7 and 1649–73). Clytaemnestra reflects on the events of the tragedy in this metre:

> μηδαμῶς, ὦ φίλτατ' ἀνδρῶν, ἀλλὰ δράσωμεν κακά·
> ἀλλὰ καὶ τάδ' ἐξαμῆσαι πολλὰ δύστηνον θέρος.
> πημονῆς δ' ἅλις γ' ὑπάρχει· μηδὲν αἱματώμεθα.
> στείχετ' αἰδοῖοι γέροντες πρὸς δόμους, πεπρωμένοις
> πρὶν παθεῖν εἴξαντες· ἀρκεῖν χρὴ τάδ' ὡς ἐπράξαμεν.
> εἰ δέ τοι μόχθων γένοιτο τῶνδ' ἅλις, δεχοίμεθ' ἄν,
> δαίμονος χηλῇ βαρείᾳ δυστυχῶς πεπληγμένοι.
> ὧδ' ἔχει λόγος γυναικός, εἴ τις ἀξιοῖ μαθεῖν.

(1654–61)

Dearest of men, please let us not do further harm. What we have is sufficient grief already: let us not get blood on our hands. Go now, honourable elders, to your homes, <yielding to fate> before you suffer. These things must <be accepted> as we have done them. If, I tell you, a cure for these troubles were to appear, we would accept it, after having been so wretchedly struck by the heavy talon of the evil spirit. Such are the words of a woman, if anyone sees fit to learn from them.[3]

Very long lines appealed to Anglophone authors writing on classical themes, as in George Chapman's *Iliad* (1611), which occurs in iambic heptameter. Experimentation with the fifteen-syllable line became popular in Tennyson's literary circle, although uncertainty lingered as to whether the form was Greek or Persian. Appropriately, it was used alike for Hellenistic and Asian subjects. Tennyson's colleague Richard Chenevix Trench adopted an 'oriental metre' of three bacchics followed by an iamb, which he used in works on both classical and Asian topics, such as 'Xerxes' (1838) and his *Poems from Eastern Sources* (1842). In 1839 *Blackwood's* magazine published William E. Aytoun's translation of *Iliad* 22, which also uses the fifteen-syllable line. The Trojan war

---

[3] *Aeschylus*, ed. and trans. Alan H. Sommerstein, The Loeb Classical Library 145, 146, and 505, 3 vols (Cambridge, Massachusetts, and London: Harvard University Press, 2008), 2:202–3.

culminates in this book. Achilles defeats Hector and reveals his intention to abuse his enemy's corpse, so denying the Trojan warrior his funeral rites. With his last breath, Hector foretells the death of Achilles:

> Then the helmed Hector, dying, once again essayed to speak:—
> "'Tis but what my heart foretold of thy nature, ruthless Greek!
> Vain, indeed, is my entreaty, for thou hast an iron heart.
> Yet, bethink thee for a moment, lest the gods should take my part,
> When Apollo and my brother Paris shall avenge my fate,
> Stretching thee, thou mighty warrior, dead before the Scaean gate!'[4]

Robert Browning would later employ fifteen-syllable lines in his version of *Agamemnon* (1877), but with no consistent metre. Victorian use of this extended line kept alive the memory of conflict between East and West, as recounted by Homer and Aeschylus. From William Jones's description, Tennyson knew that the Arabic sequence the *Mu'allaqāt* comprised fourteen-syllable half-lines with four feet, comparable to Aeschylus' trochaic tetrameter catalectic.[5] This resemblance invites the question of whether Aeschylus' departure to a different metre is itself an Orientalist device. Could the author of *Persians* have been exposed to Persian metre? An Asian verse form would be appropriate to the Orientalist theme of Agamemnon's return from Troy, and Clytaemnestra's closing speech. Agamemnon has waged war on an Asian enemy. Clytaemnestra has murdered him because he sacrificed their daughter for the Trojan war effort. Thus Aeschylus, veteran of the Battle of Salamis (480 BCE), engages with the Athenian xenophobia he treats more explicitly in *Persians*. Connections to *Agamemnon* would also remind Tennyson readers of the potential costs entailed by progress. Agamemnon ensured favourable winds for his fleet at the expense of Iphigenia's and, a decade later, his own life.

Heartbreak impels Tennyson's narrator overseas. The treatment of this theme in the Arabic text is as credibly analogous to 'Locksley Hall' as Aeschylus' Orientalism. The *Mu'allaqāt*, 'suspended odes' (compiled c. 700 CE), were authored by the winners of a Bedouin poetry contest.

---

[4] *Blackwood's Magazine* 8 (1839): 640.
[5] *The Works of Sir William Jones*, ed. John Shore, Baron Teignmouth, 13 vols (London: Stockdale, 1807), 10:8. Teignmouth exemplifies the verse form with a Latin rendering quoted from Jones's *Commentaries on Asiatick Poetry* (1774).

The poems were embroidered on cloths and displayed at the Ka'ba shrine, near Mecca. The earliest poem in the *Mu'allaqāt* is attributed to Imru' al-Qais (sixth century CE). As in 'Locksley Hall', the speaker returns to a place he frequented long ago with his beloved:

Stay—let us weep at the remembrance of our beloved, *at the sight of* the station *where her tent was raised.* . . . A profusion of tears . . . is my sole relief: but what avails it to shed them over the remains of a deserted mansion?   (1–4)[6]

Such eclectic reading distinguishes Tennyson from the ignorant and jingoistic speaker of 'Locksley Hall'. Precisely where the poem's metre originates is not so important as the range of literary associations it has. Tennyson's debt to diverse texts is evidence that the poet does not share the youth's steady commitment to the present. The variety of textual analogues for 'Locksley Hall' befits the complexity of Tennyson's responses to British affairs in China. Even aside from the question of imperialism, he was unconvinced that the Victorian obsession with progress was entirely beneficial. As an abstraction, the idea of change alarmed Tennyson. On its tangible manifestations, he was ambivalent: he loved the railway, but hated the telephone. Britain's expansion overseas was a catalyst of domestic social-change, which he would have preferred to occur more slowly. Displeasure at the rate of social transformation is often palpable in Tennyson's works. More subtly, his poems interrogate the morality of British imperialism, doing so in a manner cognate with the national values he endorses. This chapter examines a period in which discussion of China gained urgency. While Coleridge and Gibbon address Chinese themes prophetically, Keats obliquely, and Baillie, Lamb, and Lemon humorously, Tennyson approaches China with the solemnity of his moment. Using classical frameworks, he gives serious consideration to Chinese philosophy as available in recent translation, and reflects on Britain's role in China's destiny. Tennyson's sentiments on contemporary Britain are not diametrically opposite those of the 'Locksley Hall' narrator, but the two have different visions of patriotism.

---

[6] William Jones trans., *The moallakát, or seven Arabian poems, which were suspended on the temple at Mecca* (London: Elmsly, 1782), 5. Jones's italicized interpolations complete the English syntax. Jones adds his own classical aesthetic to the Arabic direction to weep, opening with a Horatian imperative to 'stay'.

Classics and Tennyson's Politics

Tennyson's politics were reactionary; he inclined instinctively towards conservatism in its literal sense. In his essay 'On Some of the Characteristics of Modern Poetry' (1831), Arthur Henry Hallam (1811–33) attempts to distance Tennyson from his radical Romantic influences, particularly Shelley. He writes that Tennyson 'comes before the public unconnected with any political party or peculiar system of opinions.'[7] Here Hallam identifies Tennyson as a common-sense man who shuns party politics. In effect, the essay aligns the poet with the Tory values of his fellow Cambridge Apostles. Tennyson himself articulates no lucid ideology in his poetry. Where he writes on patriotic themes, he communicates a perceived gulf between age-old English values and modern politics. 'Love thou thy land' (1842) is typically nostalgic but troubled. Tennyson's uncertainty as to how a retrospective patriotism might manifest now and hereafter results in awkward verse. It is difficult to identify precisely who should carry this reverence into modernity:

> Love thou thy land, with love far-brought
> From out the storied past, and used
> Within the present, but transfused
> Thro' future time by power of thought.
>
> (1–4)

From 1850, the Laureateship obliged Tennyson to compose on national subjects. Yet works such as 'Ode on the Death of the Duke of Wellington' (1852) and 'The Charge of the Light Brigade' (1854) are obliquely critical of their times. Tennyson's tribute to Wellington insists that his subject was 'the last great Englishman': 'all is over and done' (18, 43). The piece is perfunctory eulogy by the standards of the poet who wrote *In Memoriam* (1850). Of the disaster that befell the Light Brigade during the Crimean War, Tennyson portrays a brave soldiery under foolish leadership:

> Some one had blunder'd:
> Their's not to make reply,
> Their's not to reason why,
> Their's but to do and die.
>
> (12–15)

---

[7] [Arthur Henry Hallam], 'On Some of the Characteristics of Modern Poetry, and on the Lyrical Poems of Alfred Tennyson', *The Englishman's Magazine* 1 (1831): 621.

These works are useful to historians but are seldom celebrated as verse. Evidently the poet was not sufficiently inspired by these subjects. When writing in his own voice, Tennyson does not approach the 'Locksley Hall' narrator's fervent nationalism. The poet feels marginalized by, rather than swept up in, the forces of change. He cherishes the past, and wants to 'transfuse' old values 'thro' future time'.

The poet Aubrey de Vere (1814–1902) claims that Tennyson is a better poet of the 'Ideal' than the 'National'.[8] Hence it might be seen as a solution that Tennyson brings ideals sourced in ancient culture, for which he has great enthusiasm, to bear upon British politics, on which he writes poorly when explicit. For example, readers have related Tennyson's use of the paradigmatic adventurer in 'Ulysses' to the aftermath of the 1832 Reform Act. In this interpretation, Ulysses, who needs to move on from the stifling Ithaca, represents reformers' frustration at the pace of British politics.[9] Yet such classicism sat uneasily with some of the poet's contemporaries. The purpose of poetry was debated anew by Victorian commentators. They argued over what manner of verse was appropriate to the age of progress. Tennyson's classicism must be viewed as part of this discussion not only because of his reliance on ancient Greek and Roman plots and characters, but because his opinions on what poetry should offer the reader were indebted to very old models. Tennyson saw himself as heir to Homer and Virgil. In the piece 'To Virgil', the Roman poet is himself the 'Golden branch amid the shadows', granting Tennyson access to the visions of the underworld (14). Richard Jenkyns observes that the part of this poem that captures Virgil's temperament (rather than listing his achievements) is equally a self-portrait:

> Thou that seëst Universal
>   Nature moved by Universal Mind;
> Thou majestic in thy sadness
>   at the doubtful doom of human kind.
>
>   (11–12)[10]

---

[8]   Quoted in Isobel Armstrong, 'Introduction', in *Victorian Scrutinies: Reviews of Poetry, 1830–1870*, ed. Isobel Armstrong (London: The Athlone Press, 1972), 13.

[9]   Francis O'Gorman, 'Tennyson's "The Lotos-Eaters" and the Politics of the 1830s', *Victorian Review* 30, no. 1 (2004): 11.

[10]   Richard Jenkyns, 'The Classical Tradition', in *A Companion to Victorian Poetry*, ed. Richard Cronin, Alison Chapman, and Anthony H. Harrison (Oxford: Blackwell, 2002), 235.

Unfortunately for Tennyson, there was no consensus that the literary world required another Virgil. If classical subjects were part of the furniture in the Victorian mindset, many felt that they belonged in the attic.[11] William Fox was among the critics to question the use of mythical figures in poetry when real and contemporary alternatives were obvious. 'Is not the French Revolution as good as the siege of Troy?' he asks in an 1829 essay 'On the Development of Genius'.[12] In this piece, Fox explains that the extent of the Romans' achievement might at least partly be explained by their freedom from such encumbrances as the study of dead languages, leaving them time to innovate. Therefore, Britain must not *copy* its imperial predecessor, but should emulate Rome's capacity for originality. Comparably, reviewing Tennyson's 1842 collection, John Sterling declares, 'We know not why, except for schoolboy recollection, a modern English poet should write of Ulysses rather than of great voyagers of the modern world.'[13] C. P. Chretien offers an answer of sorts by implying that Tennyson chooses ancient subjects because he feels that he has been side-lined. Yet so doing, the reviewer says, the poet is not true to the spirit of his sources. Chretien claims that Tennyson can exert control over his Greek and Roman materials only by treating them as dead:

Classic art, indeed, was no lifeless thing to its contemporaries. The artist wrought from what he saw; his creatures were but a glorified image of the ordinary life of his day. The quick, energetic Greeks knew no higher praise for a picture than that it seemed on the point to speak; for a statue, than that it promised motion. But this is past now; what was a representation to them, is final to us. . . . Old associations have died off it; it is a subject for taste, not for feeling. . . .

Among these beautiful forms of the Past Mr Tennyson delights to linger. He does not attempt to animate them; he is not anxious that they should speak or move; he would not have them flush into common life. . . . But it is his pleasure to place them in the garden of the poet's mind, where the shadows or leaves may fall upon them.[14]

Chretien's Tennyson is a control freak who is at ease only when he works with inanimate matter. Chretien is right that Tennyson finds comfort in the

---

[11] I allude to Simon Goldhill: 'Classics was simply the furniture of the mind for the Victorian upper classes.' See *Victorian Culture and Classical Antiquity: Art, Opera, Fiction, and the Proclamation of Modernity* (New Jersey: Princeton University Press, 2011), 2.

[12] Quoted in Armstrong, 'Introduction', 16.

[13] 'Tennyson, *Poems*, 1842: by J. Sterling', in *Victorian Scrutinies*, 141.

[14] 'Tennyson, *The Princess*, 1847: by C.P. Chretien', in *Victorian Scrutinies*, 211.

stability of the ancient world, which is a known quantity to the poet. But the critic neglects Tennyson's ability to make classical subjects speak to contemporary concerns. Here, Chretien's analogy is inadequate. It is not that Tennyson arranges marmoreal objects in his mind and decorates them with verse, but rather that a classically informed imagination illuminates other subjects. Yes, Tennyson finds solace in the past, but he adopts this position to examine the present.

Tennyson's poetry represents prevalent British opinions on Asia, but often with critical subtext. Although he borrows devices from the literature of the Graeco-Roman world to facilitate his contemplations of British affairs in China, Tennyson is relatively uninterested in the common notion that Britain was the hegemonic successor to Athens and Rome. Unlike Gibbon or Coleridge, Tennyson does not imply that classical history offers lessons to guide British foreign policy. Nor does he use a device such as *ekphrasis* to explore how Chinese culture had been assimilated alongside classical inheritances, as I have examined in works by Baillie and Lamb. In poems such as 'Locksley Hall' and 'The Lotos-Eaters', the mythical Greek past offers Tennyson perspective. In this universe he reinvents and interrogates aspects of British affairs in Asia, such as the threat and subsequent occurrence of war against China. Tennyson's treatment of opium in 'The Lotos-Eaters' combines a study of addiction, made poignant by personal associations, with allusion to the opium trade. While family history lends emotional force to his portrayal of narcotic dependence, Tennyson perceives the hypocrisy of the opium trade in China. By smuggling opium into China, Britain both enriched itself and perpetuated the very indolence that British commentators criticized in the Chinese. Tennyson's revisions to this poem, Sara Coleridge's adaptation of the 'Lotos-Eaters', and further poems by Tennyson such as 'Locksley Hall' are alert to important developments in British activity in Asia. Initially, the respective failures of Britain's diplomatic visits to Beijing in 1793 and 1816 provoked mixtures of derision and indifference at home. Yet these embarrassments did not immediately bring about widespread hostility towards China. As the nineteenth century progressed, popular British opinions on China became more consistently negative. In this period, the cliché of a static Asia assumed new prominence. It metamorphosed from an observation that occasioned British self-congratulation to a rhetorical predicate for forcing change upon China.

Any reading of 'Locksley Hall' as jingoistic overlooks the fact that the whole made by this poem and its companion piece, 'Locksley Hall Sixty Years After' (1886), is explicitly inward-looking at its conclusion. This perspective discourages overseas expansion. As I shall argue, the conservatism with which Tennyson views British imperialism is relatively consistent. However, as he becomes more overtly moral in later works, he articulates an increasing sympathy for China. Tennyson also has a certain affinity with British Orientalism, in the sense of an imaginative interest in Asia unaffiliated with imperial ideology. Arthur Henry Hallam was among those critics who described Tennyson's 'luxuriance'; this word for abundance had some negative connotations of excess.[15] 'Luxuriant' was a word frequently associated with Asia and the trope of excess in Orientalism. There is passing reference to China in *Enoch Arden* (1864), and more substantial engagement with the place in works like *Locksley Hall*. In a late poem, 'The Ancient Sage' (1885), Tennyson responds to *Dao De Jing* (sixth century BCE), which he read in John Chalmers's 1868 translation. Tennyson felt he knew enough about China to venture an opinion when Lord Napier called on him in 1886; the visitor's father, as I discuss below, was a key figure in debate that preceded the First Opium War. Tennyson's son, Hallam Tennyson, recalls that the poet described China to Napier as a place of unrealised—perhaps frustrated—potential: 'He thought that the Chinese, who lived on a very little, could imitate everything, and had no fear of death, would, not long hence, under good leadership be a great power in the world.'[16] Thus China's 'cycles' were not necessarily unproductive. In his poetry Tennyson intimates that foreign interference stunts Chinese development. He loves his land, but bids it caution in tones that recall Clytaemnestra and Odysseus.

Time Stands Still: Asian Stagnation in a Classical Universe

Tennyson describes a splendid but static Asia in 'Recollections of the Arabian Nights' (1830). He categorized this piece under 'Juvenalia' in

---

[15] [Hallam], 'Characteristics of Modern Poetry', 623.
[16] Hallam Tennyson, *Alfred Lord Tennyson: a Memoir by his Son*, 4 vols (London: Macmillan, 1897) 2:328.

Complete Works (1871). 'Recollections' juxtaposes two clichéd European views on Asia, and finds them incompatible: this Orient is magnificent, but is such an indolent place that we wonder how the splendour came to be. As such the poem can be considered a starting point for Tennyson's views on the East. His perspective would alter vastly. He reinvestigates several ideas from 'Recollections' in 'The Lotos-Eaters', first published in 1832. His alterations to the latter poem for his 1842 collection capture both personal and national crises over opium, which had escalated in the intervening years. The progress from 'Recollections' to the respective versions of 'The Lotos-Eaters' demonstrates Tennyson's changing perspective on Asia, and his restlessness to find the correct vehicle for the subject. To supplement this discussion, Sara Coleridge's version of 'The Lotos-Eaters' (1842/43) exemplifies how Tennyson's poem might be read as explicitly about China and the opium crisis, yet simultaneously as a work that articulates personal encounters with addicts.

'Recollections' rehearses the limited movement of 'The Lotos-Eaters'. A naval landing is the only significant action in each poem. Well-known figures preside over these occurrences, men whose presences raise the reader's expectations in a manner that is ultimately frustrated by the lack of incident. In the first stanza of 'Recollections', Tennyson introduces a refrain in which he accounts for the magnificence of Baghdad:

> For it was in the golden prime
> Of good Haroun Alraschid.
>
> (10–11)

The poem concludes with a vision of this ruler on his throne:

> Thereon, his deep-eye laughter-stirred
> With merriment of kingly pride,
> Sole star of all that place and time,
> I saw him – in his golden prime,
> THE GOOD HAROUN ALRASCHID.
>
> (150–54)

To reach this point, the speaker has left a boat and ventured through the palace gardens. She/he (we might presume a nostalgic Tennyson) has used Alraschid's name on thirteen occasions, only to terminate the narrative when the Caliph actually appears. The deceptive promise of 'So, leaping lightly from my boat' towards the end of 'Recollections'—a stealthy movement, creating a suspense that is neither heightened nor fulfilled—recurs at the onset of 'The Lotos-Eaters' (92). The later poem begins in the voice of Odysseus:

> 'Courage!' he said, and pointed toward the land,
> 'This mounting wave will roll us shoreward soon.'
>
> (1–2)

The stirring exhortation for 'courage', and the dramatic gesture of Odysseus pointing to land, is immediately succeeded by submission to the agency of the 'mounting wave'.

Odysseus is curiously ill-suited to a poem about inaction. While 'The Lotos-Eaters' deviates far from its Homeric source, 'Recollections' is similarly provocative. 'The Lotos-Eaters' plays on our knowledge that in the *Odyssey*, the mariners will leave the island. The extent to which Tennyson has adopted Homer's vision is unclear: we cannot tell whether or not the closing declaration of 'we will not wander more' is ironic (173). 'Recollections' also exploits our familiarity with its materials to create uncertainty. The reader wonders to which version of the main character Tennyson will commit. With reference to the 'good Haroun Alraschid', Tennyson offers a choice between an imaginary and a historical setting for the poem. The title directs us to *Arabian Nights*, but the relevant character was based on a historical figure, Harun al-Rashid (c. 766–809). A Caliph during the Islamic Golden Age, al-Rashid is idealized in historical treatments as a patron of commerce, science, and the arts. Tennyson's Alraschid hovers between these personae. From *Arabian Nights*, Tennyson says that 'Noureddin and the Fair Persian' and 'The History of Aboulhassen' were sources for 'Recollections'.[17] In each of these stories, a young noble falls in love with the Caliph's favourite. Noureddin survives court intrigue, and the Caliph allows him to remain married to the beautiful Persian, having observed the couple while disguised as a fisherman. Less happily, Aboulhassen the jeweller proves unable to dissuade his friend from an affection that proves fatal to the lovers, who assume that the Caliph will not relinquish his claim on a woman to whom he has paid incessant attention. Consequently, the lovers die of sorrow. The Alraschid of these tales is passionate, clever, and restless, if unconcerned with affairs of state. However, Tennyson's

---

[17] *The Poems of Tennyson: in Three Volumes*, ed. *Christopher Ricks*, Longman Annotated English Poets, 2nd ed. (London: Longman, 1987), 1:225.

Caliph is entirely idle. The Alraschid of 'Recollections' is as decadent as his *Arabian Nights* counterpart; how he is 'good' is unfathomable. Evidence surrounds the narrator that Alraschid, like the historical figure, presides over a sophisticated civilization. Yet the impressive aspects of Alraschid's domain are ostentatious. Alraschid's unresolved character in the poem corresponds to a problem of nineteenth-century Orientalism: how could European accounts of accomplished Eastern societies be reconciled with conventional criticisms of a stagnant Asia?

The poem begins with a Wordsworthian breeze. This impels a mental voyage that recalls 'Alastor' (1816) but, unlike Shelley's poem, Tennyson's realm is one of escapist fantasy, lacking spiritual significance:

> When the breeze of a joyful dawn blew free
> In the silken sail of infancy,
> The tide of time flowed back with me,
>   The forward-flowing tide of time.
>
> (1–4)

This Orient becomes unreal amidst oxymoronic references to time. Asia is doubly confined to the past—the child's indulgence in old, Oriental tales is recalled by the elder poet—yet the realm becomes ahistorical or ageless in the contrary movement of time, which flows both backward and forward. The figures of the child and the Caliph represent conflicting elements of Tennyson's attitude towards Asia, a place that evoked nostalgia amongst *Arabian Nights* readers of his time, but was simultaneously the subject of disapproval in popular politics. The initial tour of Orientalist clichés is appreciative:

> Anight my shallop, rustling through
> The low and bloomèd foliage, drove
> The fragrant, glistening deeps, and clove
> The citron-shadows in the blue:
> By garden porches on the brim,
> The costly doors flung open wide,
> Gold glittering through lamplight dim,
> And broidered sofas on each side.
>
> (12–19)

Despite such grandeur, the speaker is aware that the possibilities of this environment are limited. He tells us that he 'often' undertook the same imaginative voyage (23). From this we imagine the journey to Alraschid's palace in an eternal loop, with no possibility of advancement beyond the final glimpse of the Caliph. Alongside staples of Orientalist luxuriance stand objects of vexation which correspond to an unchanging Asia:

> deep inlay
> Of braided blooms unmown, which crept
> Adown to where the water slept.
>
> (28–30)

The 'unmown' flowers—in a haphazard arrangement communicated by the field rhyme 'adown'—tell of neglected duty. The water 'slept': symbolically, it is stagnant. The only antagonistic forces in this realm occur momentarily in the nightingale's song:

> Far off, and where the lemon-grove
> In closest coverture upsprung,
> The living airs of middle night
> Died round the bulbul as he sung;
> Not he: but something which possessed
> The darkness of the world, delight,
> Life, anguish, death, immortal love,
> Ceasing not, mingled, unrepress'd,
>   Apart from place, withholding time,
>   But flattering the golden prime
>   Of good Haroun Alraschid.
>
> (67–77)

Here 'living' and 'dying', 'delight' and 'anguish' cancel each other in song without coming to being. Hence the poet describes a non-place in which time has halted or has *been* halted, 'something . . . withholding time'.

The lack of variety in Alraschid's Caliphate is accentuated formally in an extended version of the refrain. This elaboration, with its pointedly weak repetition of 'good' in 'goodly', occurs four times in the poem:

> A goodly place, a goodly time,
> For it was in the golden prime
> Of good Haroun Alraschid.
>
> (31–33)

The effect of exhaustion is compounded in the final line of each stanza. Despite Tennyson's frequent variations in the rhyme scheme of his eleven-line stanzas, the conclusive 'Alraschid' never rhymes. Each verse ends with a flat allusion to Alraschid, and the poem ends with rather a flaccid one, a vision that unites several Orientalist motifs. Narcotically the poem lulls us, as though to deeper stages of intoxication, with its repetitions and steady movement to the inner recesses of Alraschid's kingdom. There, with Keatsian voyeurism, the speaker gazes 'trancedly' upon the object of the Caliph's recent attention, a 'Persian girl alone, | Serene with argent-lidded eyes' (134–35). As in *Arabian Nights*, Alraschid devotes his energies to womanizing. The post-coital imagery of the Caliph's 'cloth of gold', which 'down-drooped, in many a floating fold' connotes depletion and incapability (149, 147). This Asia is a place for the mind of a child, who is dazzled by novelty, but Alraschid wastes his 'golden prime' here. Alraschid's silk is luxurious, but in the opening lines, silk was infantile. Hence, the speaker relegates this fantasy land to his youth.

'Recollections' represents the hackneyed but irreconcilable opinions on Asia as, respectively, accomplished and idle. Tennyson makes a more nuanced exploration of Eastern themes in 'The Lotos-Eaters'. In this poem he addresses a complex political situation by displacing contemporary controversies to a mythical past. While China was widely derided as unprogressive, the terms on which Britain interacted with the Middle Kingdom altered significantly during the 1830s. Parliament had gradually eroded the powers of the East India Company by renewing its charter with reduced privileges in 1793, 1813, and 1833. The corporate empire, with its overseas territories and standing army, was stripped of its assets. This process began with the Regulating Act of 1773, in which the Company accepted the government's rules in return for financial assistance. For all its wealth, the Company needed funds to exploit its opportunities in Asia. The Directors were willing to cede administrative autonomy. The transactions that brought the Company to this pass remain nebulous to scholars. It is clear that much of its fortune had recklessly been lavished upon returning Nabobs. John Keay draws attention to 'the relationship, as yet dimly perceived, between the financial difficulties which precipitated each dose of state intervention and the fiscal handicaps under which the Company conducted its tea trade.'[18] The most important curtailments of the Company's independence occurred in Tennyson's lifetime. Monopoly had been the keystone of

---

[18] John Keay, *The Honourable Company: A History of the English East India Company* (London: HarperCollins, 1993), 386.

Queen Elizabeth's Royal Charter in 1600. The 1813 charter ended the Company's sole right to the India trade, and claimed all sovereignty of Company possessions for the Crown. After that the China trade was the Company's sole monopoly.

While the British government wished to attenuate the Company's political power in Asia, other problems existed. Controversial reports had reached Britain about the Company's treatment of foreign natives. Pitt's East India Company Act of 1784 attempted to respond to such humanitarian concerns. The trial of Warren Hastings (1787–95) illuminated British misbehaviour overseas. Although Hastings was acquitted rather than impeached, and the government made full use of the charters to prise power from the Company, the treatment of foreigners by British traders remained an unresolved issue.

Hobbled, the Company sought new revenue streams. British parliament's failure to establish rules for the treatment of foreigners ensured that an expanded opium trade was a viable source of income. The Company produced opium by monopoly in India. Chests of the harvest were auctioned to private traders in Calcutta, who sold the opium on to Chinese dealers. Because independent merchants were involved, the Company's opium business evaded financial regulation by the British government.

Drug traffickers and corrupt officials allowed the Chinese drug trade to flourish. However, the Qing Dynasty took opium seriously. Under the edict of 1729, opium dealers were strangled. Their employees were caned, imprisoned, and subsequently exiled. Because the 1729 decree had neglected the subject of importation, a new proclamation was issued in 1799 to deter foreigners from transporting the drug into China. The possibility that the Company might cease the supply of opium to China was a concession made available to Macartney in his brief for the 1793 Embassy, but he never discussed the issue with officials. By 1804, the volume of the opium trade had cancelled out the national trade-deficit hitherto caused by tea.

Everyone involved in the opium trade knew that it was immoral. Hastings was careful to prevent local consumption in his Bengal days. He declared the drug a 'pernicious Article of Luxury, which ought not to be permitted but for the Purposes of foreign Commerce only.'[19] Evidently the problems caused by an Indian population addicted to opium

[19] Quoted in *Minutes of the Evidence Taken at the Trial of Warren Hastings*, 11 vols (London: Parliament, 1788–94), 4:2219.

would outweigh the possible proceeds. In 1830 the Company's Select Committee debated whether it was reasonable to smuggle opium to China. They concluded that 'it does not appear advisable to abandon so productive a source of revenue.'[20] Merchants continued their business in the knowledge that they broke no British laws. When Britain appointed Trafalgar veteran Lord Napier (1786–1834) chief superintendent of the China trade in 1834, the opium trade had fallen under governmental remit. Napier suggested a military solution to the closure of Canton factories by Qing officials, and summoned two British frigates. He was placed under house arrest and escorted to Macao, soon to die of a fever. The new, open aggression towards China, governmental interest in opium, and Napier's untimely death in Macao were all factors that made war on China more likely, as discussed in the next chapter.

Undoubtedly Tennyson was a more accomplished poet when he drafted 'The Lotos-Eaters' than such so-called juvenilia as 'Recollections'. He was confident enough to publish 'The Lotos-Eaters' in 1832. This poem is informed by public debates about Asia, but also by personal concerns which are absent from 'Recollections'. At the time of 'The Lotos-Eaters', the popular perception that China had made little technological or cultural progress had become complicated by recognition of Britain's responsibility for the scenario. Britain hindered China by the illicit sale of opium. The exact procedures and conditions of Chinese addicts were depicted in texts such as Davis's *The Chinese* and Robert Fortune's travel narrative (1847), which describes a day in the life of an opium den (Figure 5.1). Hence, the supposed backwardness of China was increasingly a cause of national guilt in Tennyson's lifetime. The interval between publication of the first and second versions of 'The Lotos-Eaters' was a decade in which Sino-British affairs reached crisis. Contemporaneously, Tennyson watched his father and brother become opium addicts.

Tennyson's poem had obvious relevance to contemporary debate. Early readers of 'The Lotos-Eaters' noticed Tennyson's identification of Homer's lotus with the opium poppy, *papaver somniferum*. This was not a conventional association. It is more usual to interpret the wedding at Sparta as the *Odyssey*'s opium episode.[21] Here Helen drugs the wine with

---

[20] Quoted in *East India Company's Affairs*, vol. 4 of *Reports from Committees*, 18 vols (London: H. M. Stationery Office, 1832), 8.70.

[21] Lucy Inglis, *The Milk of Paradise* (London: Macmillan, 2018), 16–17.

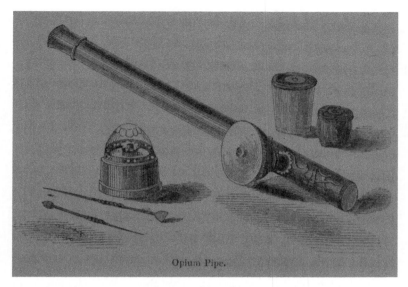

Figure 5.1 The exact procedures and conditions of Chinese addicts were depicted in texts such as John Francis Davis's *The Chinese*, which includes this picture of paraphernalia (3:31).

Photo courtesy of the Matheson Library.

Egyptian nepenthe so that Telemachus and Menelaus will forget their sorrows (4.219–30). De Quincey says nothing of the lotus-eaters in *Confessions*. The word λωτός/*lotos* referred to a variety of plants in the Hellenistic world, including the Indian *nelumbo nucifera* and the Egyptian water-lily (*nymphaea caerulea*). The notes to Alexander Pope's translation of Homer, one of Tennyson's favourite volumes, outline the confusion over the lotus that had arisen amidst the historicist inclinations of eighteenth-century Homeric studies. The belief that Homer was historically accurate provoked diverse speculations on the classification of the plant. Pope himself does not venture a solution. In 1835 Connop Thirlwall situated *Odyssey* 9 in Libya and stated with similar confidence that Homer's lotus must be the *ziziphus jujuba*.[22] In a later study, Catherine Barnes Stevenson observes that the Egyptian water-lily, which was known to Homeric Greece, resembles the opium poppy

---

[22] Connop Thirlwall, *A History of Greece*, 8 vols (London: Longman, Rees, Orme, Brown, Green, & Longman 1835–44), 1:212.

physically.[23] If Tennyson spotted this similarity, he did not say so explicitly. Hence the conflation of the two plants was an unexplained leap to some of his readers. Tennyson's early critics found it remarkable, and suspicious, that the poet appeared to identify Homer's lotus with opium so decisively. In his review of the 1832 collection, John Wilson Croker infers that Tennyson makes Homer's lotus into opium because the poet is an addict himself: 'Though the subjects are derived from classical antiquity, Mr Tennyson treats them with so much originality that he makes them exclusively his own.' He elaborates that Tennyson's mariners are 'a kind of classical opium-eaters', and continues, 'Mr Tennyson [is] himself, we presume, a dreamy lotus-eater, a delicious [for "delirious"?] lotus-eater'.[24] To the poet's irritation, he could not dispel the rumour that he was an opium addict. One distinguished by-passer described Tennyson as 'a dirty man with opium-glazed eyes and rat-taily hair.'[25]

Homer's lotus-eaters episode lends itself to contemplation of the Chinese opium trade by its narcotics, naval theme, and encounter with the Other. It is analogous to foreign interference that Tennyson used a main character whom he considered a devious meddler. In a marginal note to Euripides' *Hecuba*, the poet writes that 'Ulysses is, as usual, crafty & unfeeling'.[26] Dante's *Inferno*, in H. F. Cary's translation, was another of Tennyson's favourites. Here Tennyson encountered a version of Odysseus who, in his preoccupation with the Trojan war, ignores the mission to retrieve Helen. This Odysseus dwells on nation-building overseas and imperial legacy. Thus, Dante's version of the character strikes a chord with political concerns of nineteenth-century Britain:

> These in the flame with ceaseless groans deplore
> The ambush of the horse, that open'd wide
> A portal for that goodly seed to pass,
> Which sow'd imperial Rome.[27]

---

[23] Catherine Barnes Stevenson, 'The Shade of Homer Exorcises the Ghost of De Quincey: Tennyson's "The Lotos-Eaters"', *Browning Institute Studies* 10 (1982): 125.

[24] *The Quarterly Review* 49 (1833), 88–92.

[25] *The Diary of Lady Frederick Cavendish*, ed. John Bailey, 2 vols (London: John Murray, 1927), 2:101.

[26] Quoted in A. A. Markley, *Stateliest Measures: Tennyson and the Literature of Greece and Rome* (Toronto: University of Toronto Press, 2004), 35.

[27] Dante Alighieri, *The Vision; or, Hell, Purgatory, and Paradise*, trans. Henry Francis Cary, 3 vols (London: Taylor and Hessey, 1819), 1:228.

Shakespeare's *Troilus and Cressida*, like Dante, follows the Virgilian tradition in which depictions of the Trojan war sympathize with the defeated forces rather than the invaders.

'The Lotos-Eaters' portrays a realm in which every aspect of existence is permeated by the effects of opium. It is, like China, an addicted country. The newcomers to Tennyson's island of lotus-eaters are amazed at its stillness: 'A land where all things always seem'd the same!' (24). The description recalls the uneventful cycles of Cathay derided in 'Locksley Hall', and expresses British sentiments on China that remained conventional in the 1830s. Accordingly, Tennyson elaborates on Homer's bare portrait of the lotus-eaters with the attributes of opium addicts:

> And round about the keel with faces pale,
> Dark faces pale against that rosy flame,
> The mild-eyed melancholy Lotos-eaters came
>
> (25–27).

A sailor new to lotus-eating is struck by the immediate alteration worked upon his companion:

> His voice was thin, as voices from the grave;
> And deep-asleep he seemed, yet all awake.
>
> (35–36)

Had Tennyson not been surrounded by opium users at home, we might think these withdrawn and gormless figures had been culled from a contemporary account of Asia such as Josiah Condor's description of Turkish addicts: 'pale, emaciated, and ricketty, sunk into a profound stupor or agitated by the grimaces of delirium'.[28] While Homer's mariners are reluctant to leave the island of lotus-eaters, the thoughts of Tennyson's addicts are so muddled that what begins as a declaration of intent becomes the opposite in the space of five words: 'We will return no more' (43).

In the 'Choric Song' sub-narrative, which contains 128 of the expanded poem's 173 lines, it is redolent of the Chinese opium crisis that Tennyson explores the subject in relation to collective hindrance rather than individual dependence. If it is a stretch to associate 'yellow' too readily with China, the colour attracts attention by its unmatched

---

[28] Josiah Condor, *The Modern Traveller: Turkey* (London: J. Duncan, 1830), 138.

repetition in 'The Lotos-Eaters'. Tennyson names 'yellow' on four occasions in the poem, once with the exotic suggestion of spices: 'round and round the spicy downs the yellow Lotos-dust is blown' (49). Yellow had not acquired the xenophobic associations with the Yellow Peril that would follow later in the century. 'Yellow' was known in Britain as the term by which the Chinese defined themselves in distinction from foreigners. The Chinese were the descendants of the mythical Huangdi, the Yellow Emperor. They lived in the land of the Yellow River (Huang He), which flowed into the Yellow Sea (Huang Hai), by which Macartney's expedition had first approached the Middle Kingdom.

Tennyson's revisions to 'The Lotos-Eaters' for the 1842 publication reflect international developments as well as personal concerns. The First Opium War (1839–42) broke out after a zealous Chinese commissioner named Lin Zexu seized and destroyed £2m worth of opium. Britain attacked China for reparation. At home this was an unpopular war, which *The Times* portrayed as a massacre. For his part, Tennyson had experienced considerable turbulence since he drafted the first version of 'The Lotos-Eaters'. In 1831 the poet's father, George Clayton Tennyson died, having become dependent on opium for chest pain. In 1833 Hallam died, occasioning a protracted bereavement that inspired *In Memoriam* and much of Tennyson's canonical poetry. Coleridge's *Table Talk* was published in 1835 and included infamous criticism of Tennyson's verse. Tennyson lost the family fortune in a poor investment, and in 1840 felt compelled to release Emily Selwood from their long-standing engagement. To such personal upheaval we might attribute the so-called 'lost decade' in which Tennyson published no poetry. Yet he continued to write, and the events of this period, both international and immediate, leave their mark on poems such as 'The Lotos-Eaters', 'Ulysses', and 'Locksley Hall'.

Of personal affairs, the decline of Tennyson's brother, Charles (1808–79), is most tangible in the revised 'Lotos-Eaters' published in 1842. That Charles had acquired Davis's *The Chinese* enhances the connection between his own affairs and the opium crisis. Here Tennyson elaborates on the implications of addiction, as illustrated for him in his own household. The failure of Charles's marriage informs Tennyson's contemplation of neglected responsibility:

> Dear is the memory of our wedded lives,
> And dear the last embraces of our wives

And their warm tears: but all hath suffered change:
For surely now our household hearths are cold:
Our sons inherit us: our looks are strange:
And we should come like ghosts to trouble joy.

(114–19)

The excessive use of colons here accentuates the lotus-eaters' broken logic. They hesitate, and the words that follow colons tend not to explain those that preceded them. There is no chain of reason evident in the claims that 'our household hearths are cold: | Our sons inherit us: our looks are strange'. This sequence of images is impressionistic, and as such is entirely appropriate for its subject. The lines recall Hallam's statement that 'congruity of sentiment' has greater power to enrapture the reader than logical relation.[29] Ostensibly writing about Cicero, Hallam compares oratory to poetry. In Tennyson's poem, the mariners attempt to make a case for their inaction, but do not form the persuasive argument that they believe they do. It is a bleak vision of opium use. The addicts cannot think, cannot plan.

Finally, the sailors commit to idleness: 'Oh rest ye, brother mariners, we will not wander more' (173). The line reads ironically if the reader knows Homer, because Odysseus will soon have the men carried back aboard ship against their will. However, Tennyson gives no indication that he reproduces Homer's vision faithfully. As the poet's son, Hallam Tennyson, said of 'Ulysses', 'perhaps The Odyssey has not been strictly adhered to'.[30] 'Eating the Lotos day by day' suggests a broader temporal range than in Homer's episode, whether perceived or actual (105). If the lotus has become opium, a drug capable of destroying families and countries, it may be that the sailors never leave in this telling.

Tennyson and Coleridgean Visions of China

Two Coleridgean texts are analogous to Tennyson's 'Lotos-Eaters', illuminating the Chinese presences in that poem. These works were authored by Samuel Taylor Coleridge's children, Hartley (1796–1849)

[29] Arthur Henry Hallam, *Remains in Verse and Prose*, ed. H. Hallam (London: W. Nicol, 1834), 209.
[30] Quoted in *The Poems of Tennyson*, 1:614.

and Sara (1802–52). Like Tennyson they were omnivorous readers and personally affected by addiction.

Domestic misfortune and Homeric epic were not the only factors to colour Tennyson's treatment of China. Another credible source for Tennyson is a poem about goldfish. Hartley Coleridge's 'Address to Certain Gold Fishes' (1830) shares language and ideas with 'Locksley Hall' and 'The Lotos-Eaters'. Hartley dwells on his subject's Chinese origin. Goldfish came from Asia, and the tradition of keeping them as pets began in China. Goldfish had been introduced to Europe via Portugal in the seventeenth century. Accordingly, Hartley regards the fish as exiles. Onto them he projects a range of associations with China. On first inspection, Hartley describes the fish as ornamental and carefree, living specimens of *chinoiserie*:

> Pretty creatures! we might deem
> Ye were happy as ye seem,—
> As gay, as gamesome, and as blithe,
> As light, as loving, and as lithe,
> As gladly earnest in your play,
> As when ye gleamed in far Cathay.
>
> (26–31)

Yet the goldfish are doubly symbolic. While the creatures can be made to represent the bright gaiety of British *chinoiserie*, Hartley wonders whether they might also embody the less-happy reality of life in China. It is not only the name 'Cathay' for China that Hartley's poem shares with 'Locksley Hall', but the perspective on Asian life as fruitless in its circularity. Hartley's use of 'Cathay' marks a turning-point at which he wonders whether the experience of a goldfish resembles the unvaried misery of a Chinese coolie. If this image anticipates Tennyson's allusion to Cathay caught in a loop in 'Locksley Hall', Hartley's elaboration of day-to-day misery foreshadows 'The Lotos-Eaters'. Tennyson's mariners wish for 'rest from weariness' (59). They lament that the unproductive life spent 'enduring toil' leads many to 'suffer endless anguish' in the afterlife (166–69). To rest, the sailors conclude, is worthier than to 'labour in the mid-deep ocean' (172). Much of Tennyson's language occurs in Hartley's poem too:

> Your restless roving round and round
> The circuit of your crystal bound,—

Is but the task of weary pain,
An endless labour, dull and vain.

(38–41)

Tennyson's sailors decide that a repetitive life of addiction is superior to that of worthless 'toil'. In his lifetime the cycles of Cathay were externally effected by the supply of opium, a subject that to Tennyson demanded the gravity of Homeric epic. Yet this existence of inexorable futility was also manifest in goldfish, doomed to circumnavigate their bowl eternally.

Tennyson's Orientalism and portrayal of intoxication moved Sara Coleridge to the extent that she wrote her own version of the poem. In 'Tennyson's "Lotos-Eaters" with a new conclusion' (see appendix), Sara seeks to improve on her source. Dialogic authorship was very much on Sara's mind. At the time of drafting her version of Tennyson, she had commenced the task of defending her father from charges of plagiarizing Friedrich Schiller. This work would consume five years of Sara's life and culminate in her edition of *Biographia Literaria* (1847). Her key contention, that borrowed ideas constituted nuclei from which Coleridge developed his own ideas, applies equally to Sara's 'Lotos-Eaters'. Tennyson's poem also appealed to the love of classics that Sara developed in a remarkably rigorous home-schooling under her mother and Robert Southey. Her 'Lotos-Eaters', unpublished until 2007, revises the 1832 version of Tennyson's text, commencing with 'the lotos booms below the flowery peak' (145, in which Sara replaces 'barren' with its opposite, 'flowery'). Sara's text amplifies the moral aspects of Tennyson's poem, which had remained topical. As with Tennyson's original, personal history looms over Sara's text. She spent considerable time with her father during the Highgate period. Coleridge Senior was almost always bedridden and intoxicated at this time. Sara was an opium user too. One of her best-known poems, entitled 'Poppies' (1834), captures the dynamic between an addicted parent and an oblivious child. In this poem, the parent is Sara herself. Like Tennyson, Sara disapproved of opium on the basis of experience. It is likely that her intimacy with de Vere, a keen Tennyson reader, stimulated Sara's interest in the 'Lotos-Eaters'.

In *Table Talk*, Samuel Taylor Coleridge complained of Tennyson's tendency 'to deal in new metres without knowing what Metre means' (14.1.367). Sara's opinion of Tennyson's poetry differed from her father's; she rewrote the 'Lotos-Eaters' accordingly. In her criticism Sara does not fault Tennyson's metre, but rather finds his poetry too studied. She laments Tennyson's excessive 'intellectualism' in a letter.[31] In a draft of a review from 1848—heavily censored on publication in the *Quarterly Review* for its sympathy towards the Cockney School—Sara places Tennyson in 'the school of Sensation rather than Reflection'. She borrows this distinction from Arthur Henry Hallam's 1831 review of Tennyson. Like Hallam, Sara does not intend 'Reflection' and 'Sensation' to be mutually exclusive. Nor is it contradictory that at one point she faults Tennyson with excessive 'intellectualism', and says at another that he is too much concerned with 'Sensation'.[32] What 'intellectualism' and 'Sensation' have in common is that they risk neglecting morality, the quality of Wordsworth's and Coleridge's poetry that Sara perceives as deficient in Tennyson's. By borrowing language and imagery from 'Kubla Khan', Sara enhances the moral content of the 'Lotos-Eaters'. The same devices accentuate the relevance of Tennyson's original text to the opium trade.

In her 'Lotos-Eaters', Sara describes Tennyson's island in terms of Orientalist plenitude. The place also has a power to soothe which Sara expresses in Coleridgean language that betrays hidden dangers:

> Here are a thousand charms,
> One best of all, that every pang disarms,
> Th'enchanted lotos bloom o'er all our senses reigning
>
>   (9–11).

Like the wilderness at the edge of Kubla Khan's domain, the island is 'enchanted'. In Coleridge Senior's poem, that word corresponds to a 'savage place'; trouble in paradise. One cannot notice the shared vocabulary without recalling the dark undertones in 'Kubla Khan'. Comparably the disarmed pangs in Sara's poem are not consolatory when we remember Coleridge's 'Dejection: An Ode', which reports 'a grief without a pang' (21). This is a melancholy intoxication, which maintains awareness that pain has merely been anaesthetized. The cause of pain has not been eradicated.

---

[31] *The Regions of Sara Coleridge's Thought: Selected Literary Criticism*, ed. Peter Swaab, Nineteenth-Century Major Lives and Letters (New York: Palgrave Macmillan, 2012), 195.

[32] *The Regions of Sara Coleridge's Thought*, 104.

Sara responds to the portrayal of addiction as a communal experience in Tennyson's poem, which I related to China as an addicted nation. In Sara's version, this shared affliction entails a loss of individual identity:

> One radiant smile our trancèd gaze detaining
> Of one calm lake out of whose bosom ever,
> Drawn from many a shadowy fountain,
> In yon far distant boundary mountain
> Softly flows the travelled river
> Just heard above the stock dove's plaining:
> Or, borne upon the wave, with lilies float,
> Tranquil as they amid the slumb'rous gleam,
> Or, in the zephyr-wafted boat,
> As though we flew unpinioned in a dream
> From fragrant bank to bank pass lightly o'er.
>
> (15–25)

One smile of one lake; the mariners display only the characteristics of their surroundings. A salient Coleridgeism occurs in Sara's use of *rejet*, which invites us to read the rhyming lines together:

> Of one calm lake out of whose bosom ever,
>
>   . . .
>
> Softly flows the travelled river.

The progress of the river to the lake, to the interior of the mysterious island, here connotes a deepening narcotic trance.

Sara omits some of Tennyson's repetitions, but introduces new duplications. In the next sequence she repeats three of Tennyson's lines, then three of her own with variations. Sara cuts the mariners' declaration, 'we will return no more'. With these words Tennyson raises the possibility of volition, but Sara disallows such speculation. As such, hers is an even more pessimistic vision of addiction than Tennyson's. We might also compare Tennyson's own revision to the conclusion for the 1842 publication. In this version, the mariners flatter themselves that they might 'lie like gods together', a Lucretian image (*On the Nature of Things*, 3.18–25). They exaggerate the misery of mortal life as 'endless anguish', and the paradigm of the Olympians validates idleness. But Sara returns to the lake, river, and fountain:

> We will abide in the golden vale
> And never launch into the boundless plain,

> The watery waste where threat'ning billows roar,
> But nigh the sapphire lake remain
> In whose deep hospitable breast
> Derived from many a shadowy fountain
> In yon far distant sky-commingled mountain
> The travelled waters sink to rest,
> And there beside th'untroubled lilies float.
>
> (40–48)

The world beyond the island is entirely forgotten in this version of the poem. The sailors' consciousness is constrained within the realm of intoxication. The drug users are hopelessly lost in their trance.[33]

Sara insists on an Asian context for her study of addiction by her assimilation of 'Kubla Khan'. We might say that she anticipates Tennyson's own revised conclusion. Hallam Tennyson recalls his father's opinion that the new ending was an 'improvement':

The last paragraph setting forth the Lucretian Philosophy respecting the Gods, their aloofness from all human interests and elevated action, an Epicurean and therefore hard-hearted repose, sweetened not troubled by the endless wail from the earth.[34]

Yet Tennyson's scene of idle gods is exactly the sort of 'intellectualism' for which Sara faults him in her later correspondence. Where we might expect more palpably moral sentiments on drug use and abnegations of responsibility, Tennyson finds a vignette in classical culture that allows him to retreat, much as the sailors do. It may be because reviewers lamented this deficiency that Tennyson's later poems—including a scathing account of the consequences of Epicureanism in 'Lucretius' (1868)—contain clearly didactic elements, which indicate how Britain might justly conduct its international affairs.

---

[33] Compare Sara's assessment of her father: 'The nerveless languor . . . paralysed his powers both of rest and action, precluding by a torpid irritability their happy vicissitude,— rendered all exercises difficult for him except of thought and imagination flowing onward freely and in self-made channels.' See Samuel Taylor Coleridge, *Biographia Literaria or, Biographical Sketches of My Literary Life and Opinions*, ed. Sara Coleridge, 2 vols (London: William Pickering, 1847), 1:xix.

[34] Hallam Tennyson, *Alfred Lord Tennyson,* 2:504.

Chinese Lessons for Britain in 'Locksley Hall', 'Sixty Years After', and 'The Ancient Sage'

In light of the connections Tennyson articulates between cultural stagnation and opium in his other poems, the 'Locksley Hall' speaker's chief concern becomes more sympathetic to the reader. He does not hate Asia as a distant, lesser other. The problem is the opposite: China's condition is too close to the character's own for comfort. As such he enacts a version of de Quincey's Sinophobia which, as I argue in the next chapter, is ultimately self-oriented. The 'Locksley Hall' speaker fears that his life will replicate the unprogressive 'cycles of Cathay'. His anxiety originates in a sense of inferiority which, in turn, corresponds to the personal connection to Asia that the youth reveals in the poem. References to opium in 'Locksley Hall' accentuate the speaker's perception of himself as the Oriental outsider. Amid the hubbub of British advancement, the youth quotes Hamlet to lament that his own time is 'out of joint' (134).

The speaker knows that he drifts outside the 'grooves' that lead to attainment. This has caused his beloved Amy to favour a rival. He strikes an ominous note in his recollection of their courtship by describing Amy in terms that recall Tennyson's lotus-eaters:

> Then her cheek was pale and thinner than should be for one so young,
> And her eyes on all my motions with a mute observance hung.
>
> (21–22)

Amy, sallow and withdrawn, is not an image of ecstatic love. She is inactive but for an unsettling stare; she only hangs her gaze on the youth's 'motions'. Whatever her true sentiments for the speaker in those days, his effect is that Amy resembles an opium user. The intoxicated languor he causes shows that the suitor is unlikely to provide a positive future. Accordingly, when he imagines Amy before him years later, the youth suggests that she anaesthetize her guilt:

> Drug thy memories, lest thou learn it, lest thy heart be put to proof,
> In the dead unhappy night, and when the rain is on the roof.
>
> (77–78)

The young man envisions the solution to his problems as a concoction like laudanum, in which brandy is mixed with opium: 'I myself must mix with action, lest I wither by despair' (98). The Oriental presence of opium is a clue to the speaker's Asian identity:

> Here at least, where nature sickens, nothing. Ah, for some retreat
> Deep in yonder shining Orient, where my life began to beat;
> Where in wild Mahratta-battle fell my father evil-starred;—
> I was left a trampled orphan, and a selfish uncle's ward.
>
> (153–56)

The primal, heart-like alliteration in 'my life began to beat' distinguishes the speaker's role in Asia from the sober portrayal of a British-led 'Federation of the world' earlier in the poem (129). His father's death in India is the key circumstance by which the young man was deemed unfit for Amy. He imagines a cyclical family history in which he, if unable to slot into the groove of national advancement, would also seek his fortune in Asia. The youth does not envision that he would act as a colonial invader, but instead describes a hedonistic kind of integration:

> There methinks would be enjoyment more than in this march of mind,
> In the steamship, in the railway, in the thoughts that shake mankind.
>
> (165–66)

The 'march of mind' is restrictive. The speaker recognizes that the culture that begets invention also imposes social rules which, he feels, have cost him union with Amy. His scene of Orientalist primitivism appeals to him because it is one of unregulated impulses. Here children signify a sexual abandon that might compensate for the frustrated love-affair:

> There the passions cramp'd no longer shall have scope and breathing space;
> I will take some savage woman, she shall rear my dusky race.
>
> (167–68)

He rejects this future and derides Cathay, pledging himself to Britain instead. The poem ends, like 'Ulysses', with volition that is stirring but also ambiguous: 'the mighty wind arises, roaring seaward, and I go' (194). 'It closes, but does not cease', A. H. Japp claims in an appraisal of 'Locksley Hall' from 1865. Japp's commentary is likely to have inspired Tennyson's sequel, 'Locksley Hall Sixty Years After'. The critic continues: 'it was unsafe for the poet to leave his hero here, . . . when viewed simply for the formally moral stand-point, which requires that a direct lesson be drawn from everything.'[35] Tennyson supplies the missing instruction in the sequel to 'Locksley Hall'. The precise moral is one of several attributes that this sequel shares with another late work, 'The Ancient Sage', which explores Daoism.

While 'Locksley Hall' is '*overheard*'—to borrow John Stuart Mill's term for poetry, especially suited to the dramatic monologue—in 'Sixty Years After' the same speaker addresses his grandson.[36] This arrangement facilitates didacticism. 'The Ancient Sage' uses a similar device. As the Platonist Benjamin Jowett (1817–93) suggested that Tennyson read Laozi, it is unsurprising that the poet's treatment of the Chinese sage should take the form of a philosophical dialogue. This discourse examines the concepts of *Dao De Jing* dialectically. Undoubtedly the Greek approach betrays an Occidental perspective. Certain of the characters' comments on Daoism are anachronistic or Christian in principle. 'The Ancient Sage' is obviously a subjective interpretation of Laozi as encountered in translation. Yet by this method Tennyson makes aspects of the notoriously enigmatic Chinese text explicit. Furthermore, the piece demonstrates that his reading of Laozi compelled Tennyson to reconsider subjects such as time, progress, inaction, and the exchange between East and West.

The Daoist piece embodies a kind of literary criticism: the sage reads and responds to a poem authored by his companion, a work which poses existential questions. The philosopher's voice in blank verse is in dialogue with quotations from the youth's poem, which occurs in ballad-metre. There is some allusion here to the source of Tennyson's fascination with Daoism: Jowett had become a mentor to the poet, who often read him new work. Jowett was unsparing with his criticism and typically suggested metaphysical themes. Hence, as in 'Sixty Years After', an older man advises a younger one in 'The Ancient Sage'. The grandson in 'Sixty Years After' fears for his future; the young man in 'The Ancient Sage' voices religious scepticism. In the poem-within-the-poem, the youth reveals that bereavement has robbed him of his beloved; amorous disappointment recurs in 'Sixty Years After'. Both poems conclude with

[35] Quoted in *The Poems of Tennyson*, 3:130.
[36] *Essays on Poetry by John Stuart Mill*, ed. F. Parvin Sharpless (Columbia: University of South Carolina Press, 1976), 12.

explicit instruction. In 'The Ancient Sage' this didacticism occurs as a list
of prohibitions, more Judaeo-Christian than Daoist in tone:

> help thy fellow men,
> And make thy gold thy vassal not thy king,
> And fling free alms into the beggar's bowl,
> And send the day into the darkened heart;
> Nor list for guerdon in the voice of men,
>
> . . .
>
> Nor roll thy viands on a luscious tongue,
> Nor drown thyself with flies in honied wine;
> Nor thou be rageful, like a handled bee.
>
> (258–69)

There is no equivalent set of commandments in *Dao De Jing*. In
Chalmers's translation, which makes additions to render the terse Chinese text as syntactic English, Laozi counsels moderation by descriptions
of the exemplary sage rather than commandments: 'He is chaste, but
does not chasten others. He is straight, but does not straighten others. He
is enlightened, but does not dazzle others.'[37] Thus the two Tennyson
poems settle on conventional Christian instruction, but they do so by
way of serious engagement with Chinese ideas.

In 'The Ancient Sage', Tennyson's classicism colours his mediation of
Daoism. This poem too expresses Tennyson's antagonism towards
national progress and the atmosphere of hubris. Laozi appeals to Tennyson because the philosopher's hypothesis of an unseen, all-pervasive
substance can be used to illuminate the limitations of empiricism, the
keystone of nineteenth-century science. *Dao De Jing* is also enjoyable per
se. Tennyson responds to Laozi's playful repetition of terms, a quality of
the work that does survive translation: 'The *tau* (reason) which can be
tau-ed (reasoned) is not the Eternal *Tau* (Reason). The name which can
be named is not the Eternal Name.'[38]

Tennyson's Chinese philosopher addresses the young man's impa-
tience for knowledge of the *dao* (道), the unseen cause and substance of
all existence. Tennyson terms *dao* the 'Nameless':

---

[37] *Tau The King: The Speculations on Metaphysics, Polity, and Morality of 'The Old
Philosopher', Lau-Tsze*, John Chalmers trans. (London: Trübner & Co., 1868), 45–6.

[38] *Tau The King*, 1.

If thou would'st hear the Nameless, and wilt dive
Into the Temple-cave of thine own self,
There, brooding by the central altar, thou
Mayst haply learn the Nameless hath a voice,
By which thou wilt abide, if thou be wise,
As if thou knewest, though thou canst not know;
For Knowledge is the swallow on the lake
That sees and stirs the surface-shadow there
But never yet hath dipt into the abysm,
The Abysm of all Abysms, beneath, within
The blue of sky and sea, the green of earth,
And in the million-millionth of a grain
Which cleft and cleft again for evermore,
And ever vanishing, never vanishes,
To me, my son, more mystic than myself,
Or even than the Nameless is to me.
    And when thou sendest thy free soul through heaven,
Nor understandest bound nor boundlessness,
Thou seest the Nameless of the hundred names.
    And if the Nameless should withdraw from all
Thy frailty counts most real, all thy world
Might vanish like thy shadow in the dark.

(37–52)

The sage's interlocutor desires full knowledge of the visible world, specifically of the power that underlies all phenomena. He understands that the perceptible universe is, in a Platonic metaphor, but a 'surface-shadow'. The answer he receives is Augustinian.[39] The Chinese philosopher characterizes the Nameless as a consciousness that sustains the universe intentionally, and which might withdraw. He adds that faith is a prerequisite of knowledge: 'cling to Faith beyond the forms of Faith!' (69). *Dao De Jing* makes no reference to faith whatsoever. Other aspects of Tennyson's poem might equally be termed Daoist or Graeco-Roman: the *yin-yang* and kinds of binarity; the metaphors of cave and fountain; the relationship between nature as material Earth (*di*, 地) and as a set of processes, or Heaven (*tian*, 天), which has its counterpart in the distinction between *natura naturans* and *natura naturata*. Many of the ideas in 'The Ancient Sage' occur in Tennyson's earlier poetry, but he finds

---

[39] See Howard W. Fulweiler, '"The Argument of the Ancient Sage": Tennyson and the Christian Intellectual Tradition', *Victorian Poetry* 21, no. 3 (1983): 203–16.

Chinese equivalents in Laozi. Most importantly, however—and despite the Augustinian exhortation for faith—the philosopher's epistemological method is fundamentally Chinese. Knowledge of the universe is self-knowledge, which results from solitary introspection: 'dive | Into the Temple-cave of thine own self'. A variant of this advice is expressed in 'Sixty Years After', and the lesson has an application to Britain's affairs in China.

Both Tennyson's Chinese philosopher and the 'Locksley Hall' speaker discuss the flow of time as it relates to personal crisis. The sage's follower despairs that time seems a supreme power beyond human influence, an impersonal force that negates accomplishment with senility, bodily deterioration, and death. The Tennyson reader is reminded of 'The Lotos-Eaters', in which the sailors relinquish the possibilities of heroism or suffering in favour of stasis. Intoxicated, they halt or abandon time, refusing participation in worldly affairs. 'The Ancient Sage' tells us that anxiety over the passage of time is misdirected:

> The days and hours are ever glancing by,
> And seem to flicker past through sun and shade,
> Or short, or long, as Pleasure leads, or Pain;
> But with the Nameless is nor Day nor Hour;
> Though we, thin minds, who creep from thought to thought
> Break into 'Thens' and 'Whens' the Eternal Now:
> This double seeming of the single world!
>
> (99–105)

Change is constant in Daoist cosmology, but time itself is unknowable. Tennyson embellishes Laozi with a Romantic suggestion that time is subjective. The philosopher says his follower must bend time to his will, and explains that the effort to comprehend time by empiricism will fail.

Speculation on time in 'The Ancient Sage' is pertinent to 'Locksley Hall' and 'Sixty Years After' not simply because of allusions to Asia and progress in those texts, but because the speaker imagines his fate as the product of 'Thens' and 'Whens'. He considers Victorian accomplishment 'the long result of Time' (12) and himself 'heir of all the ages' in 'Locksley Hall' (178). But in 'Sixty Years After', the character acknowledges widespread poverty in Britain: 'Progress halts on palsied feet' (219). Here too the message is that one's condition is separable from the march of progress. This realization leads the character to mimic the Chinese sage's advice on introspection, although from a more mundane perspective. Implicitly he rejects imperialism with a recommendation that his addressee, heir to Locksley Hall, focus on local matters. The speaker praises his former rival, Amy's late husband, for his commitment to the community:

> Move among your people, know them, follow him who led the way,
> Strove for sixty widow'd years to help his homelier brother men,
> Served the poor, and built the cottage, raised the school, and drain'd the fen.

(266–68)

The formal analogues for 'Locksley Hall' include poems that explore intervention in foreign realms. The consequences to Paris's abduction of Helen are dire both in the communal experience of battle and individually, as demonstrated by the plight of figures such as Iphigenia and Agamemnon. At the conclusion to *Agamemnon*, Clytaemnestra indicates that supremacy over another culture is a hollow attainment. Viewers of the *Oresteia* know that the legacy of retaliatory violence continues beyond the scope of Clytaemnestra's vision. Thus Tennyson approached Cathay from texts that portray meddling overseas as internecine. Such wisdom manifested to Tennyson in the import of opium to Britain, where it harmed his family, and its sale in China, where its disruptive effects reached British newspapers and occasioned war. British commentators faulted the Qing Empire for insularity, and interpreted Chinese refusal to indulge British aspirations as a symptom of backwardness. But Laozi's inward gaze, as rendered by Tennyson, seems a logical extension of aspects of the *Iliad*, *Odyssey*, and *Oresteia* that caution political powers against international aggression. Qing insularity is consistent with the introspection of canonical Chinese philosophers, from the metaphysical Laozi to the family-oriented Confucius. Older and wiser, the 'Locksley Hall' speaker comes to think there's something in it.

6

A Greek Tragedy in China

Thomas de Quincey's Opium Wars Journalism

'It is not for knowledge that Greek is worth learning', Thomas de Quincey (1785–1859) declares in an article of 1823, 'but for power' (3:73). This 'power', he explains, is a state induced by certain literature 'in which I should be made to feel vividly . . . emotions which ordinary life rarely or never supplies' (3:71). The literature of 'power', which transports its audience emotionally, is comparable to the sublime theorized by Edmund Burke (1756) and de Quincey's Romantic contemporaries. In this work, entitled *Letters to a Young Man whose Education has been Neglected*, de Quincey encourages an autodidact to learn Greek and Latin. De Quincey does not name particular texts, but implies that wide study of Greek and Roman culture yields the experience of 'power'. Classics is a nebulous concept in de Quincey's works: vaguely defined yet talismanically effectual, characterized by deep textual knowledge and a sense of affinity with the ancient world.

In a survey of ancient Greek authors for *Tait's Magazine*, entitled 'A Brief Appraisal of Greek Literature' (1838), de Quincey defines classics only by the social pre-eminence of ancient literati: 'the calling them *classici*, implied that they belonged to *the* class emphatically, or par excellence' (11:7fn). While de Quincey does not outline his classical canon, it is evident that he particularly favours Greek drama, historical writing, and rhetoric. De Quincey posits that classical works are not solely to be considered literature of 'power' for their effect on the reader, but because classical knowledge obtains the scholar a greater degree of social and political influence. As with Lamb, excellence in classics comes across as a kind of exclusive club in de Quincey's work. By extension,

China from the Ruins of Athens and Rome: Classics, Sinology, and Romanticism, 1793–1938.
Chris Murray, Oxford University Press (2020). © Chris Murray.
DOI: 10.1093/oso/9780198767015.001.0001

nations that possess literatures of 'power' are superior to those which de Quincey adjudges without. He celebrates that 'within the next two centuries all the barbarous languages of the earth . . . will be one after another strangled and exterminated' by the languages of 'power' (3:60). Subsequently he invokes the classical literature of 'power' in a series of hostile articles on China. This chapter is concerned with the transposition of ideas that occurs between de Quincey's essays on subjects that are ostensibly unconnected. He produces essays on Greek tragedy that are really about British supremacy, and articles about China in which Greek tragedy substantiates bellicose rhetoric. They appeared at crucial junctures in Sino–British relations. These texts were contemporaneous with the Opium Wars, and they fit into a bigger pattern. Classics provided concepts for several types of discussion that would lead to conflict with China. These dialogues often alleged British humiliation by China, the counterpart to the Chinese national-humiliation narrative discussed in the following chapter.

Talent and disappointment underlie de Quincey's attitude to classical culture. A distinguished young scholar at Manchester Grammar School, de Quincey matriculated at Worcester College, Oxford in 1803. He was uninspired both by the academics and his fellow students, became indebted for his purchase of books and opium, and spent lengthy periods in London during term. When due to take his final exams, he absconded, never to return. Nonetheless de Quincey's circle, which included Coleridge and the Wordsworths, considered him a brilliant classicist. Accordingly in 1820 de Quincey was nominated for a Professorship in Moral Philosophy at the University of Edinburgh. The position was awarded to his colleague John Wilson, editor of *Blackwood's* magazine. Privately, Wilson confided that he was so ignorant of his supposed subject that he required assistance. Initially he implored de Quincey for advice on Plato, Aristotle, and Socrates; in practice, many of Wilson's lectures were authored entirely by de Quincey in the form of letters to his friend. De Quincey became increasingly bitter at his impoverishment in light of the impostor Wilson's well-remunerated professorship.[1] The two argued acrimoniously, but reconciled in 1823. Some years later de Quincey

---

[1] Robert Morrison, *The English Opium Eater: A Biography of Thomas de Quincey* (London: Weidenfeld & Nicolson, 2009), 199–203.

began to write about classical subjects in his journalism. This was an abrupt departure, as his plenteous output included no work on the ancient world prior to the series of six articles on 'The Caesars' (1832–34). De Quincey drew on Livy, Cassius Dio, Gibbon, and especially the 'anecdote-monger' Suetonius for 'The Caesars', which appeared in *Blackwood's* (9:38). The articles display a preference for scandal and intrigue over historical accuracy. De Quincey contributes nothing to original research on the subject, but the imagination and insight typify his later writing on the ancient world. The paranoia and fixation with surveillance are common to his works more generally:

Gibbon has described the hopeless condition of one who should attempt to fly from the wrath of the almost omnipresent Emperor. But this dire impossibility of escape was in the end dreadfully retaliated upon the Emperor; persecutors and traitors were found everywhere: and the vindictive or the ambitious subject found himself as omnipresent as the jealous or the offended Emperor. The crown of the Caesars was therefore a crown of thorns: and it must be admitted, that never in this world have rank and power been purchased at so awful a cost in tranquillity and peace of mind. The steps of Caesar's throne were absolutely saturated with the blood of those who had possessed it: and so inexorable was that murderous fate which overhung that gloomy eminence, that at length it demanded the spirit of martyrdom in him who ventured to ascend it.   (9:133)

Subsequently, classical themes became ubiquitous in de Quincey's journalism. His essays include commentaries on Homer (1841), Plato's *Republic* (1841), Cicero (1842), and Herodotus (1842).

Ostensibly it appears that de Quincey's views on China manifest a familiar motif in classical reception studies, by which British imperialists invoke the ancient world to legitimate foreign policy. Yet de Quincey's writing on Asia—particularly China—demonstrates conflicting attitudes towards empire. In reference to Gibbon, Jeremy Black notes that 'although empire would come to be seen as a site and source of manliness in the High Victorian period, it was a source of anxiety a century earlier'.[2] What is unusual about de Quincey is his tendency to oscillate between the perspectives Black indicates. The Romantic who lives too long becomes a Victorian: this is a partial explanation for his contradictory opinions on Asia. However much de Quincey's journalism appears to

---

[2] Jeremy Black, 'Responding to the Outside World', *Eighteenth-Century Studies* 45, no. 1 (2012): 319.

endorse British imperialism, his jingoism is undermined by old and personal anxieties. These are signalled, for example, by de Quincey's persistence, decades after the publication of his autobiographical *Confessions of an English Opium Eater* (1821), in writing under the pseudonym 'the English Opium Eater', even on political matters. His attempts to assert himself by reference to the literature of 'power' always intimate a fear of disempowerment. Hence, de Quincey's use of Greek tragedy to call for war on China offers evidence both of his aversion to violence, and hostility to suppressed aspects of himself which are closer to the figures of his Oriental nightmares than they are to his classical ideals. This kind of self-projection demonstrates that de Quincey fits Said's model of the Orientalist more neatly than other figures in this book. A further trait he displays in accordance with Said's hypothesis is that, motivated by a wish for Britain to conquer and homogenize foreign territories, de Quincey merges Asian cultures into a vision of a single Orient. He bemoans *feng shui*, but his example is from ancient Persia (18:123). De Quincey has ingested classical Orientalism, and likens Qing diplomacy to the courts of Darius and Xerxes (18:91–92). Yet his precise mode of self-projection undoes the political conviction. Using classics, de Quincey expresses ambivalence concerning opium, a subject that troubles him more greatly than he admits in *Confessions*.

In 1857, shortly before the outbreak of the Second Opium War (1857–60), de Quincey published two articles in the magazine *Titan*. With considerable interest in a dispute that centres on opium, he recommends that Britain attack China. In the first of these articles, de Quincey declares that the 'Mantchoo' rule invites destruction with 'the demoniac *hybris* of Greek Tragedy' (18:97). I begin detailed discussion of de Quincey's writing on China with this late essay because, as I shall clarify, 'demonaic *hybris*' encapsulates an idea that permeates his China essays. To validate his opinion, de Quincey trots out the clichés about perceived slights inflicted on British visitors by the Qing Empire over two centuries. He argues for retributive warfare. In this journalism de Quincey revives a favourite theme. Prior to the First Opium War (1840–42) he contributed a supportive article entitled 'On the Opium and the China Question' to *Blackwood's* in 1840, followed by a second essay entitled a 'Postscript'. De Quincey's reflections on China were well received. In the 'Postscript', de Quincey boasts that his first piece anticipated—and possibly influenced—the Duke of Wellington's decisive pro-war speech at the House of Lords, which he declares has 'oracular value' (18:563). In 1857 de Quincey's articles on China were sufficiently popular to be republished as an independent pamphlet.

De Quincey adopts warmongering rhetoric on China. 'So arrogant a people must be brought to their senses,' he declares in 1840. 'Thump them well . . . it is the only logic which penetrates the fog of so conceited a people' (18:541). The crisis arose from Qing officials' newfound determination to block the import of opium. Britain waged both Opium Wars with the intention to force its opium *into* China—more broadly to achieve free trade—and thereby compensate for the outflow of funds spent on tea. A decade of rising anti-Chinese sentiment in Britain culminated in 1839. Qing authorities had confiscated a year's harvest of opium, valued at £2m. The opium trade was under assault, to the dismay of the English Opium Eater. Furthermore, de Quincey's son Horace had been dispatched to Canton earlier in 1840 as a lieutenant in the army, where he would die from a fever in 1842. Horrified by the loss of so much opium, personally aggrieved, and with his national pride insulted, de Quincey advises war without hesitation. Charles Elliot (1801–75), British Superintendent of Trade in China, allowed Lin Zexu's officials to destroy the opium, but promised the traders compensation. The Foreign Secretary, Viscount Palmerston (1784–1865), issued a letter of demands. Britain attacked China in June 1840, with Elliot effectively holding Canton to ransom. To some extent de Quincey find the situation in China absurd, and he blames the Superintendent for the destruction of the opium chests in 1839: 'the total loss—every shilling of it—was a pure creation of Elliot's' (11:540). His argument for war captures a cumulative sense of outrage at China rather than resentment over a single incident.

Similarly in 1857 de Quincey claims that the Qing empire prompts British retaliation with 'the spirit of insult and arrogant self-assertion' (18:85). In 1856 Chinese officials captured a British merchant-ship, the *Arrow*, for its involvement in piracy. The Royal Navy shelled Canton in retaliation. Eventually the authorities released the vessel and crew, but Britain felt an apology was due from the Qing Empire, which was not forthcoming. Hence in the 1857 journalism de Quincey urges war again, with further reference to 200 years of supposed insults suffered by British visitors to China. Prime Minister for a second time, Palmerston won the general election that year—which became known as the 'Chinese election' for the central debate—largely on account of promises to restore British pride by attacking China. His was an especially xenophobic campaign. Palmerston's supporters used explicitly violent imagery to persuade the public that the Qing regime was evil.[3]

Although de Quincey's choice of the phrase 'demoniac *hybris*' appears to be a fleeting allusion to the classical *daimon*, the concept haunts de Quincey's sentiments on China and his Orientalism more widely. Few readers would expect de Quincey's Opium Wars commentary of 1857 to commence with a reflection on classical Athens and ancient Greek theatre. In this context, de Quincey associates literature of 'power' not solely with personal status, but extends it to the British Empire, whose cultural predicates lie in ancient Greece and Rome. Drama, de Quincey begins, induced 'moral regeneration' in the Athenian audience; a constant renewal of the principles that distinguished the city's enlightened populace (18:85). De Quincey contends that China is without morality because it lacks such culture. Moreover, China resembles the protagonist in a Greek drama; hence de Quincey complains that the Qing officials have acted with 'the demoniac *hybris* of Greek Tragedy'. Thus de Quincey invokes the severity of classical tragedy to emphasize the importance, as he sees it, of a punitive attack on China. With the literature of 'power' he calls for a display of imperial might that will champion the opium trade and nullify the threat of the Orient.

Critics have tended either to avoid de Quincey's China journalism entirely or to treat its ostensible racism as a cheap holiday. Anne Veronica Witchard attributes to de Quincey a 'pathological loathing of China'.[4] Diane Simmons terms the Opium Wars journalism the 'vengeful fantasy' of a 'bully'.[5] To an extent such claims are valid, but they miss significant nuances. Some of the tragic ideas that de Quincey introduces

---

[3] Julia Lovell, *The Opium War: Drugs, Dreams and the Making of China* (London: Picador, 2011), 255.

[4] Anne Veronica Witchard, *Thomas Burke's Dark* Chinoiserie: Limehouse Nights *and the Queer Spell of Chinatown* (Farnham: Ashgate, 2009), 62.

[5] Diane Simmons, *The Narcissism of Empire: Loss, Rage and Revenge in Thomas De Quincey, Robert Louis Stevenson, Arthur Conan Doyle, Rudyard Kipling and Isak Dinesen* (Eastbourne: Sussex Academic Press, 2006), 42–3.

to his commentary on China compromise the interpretation that he is entirely in favour of conflict. I contend that by 'demoniac *hybris*', he means specifically to invoke the idea of the classical *daimon*, by which evaluation of agency and responsibility is problematic. The *daimon* or 'allotter' is the 'operator of more or less unexpected, and intrusive, events in human life' (OCD4). By this device the Qing Empire is not entirely culpable for its actions. Furthermore, this comprehension of the *daimon* can allegorize both the Malay amok in *Confessions*, and opium addiction: all entail an individual's loss of volition, a surrender of agency to an outside force. Such creative reinterpretations of the *daimon* were popular among de Quincey's acquaintance and their followers. Coleridge's *daimon*, as I have discussed elsewhere, is comparable to de Quincey's.[6] Shelley's *daimon*, like Socrates', is a guiding voice, while Yeats's is an alter-ego. I think that such readings of the Greek tragic *daimon* appealed to de Quincey's circle because of parallels in contemporary debates on philosophy and science. Feelings of power and helplessness associated with daimonic activity are adaptable to political allegory. Discussions of creative inspiration, religious enthusiasm, Mesmerism, and Necessitarianism all entailed reflection on predestination and personal agency, as did conceptualization of the *daimon* as an instrument of fate, typical of the anachronistic and rather Shakespearean reading of Greek tragedy amongst de Quincey's contemporaries. For example, Coleridge explains the skill with which an ancient tragedian was required to relate the chorus to the interests of the plot: 'you may take people to a place, but only by a palpable equivoque can you bring Birnam Wood to Macbeth at Dunsinane . . . . Fine instance in Eschylus—Agamemnon' (5.2:317). In the Romantics' tragic universe, the classical *daimon* serves destiny.

Allusions to tragedy in de Quincey's journalism on China suggest symbolic violence rather than a literal call-to-arms. More specifically the *daimon* as metaphoric of his own helplessness reveals how the Opium Wars journalism continues the work of *Confessions*: it is an encoded expression of de Quincey's neurosis as addict. Hence the China articles resume a wider, paradoxical pattern in which the literature of 'power', invoked to defy an Oriental threat, communicates de Quincey's perception of his own vulnerability.

---

[6] Chris Murray, *Tragic Coleridge* (Farnham: Ashgate, 2013), 25–41.

Classics, *Confessions*, and de Quincey's Orient

As we saw in the previous chapter, for de Quincey to invoke the ancient world in reference to the opium controversy was not unique. As with the drug trade, rhetoric on both sides of the war debate alluded to classics in ways that typify responses to Victorian imperialism more generally. An article in *Blackwood's* magazine adopts a fatalistic attitude to the proposed war, and twice makes use of Suetonius' attribution to Caesar, 'the die is cast'. The journalist opines that Qing officials display the 'melancholy immortality of the last of the Romans'.[7] Gladstone refers to 'the story of the siege of Troy that Neptune swept away the bulwark of the Greeks' to complain that Lord Chancellor Cranworth has unfairly dismissed anti-war argument.[8] Sympathetic with the Chinese, his choice of allegory intimates Gladstone's fears for the likely consequences of conflict. Clergyman Algernon Sydney Thelwall claims that the British Empire has succeeded the Roman, and should therefore adopt a greater sense of responsibility for its actions in China.[9] The accomplished Sinologist and diplomat Thomas Taylor Meadows (1815–68), whom de Quincey cites as provoking his resumption of interest in China in 1857, cites the prevalence of 'legal slavery' in China. Surveying China's recent insurrections, the erosion of Qing authority, and the low status of Chinese natives under their Manchu rulers, Meadows reasons that the cultural superiority he attributes to ancient Athens and Rome relates directly to their greater proportions of 'free men'.[10]

In a convergence of de Quincey's pursuits, part of the anti-Chinese sentiment in Britain during the 1830s reflected a dispute, stoked by opium traders, which involved comparative Greek and Chinese etymologies. The *Canton Register*, owned by opium merchant James Matheson (1796–1878), began to complain that official Chinese documents referred to the British merchants as *yi* (夷), which the *Register* translated as 'barbarians'. This interpretation was reasonable given that historically

---

[7] 'The Opium and the China Question', *Blackwood's Edinburgh Magazine* 47 (January–June 1840): 368–83.

[8] William Ewert Gladstone, *War in China* (London: Rivingtons, 1857), 19.

[9] Algernon Sydney Thelwall, *The Iniquities of the Opium Trade with China* (London: H. Allen & Co., 1839), 134.

[10] Thomas Taylor Meadows, *The Chinese and their Rebellions* (London: Smith, Elder & Co., 1856), 630–7.

the word, rather like Gibbon's sense of what was barbaric, denoted those excluded from the culture of the Central States. *Yi* had passed by Macartney's translators unremarked. Many found the term unobjectionable. However, the *Register*'s letters page debated the justness of calling Britons *barbaros*, and the scandal spread home. Although journals such as the *Quarterly Review* and the *Asiatic Journal* claimed that 'barbarian' was a mistranslation of *yi*, Matheson alleged insult in order to press for war. Ultimately 'the idea that the Chinese called the British "barbarian" was appealing and had . . . purchase in the print media in 1830s Britain.'[11] The word 'barbarian', with variants, occurs no fewer than fifty times in *Register* editor John Slade's *Narrative of the Late Proceedings and Events in China* (1839). He translates *yi* as 'barbarian', and rages that the Britons are so treated. Meanwhile he refers to the Chinese freely as 'barbarians'. In the 1834 memoir of Dutch Missionary Society envoy turned East India Company interpreter Karl Gützlaff, the word 'barbarians' is repeatedly passed back and forth between the narrator and the Chinese sailors he meets, without analysis. The debate over *yi* continued. In 1851 Thoms—whom Morrison had enlisted at Macao to print his Chinese dictionary, and who translated *Chinese Courtship*, discussed in Chapter 4—published a pamphlet entitled *Remarks on rendering the Chinese word man 'Barbarian', showing that the Chinese do not call Europeans Barbarians*. Here Thoms investigates the character 蠻, *man*, which was also applied to Europeans and whose popular translation as 'barbarian' Thoms disputes. He forgets, strangely, that he himself translated *man* as 'barbarian' in *Chinese Courtship*.[12] Meadows rebutted Thoms in the *Shanghae Almanac* in 1854. Thus when de Quincey counts Chinese among 'barbarous languages', he participates in an ongoing argument about translation, barbarism, and national humiliation which joined modern Canton to ancient Greece.

Depth of emotion distinguishes de Quincey's use of classical knowledge from the above commentators in his reflections on China. He expresses lifelong fears of Asia, and unspoken ambivalence towards

[11] Song-Chuan Chen, *Merchants of War and Peace: British Knowledge of China in the Making of the Opium War* (Hong Kong: Hong Kong University Press, 2017), 90 and see 82–102.

[12] See K.C. Leung, 'Chinese Courtship: The *Huajian Ji* in English Translation', *CHINOPERL* 20, no. 1 (1997): 285.

opium. Repeatedly he relies on ideas from Graeco-Roman culture to support political arguments that are informed by these personal sentiments. De Quincey's gaze does not classicize casually in the manner of, for example, the *Blackwood's* journalist's rhetorical stroke that the 'die is cast' in China, nor does he quote from a particular text simply to achieve an emotional tone. De Quincey perceives his command of classical learning as a source of authority and even the dominant trait of his identity. Hence, allusions to classics serve multiple, interrelated functions within de Quincey's journalism on China, some of which I think are unintentional: to establish him as a learned commentator; to exemplify the culture of 'power' championed by British imperialism; as a form of resistance to alternative civilizations; to impart his awareness (at some level) that his aggressive tone is unwarranted and originates in personal experience; to hint how his own weakness resembles the frailty he attributes to China. De Quincey's China is substantially built from the materials of classical Athens, and so demonstrates that even political journalism could be based on imaginative works, pitted against reliable information about Asia.

In *Confessions*, de Quincey establishes the pattern that characterizes his journalism on the Opium Wars, by which the Orient poses a threat to him, while classical culture offers a solution. De Quincey recalls an idyllic time in the Lake District, where he enjoys the company of the Wordsworths, reads at his leisure, and ingests vast quantities of laudanum without adverse effects. Sadly the euphoric haze dissipates and is succeeded by a phase of drug-induced nightmares. De Quincey associates the transition with an unexpected visitor, whom he describes in one of his most famous passages. 'One day,' he writes, 'a Malay knocked at my door. What business a Malay could have to transact amongst English mountains, I cannot conjecture: but possibly he was on his road to a seaport about forty miles distant' (2:56).

De Quincey's servant is unable to communicate with the visitor. She fetches the master of the house, hoping that the scholar may speak the stranger's language. De Quincey descends to find his servant and the newcomer side by side as though to facilitate contrast. In his exotic 'turban and loose trowsers' the visitor elicits suspicion and fear, emotions that typify de Quincey's xenophobia towards the Orient:

A more striking picture there could not be imagined, than the beautiful English face of the girl, and its exquisite fairness, together with her erect and independent attitude, contrasted with the sallow and bilious skin of the Malay, enamelled or veneered with mahogany, by marine air, his small, fierce, restless eyes, thin lips, slavish gestures and adorations.   (2:57)

The narrator does not perceive the Malay as a visitor to welcome, but a threat that must be neutralized. De Quincey uses the literature of 'power' to approach this threat:

I addressed him in some lines from the Iliad; considering that, of such languages as I possessed, Greek, in point of longitude, came geographically nearest to an Oriental one. He worshipped me in a most devout manner, and replied in what I suppose was Malay. In this way I saved my reputation with my neighbours: for the Malay had no means of betraying the secret. . . . On his departure, I presented him with a piece of opium. To him, as an Orientalist, I concluded that opium must be familiar: and the expression of his face convinced me that it was. Nevertheless, I was struck with some little consternation when I saw him suddenly raise his hand to his mouth, and . . . bolt the whole. . . . The quantity was enough to kill three dragoons and their horses.   (2:57)

De Quincey sends the visitor on his way. To his relief, he hears no subsequent report that a Malay has overdosed in the Lake District. However, the Malay returns in de Quincey's dreams. The narrator declares that 'if I were compelled to forego England, and to live in China, and among Chinese modes of manners and modes of life and scenery, I should go mad'. Although we presume he is Malayan rather than Chinese, the Malay is the agent of this dreaded change. He becomes a 'fearful enemy' who spirits de Quincey away to the Orient, a place of unaccountable horrors where 'man is a weed' (2:70). In his accounts of these nightmares, de Quincey enacts imperialistic fantasies in which he subjects Oriental creatures and gods to his rule. Yet there ensues a series of submissive images in which de Quincey undergoes a loss of power. Transformed into a crocodile, the Malay pursues the dreamer through a dense and almost incoherent succession of Orientalist clichés. Identifiably Egyptian, Indian, and Chinese images are blurred into a hellish vision of an Asia that should be feared and conquered, and its foreignness eradicated:

I was stared at, hooted at, grinned at, chattered at, by monkeys, by paroquets, by cockatoos. I ran into pagodas: and was fixed, for centuries, at the summit, or in secret rooms; I was the idol; I was the priest; I was worshipped; I was sacrificed. I fled from the wrath of Brama through all the forests of Asia: Vishnu hated me: Seeva laid wait for me. I came suddenly upon Isis and Osiris: I had done a deed, they said, which the ibis and the crocodile trembled at. I was buried, for a thousand years, in stone coffins, with mummies and sphynxes, in narrow chambers at the heart of eternal pyramids.   (2:71)

Amid the rush through exotic images, one might barely notice that the dominant emotion of the dream turns from fear to guilt. What is de Quincey's deed, at which his persecutors tremble?

Critics tend to interpret de Quincey's Orientalism with reference to key incidents in the writer's life. Modern scholarship on de Quincey has been dominated by John Barrell's study *The Infection of Thomas de Quincey: A Psychopathology of Imperialism* (1991). Barrell explains de Quincey's attitudes to Asia, and his works more generally, by reference to two key and interrelated ideas. The first component of Barrell's model is the death of Elizabeth de Quincey, the writer's nine year-old sister, when de Quincey was aged six.[13] In *Suspiria de Profundis* (1845), a sequel to *Confessions*, de Quincey is haunted by a memory of his secret visit to view and kiss Elizabeth's corpse. There are hints of Orientalism in this scene. De Quincey reflects that bereavement is more powerful when death occurs, incongruously, amidst the vibrancy of summer. These sensations are magnified proportionally; in recollection de Quincey's grief is contrasted with weather so glorious that it assumes exotic quality, intensifying the 'antagonism between the tropical redundancies of life in summer and the dark sterilities of the grave' (15:42). Additionally, de Quincey believed that Elizabeth died from hydrocephalus, an accumulation of blood in the brain. Peter J. Kitson notes that Elizabeth's autopsy was conducted by Charles White (1728–1813), an eminent theorist of polygenism, including racially divergent craniometry. Hence one likely cause of de Quincey's xenophobia is the association of Elizabeth's posthumous cranium, distorted by disease and surgery, with the variant skull-shapes and trepanation practices he associates with exotic cultures.[14]

The second major constituent of Barrell's interpretative model is de Quincey's conception of the Orient. In reality de Quincey never travelled further afield than Ireland. Topographically variable, his Orient is

---

[13] John Barrell, *The Infection of Thomas de Quincey: A Psychopathology of Imperialism* (New Haven and London: Yale University Press, 1991), 33.

[14] Peter J. Kitson, 'The Strange Case of Dr White and Mr De Quincey: Manchester, Medicine and Romantic Theories of Biological Racism', *Romanticism* 17, no. 3 (2011): 278–87.

primarily derived from a narrow selection of books such as *Arabian Nights* and contemporary Biblical criticism, although his knowledge of works by Walter Henry Medhurst (1796–1857) indicates that de Quincey took particular interest in contemporary China. Additionally, as mentioned in the previous chapter, the British viewed opium use as a Turkish habit, or more generally as an Oriental one. Hence while he imagines the Orient as represented by miscellaneous threats such as tigers and crocodiles, it is clear from his reliance on the Asian habit of opium use that de Quincey associates the Orient with an aspect of himself. I will return to de Quincey's inadmissible awareness that he is somehow Oriental. For now, I distil Barrell's study into two anxieties that haunt a range of de Quincey's works. The first is the vague danger of the Orient, an exotic nightmare-world that threatens to transform what is familiar, including de Quincey himself. The second is the fear of losing a woman, which recurs with de Quincey's inability to find Ann, the prostitute who befriended him, and the death in 1812 of Wordsworth's daughter Kate. I add that literature itself warrants inclusion as a third, major idea to interpret de Quincey. He invokes his knowledge of classical texts to resist his phobias, but inadvertently reveals profound self-doubt in the process.

Barrell's model fits de Quincey's encounter with the Malay neatly. To the narrator, the servant next to the suspicious newcomer is a young girl in peril, like Elizabeth. There is an Oriental threat in the man de Quincey classifies, questionably, as Malay. De Quincey's gift of opium to the visitor is doubly symbolic. The potentially fatal dose of opium constitutes attempted murder of the Malay. Yet for de Quincey to rid himself of his opium is also a self-corrective gesture.

Furthermore, literature exerts a salient presence in the Malay episode. Twice de Quincey alludes to his scholarly reputation. 'The girl, recollecting the reputed learning of her master', assumes de Quincey can converse with the stranger. Fortunately the Malay responds appropriately to his Greek: 'In this way I saved my reputation.' De Quincey addresses the stranger in ancient Greek with the comic explanation that this is geographically the most eastern of the languages he possesses. Yet the mode of communication is also richly suggestive of how de Quincey perceives the dynamics of the relation between himself, the servant, and the Malay. Attainment in classical scholarship was an achievement by which de Quincey distinguished himself intellectually throughout his lifetime, even amongst accomplished peers.[15] He tells that his schoolmaster once bragged to a stranger, 'That boy could harangue an Athenian mob, better than you or I could an English one' (2:14). It is remarkable, in consideration of de Quincey's Philippic tone in his China journalism, that his own indecorous but effective 'harangue' recalls his 1839 depiction of Demosthenes as a speaker who lacked rapturous eloquence but possessed the necessary 'fretful irritability' to retain the attention of 'an excitable or tempestuous audience' (11:31). De Quincey feels the same contempt for his audience that he portrays in Demosthenes. Throughout his works de Quincey displays his knowledge of classics to assert superiority over his addressee, whether a readership or, as in the case of the Malay, an interlocutor. De Quincey affirms his expertise with particular force in reflections on the Orient because the place where 'man is a weed' threatens his individuality. Furthermore, Asia's antiquity sustains an alternate civilization in which de Quincey's scholarship is redundant; thus he may be disempowered.

Overtly there is a humorous tone to de Quincey's encounter with the Malay. The self-confident Englishman who, ignorant of the foreigner's language, holds forth in Greek anticipates Alexander Kinglake's satiric portrayal of British visitors to Asia in *Eothen* (1844). Yet Leask notes the imperialistic gesture of de Quincey forcing a European language onto an Asian visitor, and refers us to the literature of 'power'.[16] To address the Malay in ancient Greek is thus a challenge to his status as a gentleman. The paradigm of classical attainment is comically inappropriate to the scenario yet is palpably serious to de Quincey. The stranger's answer in non-Greek language appeases de Quincey's fear that his intellectual supremacy is under threat. Meanwhile de Quincey's rustic neighbours assume that he speaks an Eastern language, and they marvel at his cultivation.

By quotation from the *Iliad* de Quincey refers us to the Trojan War, the archetypal European narrative of West versus East. That Britain's opium supply was predominantly Turkish encouraged such association. If the visitor assumes on arrival the role of a supplicant Priam to de

---

[15] Simon Goldhill, *Who Needs Greek? Contests in the Cultural History of Hellenism* (Cambridge: Cambridge University Press, 2002), 178.

[16] Nigel Leask, *British Romantic Writers and the East: Anxieties of Empire* (Cambridge: Cambridge University Press, 1992), 211.

Quincey's Achilles, the narrator gives no indication that he empathizes with the Malay as the Achaean hero did with his Trojan opponent. The Malay remains an object of suspicion. With the exchange envisioned on the plains outside Troy, the 'beautiful' servant becomes Helen in need of rescue from an exogenous enemy.

To dispel the threat of the Malay, de Quincey transfers their encounter to a literary realm in which the West triumphs over the Orient. When he invokes the *Iliad*, de Quincey establishes himself as an Achaean champion and the Malay as a Trojan opponent who faces inevitable defeat. Thus from the literature of 'power' he re-enacts a precedent that ensures he will prevail. With ancient poetry de Quincey intimates violence towards the Malay. In his journalism on the Opium Wars, de Quincey's aggression appears to have escalated to fantasies of bloodshed on a massive scale. Yet just as the violence of the Malay episode is subverted by de Quincey's self-corrective riddance of his opium supply and remembrance of Elizabeth, so too the belligerence of the China articles is tempered. The opium journalism, like the Malay episode, reflects on the reception of guests with elements of humour. As he recalls the failed Macartney and Amehurst embassies, de Quincey focusses on the visitors' refusal to kowtow before the Qing ruler. He cites Plutarch's story of Ismenias, a Spartan in Persian court who dropped a ring and ducked to retrieve it, to give the impression that he prostrated himself before the emperor (18:92fn). Furthermore, de Quincey proposes war on China, where the cost in human life would be real, by allusion to works of tragedy in which slaughter is symbolic; the audience of a play understands that violence portrayed onstage is merely representative. I wish to explore these ideas by reference to a dialogue between de Quincey's China journalism and an essay in which he purports to analyse the principles of tragedy.

The Opium Wars and de Quincey's 'Theory of Greek Tragedy'

In 1840 *Blackwood's* published de Quincey's 'Theory of Greek Tragedy', a contemplation of classical drama in comparison with English theatre. He transfers ideas from this work onto the 1840 China journalism, and vice versa. When de Quincey wrote on China again in 1857, he drew on his Opium War material from 1840, but also on the contemporaneous 'Theory of Greek Tragedy'. Hence there are two products of de Quincey's conceptual exchange between political commentary and literary criticism. The first is a set of articles on China that rely rhetorically on allusions to Greek tragedy and to Shakespeare. The second is a 'Theory of Greek Tragedy' whose characteristic inflection is jingoism. In fact de Quincey never really advances a theory of tragedy, but belittles Athenian drama from political motives. In addition to de Quincey's customary reliance on classical 'power', two further factors inspire his conceptual exchange between China and Greek drama. The first is that China was increasingly the subject of theatrical representation in Britain during his lifetime. Panoramas and plays responded to British experiences in China and invoked stereotypes of a childlike Chinese population under an inhumane Qing government. Light entertainments such as *The Chinese Junk, or the Maid and the Mandarin* (1848) and *The Mandarin's Daughter!* (1851) invoked Orientalist tropes in critiques of Britain. Such plays continued the tradition of Oliver Goldsmith's *The Citizen of the World* (1760–61), in which the Chinese mask facilitates self-scrutiny. While China had become material for popular drama, de Quincey extends the conceit to contemplate the Qing Empire by reference to ancient theatre.

The second reason for de Quincey to interpret events in China as tragic is that, particularly ahead of the First Opium War, the pro-war lobby justified the proposed attack in terms that were identifiable with the strife of tragedy, which ultimately yields benefit in de Quincey's interpretation of the mode. Initially, war with China was an unpopular prospect in Britain. Sceptics argued that the problem of a few self-interested merchants—whose drug trade, in any case, was immoral—was not a matter of national interest. Then Foreign Secretary, Palmerston was under pressure from Charles Elliot, who had promised the traders reparations for their lost opium. Additionally the merchant William Jardine (1784–1843) had arrived in London to agitate for the military strike and advise on China's topography. The government did not want to pay for the lost opium itself. Military strength appeared the only means to persuade the Qing Empire to recompense. To make the opium squabble a national concern, Palmerston contended that British dignity had been insulted. Additionally, to provide moral justification for an assault on China, Palmerston portrayed the Qing Empire as an antiquated and barbaric regime. Skirting around the immorality of the opium trade itself, Palmerston argued that an efficiently waged war would have purgative effect in China. The pro-war lobby posited that their attack would not only achieve free trade for Britain but prevent further unrest in China.[17] Although the motion for war won support by a very slim majority, Palmerston's rhetoric appears to have been crucial to the general change of British opinion on China from positive to negative in the following years.[18]

Aggravation by a foreign power occasioned reflection on Britain's identity. This did not occur only as reflexive self-assertion in political debate. Britain's standing as an international force was such a pervasive conversation that it could even define an essay on ancient literature. Although de Quincey is usually reverential towards classical culture, in the 'Theory' he sets out to establish the supremacy of British civilization. In *Confessions*, de Quincey became the Achaean hero, European conqueror of an Oriental threat. But in the 'Theory of Greek Tragedy', Greece becomes, like China, a lesser culture compared to Britain. I propose that the extended critical analysis of Greek drama in the 'Theory' illuminates both the symbolic thought de Quincey uses to justify the Opium Wars and the personal turmoil beneath his political commentary.

De Quincey argues that tension in China necessitates tragic resolution: ritual destruction that eventuates purgation. Accordingly, de Quincey's claim that the 'Mantchoo' rulers of China incite war with 'demoniac *hybris*' is not only a charge of hubris in its modern meaning of pride, but the tragic protagonist's wanton provocation of the gods, the obnoxious behaviour that results in annihilation. I argue that by the phrase 'demoniac *hybris*', de Quincey casts the hybristic China as an Oedipus who ridicules Tiresias, or a Pentheus who dismisses Dionysus. These characters are undone, their downfalls educative to spectators. To de Quincey the Qing Empire likewise tempts retaliation: 'thump them well'. He bemoans the 'inhuman insolence of this vilest and silliest of nations' (18:85). To cast the Qing Empire as tragic protagonist defines Britain's role too. In de Quincey's tragedy, Britain is an Apollonian force that restores order, 'a conquering power, a harmonizing power' (18:535). De Quincey's invocation of literary formula exempts Britain from

---

[17]   HC Deb 7–9 April 1840, vol. 43, cols 673–948.
[18]   Lovell, *The Opium War*, 78–81.

responsibility for its actions in China. De Quincey claims mysteriously, and without elaboration, that Canton is 'indissolubly connected' with Britain (18:154). Of British presence in Asia he claims that it is '*not* in their power' to avoid contact with China. Britain is an agent of necessity in this drama rather than an aggressive empire.

De Quincey identifies anti-war dissenters and those who esteem Chinese culture as his opponents. In 1840 he terms these 'moral sentimentalists' who would form an 'anti-national party' (18:568). In 1857 he laments that 'ignorance about China manifests itself everywhere' (18:120). De Quincey discounts reports that Chinese culture possesses 'erudite sciences' and mathematics as 'errors' (18:122). His chief adversary in 1857 is the missionary Walter Henry Medhurst, who protested British plans to attack China. De Quincey pronounces Medhurst to be 'wrong . . . upon various Chinese questions' and claims that he 'palliates the Chinese follies' (18:136). Yet Medhurst had spent twenty years in Malacca and fourteen in Shanghai.

To mount a case that China has provoked Britain, de Quincey portrays an incident from 1848 as an exemplary outrage. A group of missionaries was, as de Quincey terms it, 'hustled by a mob', robbed and held to ransom near Shanghai (18:126). Consequently a British gunboat prevented Chinese junks from transporting rice until arrests were made. Finally the Chinese authorities charged ten men with abduction. Medhurst was one of the missionaries captured. Hence Medhurst's pleas for a more tolerant British attitude to China arose from personal experience.

De Quincey does not comment upon the details of the ransom episode, but celebrates that 'the drama (at one time looking very like a tragedy) closed in a joyous and triumphant catastrophe'. In allusion to the prosecution of ten suspects, de Quincey reports that 'There was an anagnoresis . . . just such as the Stagirite approves' (18:135). Here de Quincey imagines the missionaries' tormentors are unmasked. He does not consider whether the correct ten men were arrested. De Quincey implies that events in China have validated his assumption of authority on the country by satisfying a literary formula. His logic is that because the Shanghai incident can be said to conform to Aristotelian conventions of Greek tragedy, it falls within de Quincey's expertise. Thus the uninformed Orientalist refutes the experienced Sinologist. It appears that de Quincey dismisses pacifism contemptuously. Yet his criticism on tragedy contains evidence that de Quincey's proposed violence in China is strictly symbolic, in the manner that a murder onstage is one actor's gesture towards another, intended to depict strife without the necessity of actual harm.

The strength of de Quincey's views on China accounts for his inconsistent treatment of classical tragedy. The essay 'The Sphinx's Riddle' (1850) exemplifies his customary respect for Greek drama: 'Perhaps in the whole history of human art . . . there is nothing more perfect than the management of this crisis by Sophocles'. In this work de Quincey contends that he has devised a more satisfactory solution to the Sphinx' riddle than Oedipus provides: that Oedipus himself most emphatically 'fulfilled the condition of the enigma' in his extremes of dependence and self-assertion, and with Antigone his third leg by evening. Oedipus' answer to the riddle, de Quincey declares, is '*a* solution', not '*the* solution'. It is the response of a younger man, who 'shouted before he was out of the wood'. The Sphinx, for its part, is 'too easily satisfied with the answer given' (17:15–18). This is a sportive work by a man who loves his subject and is at ease with the literature of 'power'. The essay blends penetrating analysis of Sophocles' *King Oedipus*—which de Quincey argues is based on historical fact—with gentle self-parody of the excessive pride in his own expertise. However, in his 'Theory of Greek Tragedy' de Quincey makes exception to his usual exaltation of classics. In this essay he responds to Gotthold Ephraim Lessing, Friedrich Schiller, and A. W. Schlegel's attempts to theorize how ancient drama should be accommodated within their own aesthetics, which they styled as innovative rather than derivative. De Quincey sets out to address the 'problem' of how Greek drama relates to English theatre:

The tragic muse of Greece and England stand so far aloof as hardly to recognise each other under any common designation. Few people have ever studied the Grecian drama – and hence may be explained the possibility that so little should have been said by critics upon its characteristic differences, and nothing at all upon the philosophic grounds of those differences.   (11:490)

Thus de Quincey, despite the title of his essay, does not purport to theorize Greek tragedy per se, but the nature of its relationship to English tragedy. The 'philosophic grounds' he explores concern the practicalities of stage production. De Quincey's essay is a disappointing document to the scholar who hopes that, from the contentious claim that 'few people have ever studied the Grecian drama', a life-long dedicate to the ancient world would delineate his opinions on the methods, philosophy, and

significance of Greek tragedy. The piece is more valuable as an exploration of how 'power' culture could be applied to assess Asia.

Compared to British civilization, and in the absence of a more acutely
foreign culture, de Quincey depicts Greek antiquity as alien and inferior
in his 'Theory'. For demarcations of the Orient so to shift is a familiar
Orientalist trope. I suspect that Barrell's proposed fear of infection
motivates de Quincey's uneven treatment of Greece, because in some
Orientalist contexts Greece is considered Oriental. In de Quincey's
lifetime, for example, Greece remained under Ottoman rule until 1832.
This unsettles de Quincey, who fears the taint of foreignness. Hence he
invokes Greece in the *Confessions* as a part of Europe that stands between
England and the Orient, and conquers the foreign realm of Troy. However, juxtaposed solely with Britain, Greece becomes Oriental, and as
such a vehicle for de Quincey's evaluations of Asia.

Within Shakespeare's drama *Hamlet*, de Quincey sources an allegory
for the gulf he articulates between ancient Greece (or China) and modern
Britain. He cites *The Murder of Gonzago*, the play-within-a-play, as a
lesser form of drama contained within a greater one. In this scene (3.2),
the characters of *Hamlet* watch a staged performance. Hamlet suspects
that Claudius murdered his father. Hence the prince attempts to stimu-
late the usurper's conscience with an entertainment that narrates
regicide.

The play-within-a-play is a dumb show. De Quincey likens this mime
to a picture of a picture, and comments that 'we might imagine this
descent into a life below going on ad infinitum' (11:491). He does not
mean simply that *The Murder of Gonzago* scene creates a *mise en abyme*
in which a larger work contains a smaller copy. De Quincey claims that
each phase of descent is qualitatively different and should be clearly
distinguished from its predecessor:

Something must be done to differentiate the gradations. . . . Each term in the
descending series, being first of all a mode of non-reality to the spectator, is next
to assume the functions of a real life in its relations to the next lower or interior
term of the series.   (11:491)

De Quincey argues that the effect of these gradations is that each degree
of artistic removal is 'more intensely unreal'. *The Murder of Gonzago* is
not a synecdoche of *Hamlet*, in which a component represents a nuanced
whole, but a simplification.

To de Quincey, Greek tragedy is basic, 'it is a life below a life' (11:493). Athenian drama is comparable to Shakespeare's dumb show, while *Hamlet* epitomizes the complexity of British literature. Furthermore, *Hamlet* embodies the lesser theatre-form as a device that accentuates the sophistication of Shakespearean drama and, by extension, British culture as a whole. As evidence for his opinion de Quincey catalogues supposed limitations of Greek tragedy. He complains that any subtlety of presentation was impossible in the Theatre of Dionysus, and that the actors' facial expressions and voices would be 'lost' in the viewer's remoteness from the stage:

Hence the cothurnus to raise the actor; hence the voluminous robes to hide the disproportion thus resulting to the figure; hence the mask larger than life; . . . hence the mechanism by which it was made to swell the intonations of the voice like the brazen tubes of an organ.   (11:492)

De Quincey contends that Greek tragedy descends below Shakespearean drama both by its textual simplicity and the manner of its production. He reasons that the effect of this descent from reality is that the original audience found the events depicted to be distant 'from the ordinary life even of kings and heroes' (11:493).

In his Opium Wars journalism de Quincey urges a military campaign not solely to punish China, but to establish a British rule that will absorb and surpass Chinese civilization in the manner that he believes *Hamlet* assimilated Greek tragedy to produce higher drama. Such imperial absorption would eradicate cultural difference and prevent de Quincey's own effacement by a nation in which 'man is a weed'. Yet the foreign society is not only primitive in de Quincey's opinion, but 'intensely unreal'. I think that the most significant aspect of the correspondence de Quincey creates between Greek tragedy and the China question is this implication that China is somehow a lesser reality: if Greek tragedy is 'intensely unreal', and events in China constitute a *kind* of Greek tragedy, the Opium Wars must likewise be unreal. A war waged in China as a version of Greek tragedy would therefore remain strictly representative, a political demonstration that stands apart from 'ordinary life' without a human cost, like a murder portrayed onstage. Despite his rhetorical tone, I think that de Quincey does not really want war, because he does not acknowledge its authenticity. De Quincey wants the opium trade to survive, and the supremacy of British culture to be verified. He invokes the literature of 'power' to justify his intervention in the debate, but his use of Greek tragedy hints also at a commonality de Quincey perceives between himself and China. Ultimately tragedy offers a possibility that the dispute in China could be resolved by a conflict that is not real, but symbolic. To clarify this point I return to opium use, the Oriental habit by which de Quincey resembles the exotic other he despises, and the manner in which narcotic thraldom recalls Romantic interpretations of the *daimon*'s agency in tragedy.

De Quincey's *Daimon* Amok in China

To suggest why de Quincey conceives of Manchurian *hybris* as daimonic, I want first to consider another question: by what means does de Quincey decide that his visitor of 1817—real or imagined—is Malay? He portrays the stranger in 'turban and loose trowsers', but this is not specifically indicative of Malay culture. I think that de Quincey's treatment of this episode is influenced by historical narratives of Malay behaviour which resonate with his fear of the Orient. Furthermore, contemporary scholarship on Malays recalls de Quincey's opium experiences in a manner that is simultaneously reminiscent of the tragic *daimon*.

Ironically, soon after de Quincey claims to speak no Malay in *Confessions*, he uses a Malay word: 'This Malay . . . brought other Malays with him worse than himself, that ran "a-muck" at me' (2:58). De Quincey's disavowal appears contemptuous of a culture that lacks the literature of 'power' and which might even be corrosive. 'Amok' had been established as a loan-word in the early seventeenth century, during which Sumatra and Java were crucial to Britain's trade with eastern Asia. Britain governed Java from 1811 to 1817 and encountered Chinese immigrant communities in the region. William Marsden, who compiled a Malay dictionary after residence in Sumatra, defines 'amuk' as 'a state of frenzy, to the commission of indiscriminate murder'.[19] A likely influence on de Quincey's adoption of the term 'amok' is Stamford Raffles (1781–1826), whose *History of Java* (1817) was excerpted in *The London Quarterly Review*. De Quincey read periodicals keenly and was invited to contribute to the *Quarterly* by its publisher, John Murray, in 1818. De Quincey

---

[19] William Marsden, *A Dictionary of the Malayan Language* (London: Cox and Baylis, 1812), 16.

dates his encounter with the Malay as 1817—the year Raffles's *History* was published—and the onset of his nightmares as 1818.

The Javanese tribes as surveyed by Raffles, while all broadly classified 'Malay', do not strictly corroborate the 'turban and loose trowsers' of de Quincey's visitor:

> The men of the lowest class usually wear a pair of coarse short drawers, reaching towards the knees, with the *járit* or cloth folded round the waist, and descending below the knees like a short petticoat. . . . A handkerchief or tie (*íkat*) is always folded round the head. With the *Maláyus* this handkerchief is generally of the Tartan pattern, but among the Javans it is of the *bátek* cloth, and put on more in the manner of a turban than the handkerchief of a *Maláyu* is: the crown of the head is covered with it, and the ends are tucked in. While abroad, they generally wear over it a large hat of leaves or of the split and plaited bamboo.[20]

The detail in the *History* most likely to capture de Quincey's imagination is the description of Malay warriors amok. Raffles refers to 'those acts of vengeance, proceeding from an indiscriminate phrenzy, called *mucks*, where the unhappy sufferer aims at indiscriminate destruction, till he himself is killed like a wild beast, whom it is impossible to take alive'.[21] I suggest that in light of Raffles's account, de Quincey assumes that his Asian visitor is the most fearsome Oriental of all, a Malay. Secondly, I argue that to de Quincey, the Malay amok recalls the daimonic agency of tragedy: the 'indiscriminate phrenzy' in which Heracles massacres his children, or Oedipus blinds himself. Yet thirdly, the Malay amok represents not only violence that is frightful to de Quincey, but a surrender of volition that is familiar to the English Opium Eater. To imbibe laudanum cedes one's agency to an invasive force. Hence Coleridge laments opium as 'that, to which there is no Near, the γυιλτ and the avenging Daemon of my Life' (12.4:236).

Opium was not the only addiction at stake in China. Britain's thraldom to tea was a catalyst for the opium crises. De Quincey perpetuates the assumption that Britain could not forego tea, and was therefore a victim in its unwanted relations with China. His fatalistic reading of tragedy offers de Quincey philosophical tools to ennoble that victimhood as necessary. That the Qing Empire acts with 'demoniac *hybris*', in a

---

[20] Thomas Stamford Raffles, *The History of Java*, 2 vols (London: Black, Parbury and Allen, 1817), 1:87.

[21] Raffles, *The History of Java*, 1:250.

tragic context, absolves it from responsibility because it too is a victim. Like the Malay amok, the Manchus and Chinese act under compulsion, and it is the same that afflicts de Quincey: addiction to opium. The Qing officials' destruction of opium shipments is a similar gesture to de Quincey's disposal of his opium supply in the hands of the Malay, a futile attempt to avert destiny. In this tragic schematic the Opium Wars are inevitable. Where de Quincey declares that Britain should 'thump them well' I think he displays self-contempt, given the addiction he shares with China. Moreover, Britain is 'indissolubly connected' to China because it too is in thraldom, but to tea rather than opium.

De Quincey never admits his unbreakable dependence on opium explicitly. *Confessions* contains subtle refutations of Thomas Trotter, who hypothesized the existence of addiction in his *Essay, Medical, Philosophical, and Chemical on Drunkenness* (1804). In the 1856 revision of *Confessions* de Quincey removes much negative commentary on opium and exalts the drug even more. Yet he reveals ambivalence in the China journalism. His allusions to the *daimon* and running amok clarify that de Quincey understands the destruction wrought by an addict's compulsion. It is credible that the ferocity of de Quincey's prose on the Orient reflects his refusal to acknowledge the negative aspects of opium use explicitly. These two grow proportionately: the more unadulterated praise de Quincey bestows on opium, the more heinously he depicts Asia. Ironically, classics provides evidence for de Quincey's likeness to the 'barbarous' Orientals who run amok and share his narcotic dependence. The elitist literature of 'power' is appropriate to rally imperial force, but within classical literature de Quincey chooses an idea that connotes helplessness. He cites classics to rationalize his intervention in debate on the Opium Wars, yet his allusion to the *daimon* intimates that his true entitlement lies in his similarity to the addict China. Hence both de Quincey and China correspond to the tragic hero. In particular, de Quincey's suppressed self-knowledge recalls his perspective on Oedipus in 'The Sphinx's Riddle'. In de Quincey's interpretation, it is Oedipus who, unknowingly, will come to match the three phases described in the riddle more closely than the answer he gives the Sphinx. Similarly, de Quincey's accounts of Chinese victimhood form an unwitting portrait of himself. He longs not for Britain to destroy China, which would symbolize his own obliteration. Instead de Quincey wishes for a process akin to the performed violence of a stage tragedy, with the hope that Britain would control, Anglicize and surpass China. Thus the Oriental aspects of himself that de Quincey despises might survive unchallenged, in the manner that earlier tragedy is contained almost unnoticed within the higher achievement of *Hamlet*. Exploration of the dialogues de Quincey creates between classics, Asia, and opium reveals contradictions that undermine his credibility as a journalist, but from their complexity a more sympathetic man emerges than the warmonger the Opium Wars commentator first appears. The 1858 settlement Treaty of Tianjin ensured that official documents could never again refer to Britons as *yi*. But Britain was not finished with China yet. British forces pressed on into China, taking classical baggage with them as they ruminated on their actions, and ensuring that debates over barbarism and national humiliation continued.

7

'From Those Flames No Light'

The Summer Palace in 1860 and Beyond

What do the things in your home say about you? Eugenia Zuroski Jenkins observes that the early fad for *chinoiserie* coincided with the advent of British consumerism in the eighteenth century. This was the point at which the average home became filled with *stuff*, objects of decorative and diverting kinds, and the earliest such stuff commonly iterated the popular, Chinese aesthetic. These developments were also contemporaneous with Lockean interpretations of the acquisition and arrangement of objects as psychological indicators.[1] By this logic, possessions revealed how their owner had inscribed the mental *tabula rasa*. This chapter follows the line of thought to a later date, and onto a national scale. British and French collectors obtained significant Chinese treasures in the wake of the Second Opium War, for which their armies had allied to attack China. What the proceeds of this war communicated of its protagonists became contentious.

When the Second Opium War commenced in 1857, the superiority of the foreign armies was immediately evident. French forces had joined the British in response to the execution of a French missionary in 1856. Much of the war period was spent in negotiation, with British, French, and other foreign powers demanding territory, reparations, and increased freedom to trade. The Xianfeng Emperor (r. 1850–61) agreed to some of these demands but dragged his heels over others. He became emboldened by the sheer protraction of the negotiations. He gained confidence that he could refuse to meet further demands and back out

---

[1] Eugenia Zuroski Jenkins, *A Taste for China: English Subjectivity and the Prehistory of Orientalism* (New York: Oxford University Press, 2013), 45–6.

China from the Ruins of Athens and Rome: Classics, Sinology, and Romanticism, 1793–1938.
Chris Murray, Oxford University Press (2020). © Chris Murray.
DOI: 10.1093/oso/9780198767015.001.0001

of prior agreements. In 1860, British and French soldiers moved north to confront the Emperor.

The Anglo-French campaign culminated at the imperial retreat, Yuanmingyuan, six miles northwest of Beijing, in the autumn of 1860. To attack this property was symbolic rather than strategic, but even the symbolism was not obvious. Yuanmingyuan was a private paradise for Qing emperors. A place for retreat, it did not have the iconic value that, for instance, the Bastille had in 1789. As the British contingent's Chaplain to the Forces, R. J. L. M'Ghee describes, it was a peculiar setting for a military operation:

You must imagine a vast labyrinth of picturesque rocks and noble timber, lakes and streams, summer-houses roofed with porcelain of the imperial yellow, theatres and their store-houses; . . . then deck the scene with all the world-famed skill of the Celestial in landscape gardening, thrown in here and there so well that it looks like nature's own hand; . . . see, there is an imperial stag bounding across your paths; conjure up the quaint old Chinese bridge here and there, to carry you across the feeder of some placid lake, with its ornamental waterfowl.[2]

There was no-one to fight. By the time the foreigners arrived, the Emperor and his retinue had left. The armies found Yuanmingyuan near-deserted and, in short, helped themselves to whatever was inside. While discussion of this episode usually focuses on particular valuables, the quantity of acquisition was also considerable, with no fewer than one million objects taken from the Summer Palace at Yuanmingyuan.[3] Later, British troops razed the thousands of buildings dotted around the complex. These structures constituted what European discourse knows metonymically as the Summer Palace.

The events of 1860 made some British commentators uneasy. To defeat and despoil China signified imperial greatness to many but induced an identity crisis in others. British participants in the military campaign recognized the significance of their historical moment. This

[2] R. J. L. M'Ghee, *How We Got Into Pekin: A Narrative of the Campaign in China of 1860* (London: Richard Bentley, 1862), 211–12.

[3] Some sources estimate that up to 1.5 million objects were removed from Yuanmingyuan. For example, 'Chinese netizens call for return of stolen ancient bronze vessel set for auction in UK', *Global Times*, 28 March 2018. http://www.globaltimes.cn/content/1095620. shtml (accessed 18 June 2019).

was a process of British domination of Asia that would lead Victoria to assume the title Empress of India in 1877. Yet it proved controversial to burgle and burn an imperial residence, even one that belonged to an adversary. There were veterans of the 1860 China campaign who wondered whether their achievement confirmed them as heirs to those who founded Rome or those who sacked it. The conclusion to the Second Opium War was especially poignant because Britain had been there before, so to speak, in two senses. With the destruction of the Summer Palace, British troops returned to the scene of Macartney's humiliation in 1793. Secondly, the removal of precious Chinese artefacts by British and French troops precipitated a debate over repatriation that would parallel the Parthenon Sculptures controversy.

Pressed upon by a military acquaintance to give an opinion on the Anglo-French campaign in China, Victor Hugo (1802–85) answered frankly in a letter of 1861:

There was, in a corner of the world, a wonder of the world; this wonder was called the Summer Palace. . . . The Summer Palace was to chimerical art what the Parthenon is to ideal art. All that can be begotten of the imagination of an almost extra-human people was there. It was not a single, unique work like the Parthenon. It was a kind of enormous model of the chimera, if the chimera can have a model. . . . People spoke of the Parthenon in Greece, the pyramids in Egypt, the Coliseum in Rome, Notre-Dame in Paris, the Summer Palace in the Orient. If people did not see it they imagined it.

This wonder has disappeared.

One day two bandits entered the Summer Palace. One plundered, the other burned. Victory can be a thieving woman, or so it seems. The devastation of the Summer Palace was accomplished by the two victors acting jointly. Mixed up in all this is the name of Elgin, which inevitably calls to mind the Parthenon. What was done to the Parthenon was done to the Summer Palace, more thoroughly and better, so that nothing of it should be left.[4]

Literary responses to Britain's acquisition of Asian treasures were polarized in the age of empire. Unusually sympathetic to the rights of Asian peoples, Wilkie Collins's *The Moonstone* (1868) advocates returning the illicit gain of imperialism to former owners. By contrast, the museum curator in Rudyard Kipling's *Kim* (1901), based on the author's father,

---

[4] Victor Hugo, 'The Sack of the Summer Palace', trans., *The UNESCO Courier: A Window Open on the World* 38, no. 11 (1985): 15.

exemplifies a belief that foreign artefacts were more responsibly handled by British curators in British-owned repositories. In a comparable scenario, W. B. Yeats would say that such logic was 'exactly as if the Forty Thieves were to say they had a right to their treasure because they had been to the trouble of digging a cavern to contain it.'[5]

Hugo pulls no punches when he calls Queen Victoria—whose gifts from the Summer Palace takings included a small dog named Looty—a thief. His letter identifies the heart of the matter. Appraisal of British and French behaviour at the Summer Palace entails reflection on what it is to be civilized: 'We Europeans are the civilized ones, and for us the Chinese are the barbarians. This is what civilization has done to barbarism.'[6] In the 1830s fury had erupted among the Canton British that official Qing documents referred to them as *yi* (夷), which they translated as 'barbarians'. If by destruction of the Summer Palace the British forces intended revenge for past embarrassment, it was an ironically wrongheaded gesture. To sack fine buildings does not disprove allegations of barbarism. Hugo knows too that the British and French were mindful of predecessors when they evaluated their own empires. For example, Charles Trevelyan says that Britain would do well to follow the model of Rome, which 'civilised the nations of Europe'.[7] Britain must even improve on Rome, where slavery, paganism, and violence were central to imperial history. In light of this association, to mention a debate over classical artefacts is irresistible to Hugo: James Bruce (1811–63), the British High Commissioner to China who ordered the controversial incineration of the Summer Palace, was the eighth Earl of Elgin. Those who characterized Elgin Senior as plunderer of the Acropolis were quick to suggest a family likeness. Hugo ends his letter expressing hope that the Summer Palace treasures will one day be returned to their rightful owners, the Chinese. That international conversation continues, and so the fall of the Summer Palace begets curious forms of classical reception: further conversations over barbarism and civilization which are often historically informed; the theft of Chinese treasures arguably re-enacting Elgin's

---

[5] Quoted in *Lady Gregory's Journals 1916–1930*, ed. Lennox Robinson (London: Putnam, 1946), 306.

[6] Hugo, 'The Sack of the Summer Palace', 15.

[7] Charles Trevelyan, *On the Education of the Peoples of India* (London: Longman, Orme, Brown, Green & Longmans, 1838), 196–7.

acquisition of the Parthenon Sculptures; and Britain's repatriation dispute with China echoing the counterpart with Greece.

'You're Getting Sacked in the Morning': Trojan Victory and Virgilian Melancholy in China

Tennyson's ambivalence towards British progress corresponds to widespread scepticism about the country's activities in China. Analysis of certain incidents, such as the Opium Wars, often invoked ancient models, with particular reference to Virgil. In 1839 Charles William King, an American merchant based in Canton, published a pamphlet protesting Britain's planned attack on China, which came to pass as the initial conflict of the First Opium War. King imagines the aftermath of war in this text. A British visitor demands information from a Chinese subject:

> 'You idle son of Han! How name you this spot—that hill?'
> 'Afooyung-shan.'
> 'Ah! the place of the funeral pile.'
> 'Afooyung-shan,' the echo repeats, and a voice adds, ' . . . aeternumquae
> tenet per saecula nomen.'[8]

The mysterious, disembodied voice quotes the part of the *Aeneid* that describes Misenus' funeral. Thus King implies that Canton will become a landmark of sorrow during the war. Yet memory will occur in Occidental, classicist terms which, by following the Chinese name in the dialogue, suggest the power to efface Chinese culture. King's quotation therefore plays on the irony within the Latin text, and its potential use for commentary on imperialism. While Virgil refers to preserving a name eternally, the fact that the hill has been renamed indicates impermanence: surely the Cumaeans had their own name for the hill that Aeneas would call after Misenus (*Aeneid*, 6.235). King may have foreseen that within the next decade, parts of Hong Kong would be renamed after Opium War aggressors.

The Chinese will assist the British because, like the Rutuli later in Virgil's poem, they are desperate for peace. That places are forever

---

[8] Charles William King, *Opium Crisis: A Letter Addressed to Charles Elliot* (London: E. Suter, 1839), 26–7.

altered by conflict is one of several *Aeneid* themes that resonated with respondents to the Opium Wars. When Turnus launches a rock at Aeneas in the climactic duel, he misses his target, but also destroys the cultural significance of the object (12.896–902). The boundary stone, once removed from its place, is simply a stone. Its removal also symbolizes the imminent redistribution of Italian territory. The Summer Palace treasures have comparably been redefined as emblems of British supremacy, and Yuanmingyuan as a monument to suffering rather than an imperial retreat. To preserve the memory of the attack in October 1860, the grounds and buildings are today curated ruins. It is here that in 1997 the Chinese Communist Party erected a wall that reproduced Hugo's comments alongside photos of Summer Palace treasures on display in European museums, and the famous inscription *wu wang guo chi* (勿忘國恥): 'Never Forget National Humiliation'.

The Virgilian melancholy that infuses Tennyson's work and King's pamphlet was a common response to the Opium Wars. I mean 'Virgilian melancholy' in the sense that Matthew Arnold describes in his lecture, 'On the Modern Element in Literature' (1857): 'a sadness, a melancholy, which is at once a source of charm in the poem, and a testimony to its incompleteness.'[9] A 'modern' epoch, to Arnold, is one that faces a 'copious and complex' past and present; in these qualities he finds that Victorian Britain has more in common with Periclean Athens and Augustan Rome than it does with Elizabethan England. Such an age requires 'deliverance', an interpretation of its complexity.[10] Arnold sees Virgil as a failure in this task. He thinks that the Roman poet was not 'adequate' to supply the correct perspective on his times, a viewpoint which should be sympathetic and positive. He contrasts Virgil's inadequacy with the 'serious cheerfulness of Sophocles, of a man who has mastered the problem of human life.'[11] In his study *Darkness Visible* (1976), W. R. Johnson pursues Arnold's thesis that the air of irresolution in the *Aeneid* owes to Virgil's 'ineffable melancholy'. Johnson observes that characters like Turnus miscomprehend their own actions, that neither of the famous combatants retains his dignity at the poem's conclusion, and that Turnus' final helplessness enacts a 'larger despair

---

[9] *Matthew Arnold: Poetry and Prose*, ed. John Bryson (London: Rupert Hart-Davis, 1954), 282.
[10] *Arnold: Poetry and Prose*, 269.   [11] *Arnold: Poetry and Prose*, 282.

that haunts the entire poem and threatens to engulf it'.[12] He finds the *Aeneid* ambiguous about Roman achievement. Johnson posits Virgil's inability to reconcile an Epicurean belief that the social order is harmful with his conviction that history is a redemptive process, in which the collaborative entity of society itself betokens improvement.[13] Johnson takes his title from Milton's description of hellfire, 'from those flames | No light, but rather darkness visible' (*Paradise Lost*, 1.61–62). Appropriately, one memoirist of the Summer Palace campaign, to be discussed in this chapter, likens the British soldiers to devils. As the Palace burns he watches the flames flicker across the troops' faces and wonders whether an enlightened culture could perform such an act.

Clearly, progress came at great cost. To a Britain that appeared set to emulate Roman hegemony, a decisive victory in Asia recalled Aeneas' defeat of Turnus. The *Aeneid*, which so often re-enacts Homer in modified form, itself invites forms of re-enactment. Anchises' revelations to Aeneas in the underworld, in which the father informs his son that merciful rule and imposition of culture will be duties of the Roman Empire, entailed that the British Empire must do likewise. The point at which Aeneas fulfils his destiny, and secures the settlement that will be celebrated as the foundation of Roman civilization, was identifiable with the military campaign that marked British dominance of China emphatically. The *Aeneid* was fertile as a model for the clash between Britain and China for other reasons. Like Aeneas and Turnus—each of whom, reasonably, believes himself fated to succeed—the British and Chinese governments were motivated by narratives of national greatness. In Virgil's closing books, the Rutuli realise that cooperation with foreign invaders might prevent their own destruction; a compromise with a certain relevance to the Chinese situation.

The notoriously uncertain tone with which the *Aeneid* concludes has a counterpart in British officers' doubts of their own morality in light of the Summer Palace incident. In this reflective tendency, memoirs of the Anglo-French campaign are very unlike the empiricist narratives by Macartney and his companions. The later visitors were not concerned with recording information about China. Instead, they were obsessed

---

[12] W.R. Johnson, *Darkness Visible: A Study of Vergil's Aeneid* (Berkeley: University of California Press, 1976), 98.

[13] Johnson, *Darkness Visible*, 150–4.

with how their own characters, both individually and as a British collective, were defined by their actions in China. While records of the
Macartney Embassy used classical ideas to introduce Chinese culture,
accounts of the Summer Palace in 1860 invoke Graeco-Roman antiquity
for purposes of self-evaluation. Summer Palace memoirists treat China
as a known subject. Their obsession with the verdict of posterity might
strike a modern reader as Blairite. Ancient precedents could be used to
ascertain how Britain measured up as an imperial power, and its individual actors as heroes or villains. Judgment of the 1860 campaign
entailed negotiation of dissimilar concepts, such as the nebulous idea
of 'civilization' and a recent coinage, 'looting'.

Victor de Riquetti, Marquis de Mirabeau, coined 'civilization' in an
economic treatise, *L'Ami des Hommes* (1756). At first 'civilization',
derived from *civitas*, was a French term of jurisprudence. Gradually it
became a word for collective attainment. 'Civilization' was the aggregate
of activities including commerce, consumerism, the arts, religion, and
science. In the late eighteenth century the term 'civilization' was 'used to
describe both a process through which individual human beings and
nations became civilised, and the cumulative outcome of that process'.[14]
'Civilization' meant a society whose people were mannered, and virtu-
ous, and 'a civilization' restrained violent impulses. Of course, 'civilization' understood as the process of becoming 'civilized' indicates an
antithesis. In his essay on 'Civilisation' (1836), John Stuart Mill identifies
'the direct converse or contrary of rudeness or barbarism'.[15] Especially
pertinent to Britain's relations with China are Mill's Benthamite belief
that trade is morally uplifting, and his disregard for parallel social
structures in non-European cultures, such as Asian legal systems; exclud-
ing these facilitates a simple model of civilization and its opposite,
barbarism. Commerce, cooperation, and Christianity were cornerstones
of the Victorian definition of civilization. The sense of a divinely
ordained Protestant destiny encouraged a belief that Britain should
impart civilization to other societies. Empire came naturally to Britain,
proponents said; imperialism was an extension of the British character.

---

[14] Brett Bowden, 'The Ideal of Civilisation: Its Origins and Socio-Political Character',
Critical Review of International Social and Political Philosophy 7, no. 1 (2004): 30.

[15] John Stuart Mill, 'Civilisation', *The London and Westminster Review* 25 (April
1836): 2.

Despite having acquired some territories by dubious means, and losing colonies such as America by misrule, it was to be hoped that Britain was growing into its role, improving at the business of empire.[16] This argument for territorial retention is roughly analogous to one that artefacts acquired in dubious circumstances are better cared for by British curators than those elsewhere.

It is perhaps too easy to dismiss the idea of Britain's civilizing mission as hypocrisy, the disguise of imperialist greed. Such an evaluation overlooks those who believed sincerely, and without selfish motives to endorse international expansion, that empire had a responsibility to impart civilization, and who were concerned that Britain might neglect this duty. Furthermore, conscientious statesmen knew that military campaigns overseas threatened Britain's own status as civilized. Opponents to the Second Opium War, such as Gladstone and Benjamin Disraeli, knew that it was a contradiction for a so-called 'civilized' nation to resort to violence. Gladstone promoted non-interventionist policies overseas, in which context we might also consider his citation of Homer in relation to the First Opium War, discussed in the previous chapter, as relevant to (broadly viewed) Greek alternatives to Roman models of foreign policy.[17] Liberal MP Richard Cobden told Parliament that intervention for social betterment was unnecessary in China. The Qing Empire was 'the only relic of the oldest civilization of the world', and warfare was the only field in which China was inferior to Britain.[18]

Arnold's definition of a 'modern' epoch allows for 'warfare and bloodshed' at the margins of society; mass violence exists but does not interfere with 'civil life'.[19] To other thinkers, ancient precedents for the Opium Wars became stumbling blocks because Britain was supposed to do better. Mill insists that Britain has greater humanity than the Greek and Roman powers did: 'the pain they inflicted . . . did not appear to them as great an evil, as it appears and as it really is, to us'.[20] Could civilization be imparted by force? Regardless of the China campaign, the

---

[16]   Peter J. Cain, 'Character, "Ordered Liberty", and the Mission to Civilise: British Moral Justification of Empire, 1870–1914', *The Journal of Imperial and Commonwealth History* 40, no. 4 (2012): 559–61.

[17]   Krishan Kumar, 'Greece and Rome in the British Empire: Contrasting Role Models', *Journal of British Studies* 51, no. 1 (2012): 14–15.

[18]   HC Deb 26 February 1857, vol. 144, col. 1391.

[19]   *Arnold: Poetry and Prose*, 272.   [20]   Mill, 'Civilisation', 12.

concept of British civilization was under threat of disintegration. This debate was analogous to Gibbon not only for the opposition of barbarism to civilization, but also because of shared concerns about the balance of *libertas* and *imperium*. Territorial over-reach posed a risk to Britain as empire, but so did ideological incoherence. Coleridge's detection of prophetic elements in the *Decline and Fall* became more fully validated as the extent of the British Empire increased.

Voices that argued for Chinese rights would be drowned out by the scientific racism of the following decades, in which texts such as Robert Knox's *The Races of Men* (1850) gained influence. More immediately, pacifist opposition to Palmerston's foreign policy was overpowered by the anti-Asian sentiment that followed the Indian Mutiny of 1857. As discussed in the previous chapter, Palmerston won the general election of 1857 largely due to promises that he would punish China. He and his ministers termed China barbarous, and claimed that it was acceptable for Britain to civilize China forcibly despite resistance. The long-term bene-fits of free trade, Palmerston contended, would compensate for the temporary trauma of war. His sense that China should be taught a lesson, as taken up by de Quincey, was an opinion shared by commanders of the 1860 campaign. In his memoir, Lucknow and China veteran Field Marshal Garnet Wolseley is explicit that the Second Opium War was a punitive mission:

[The Chinese] drove us, much against our wish, into this war. In fact, they brought upon themselves our occupation of Pekin and the subsequent destruc-tion of the Summer Palace. They are an inconsequent people, and it would seem as if their rulers never can learn wisdom from experience.[21]

Reflecting on a life in the military in his introduction, Wolseley remarks, 'War may cause havoc, but the ruins of Thebes, of Carthage, of Greece and of Rome, remind us that unmanly vices killed the races which built these once famous and powerful cities.' Such peoples 'would not have been subdued had they retained the manly virtues that made their forebears great.'[22] Wolseley does not place the blame for destruction with the aggressors. Rome fell; shame on the Romans.

---

[21] Garnet Wolseley, *The Story of a Soldier's Life*, repr., 2 vols (New York: Charles Scribner's Sons, 1904), 2:4.

[22] Wolseley, *A Soldier's Life*, 1:20.

Although theft and total destruction at the Summer Palace merge as a single occurrence in certain eyewitness and historical narratives, they were separate events. The two actions had different significance, and the attitudes of certain protagonists towards the respective acts of violence were in stark contrast. Despoliation of the Summer Place occurred in atavistic wildness, but its ruin was calculated. Elgin was explicit that he ordered his men to burn the Summer Palace as retaliation for the torture and execution of British prisoners. While memoirs of looting the Palace portray those actions as impulsive, Elgin reports much deliberation over the fire:

I came to the conclusion that the destruction of Yuen-ming-yuen was the least objectionable of the several courses open to me, unless I could have reconciled it to my sense of duty to suffer the crime which had been committed to pass practically unavenged. I had reason, moreover, to believe that it was an act which was calculated to produce a greater effect in China, and on the Emperor, than persons who look on from a distance may suppose.

It was the Emperor's favourite residence, and its destruction could not fail to be a blow to his pride as well as to his feelings. To this place he brought our hapless countrymen, in order that they might undergo their severest tortures within its precincts.[23]

The fires that consumed the Summer Palace could be explained by participants—possible objections to Elgin's decision notwithstanding—as a punishment. It was more difficult to account for what had taken place some days previously, from which a controversy arose that centred on the word 'looting'. There was a consensus among witnesses and commentators that looting exceeded the accepted means by which the armies enriched themselves in wartime. Many were attracted to the armed forces by the prospect of prize, the spoils which defrayed the costs of war and rewarded the men for their service. For example, the brass remnants of Chinese guns were taken from Yuanmingyuan as prize, with proceeds from the sale of the metal divided amongst the company. Trophies, meanwhile, were items taken from the battlefield as souvenirs, such as enemy banners or weapons. But 'looting', a verb that signifies wanton pillage, was a new concept.

---

[23] *Letters and Journals of James, Eighth Earl of Elgin*, ed. Theodore Walrond (London: John Murray, 1872), 366.

The word 'looting' had only entered parlance via British India in the mid nineteenth-century. The term appears to have Hindi etymology, originating in the Sansrkit *lunt* meaning 'to rob' and *rup* 'to break' (*OED*). The neologism captured a sentiment that looting was at odds with popular consensus on military entitlements to prize and trophies. Often looting occurred in tandem with extortion, rape, and murder of civilians. In his study of British and French behaviour at Yuanmingyuan, Erik Ringmar theorizes an 'Oriental sublime', an 'orgiastic' experience in which the sheer otherness of Asia caused Europeans to abandon their values. The Oriental sublime, to Ringmar, entails a kind of possession— his word is *entheos*—opposite the awestruck paralysis of the Burkean sublime.[24] To identify such temporary insanity as the effect of an exotic environment accounts for the new word, 'looting': the psychology was unique, beyond the opportunism of conventional pillage. Eighty years earlier, newspaper reports on the trial of Warren Hastings had mentioned Edmund Burke's frequent references to Cicero's Verrine orations. Gaius Verres was tried for extortion in 70 BCE. As evidence of character in speeches for the prosecution, Cicero refers to Verres' many acts of pillage, which included taking gold from the Temple of Athena at the Parthenon. Commentators felt that the misbehaviour of British visitors to India and other parts of Asia was different in character from the pillage found acceptable in the records of antiquity. It even exceeded Verrine greed, which was at least an intelligible kind of wickedness. Looting was something new, and it was frighteningly animal.

Particular concern arose over looting because its consequences could reach far beyond the moments of theft and destruction. Wolseley reflects dubiously on the practice when he recalls looting that took place in India during the 1850s. As in his account of the destruction of the Summer Palace, his sentiments do not proceed from sympathy for the natives. Looting posed a threat to military integrity:

I have never been a looter. Not from any squeamish notions as to the iniquity of the game, for I believe that, as a rule, to the victor should belong the spoils of war, but in the interests of order and discipline. It is destruction to all that is best in the

---

[24] Erik Ringmar, 'Liberal Barbarism and the Oriental Sublime: The European Destruction of the Emperor's Summer Palace', *Millennium: Journal of International Studies* 34, no. 3 (2006): 926.

military training of the British Army for the officer to pillage alongside the private and possibly to dispute for the ownership of some valuable prize.[25]

Wolseley, who speaks of 'the ruins of Thebes, of Carthage, of Greece and of Rome', knows the old saying that it is just for victors to claim goods from a captured city, although Xenophon goes on to say that they might well not do so as an act of *philanthropeia* (*Cyrus* 7.5.73). More pressingly, Wolseley knew that he had witnessed utter disorder in China. Presumably it was his anxiety over exemplary behaviour that led Wolseley to choose his verb carefully when he inscribed an album of Chinese landscape scenes, later donated to the National Army Museum: 'I found this in the Summer Palace near Pekin 1860. Wolseley.'[26] Comparably, signage at the Royal Engineers Museum in Gillingham invariably accounts for the presence of Summer Palace treasures with the verb 'removed'.[27] Such language betrays anxiety over public scrutiny. Thus looting posed a twofold risk for the army by creating disorder within and inviting criticism from without.

In his own memoir of the 1860 campaign, interpreter Robert Swinhoe validates the Field Marshal's fear that looting might destabilize the army. The Summer Palace is a chaotic scene:

Officers and men, English and French, were rushing about in a most unbecoming manner, each eager for the acquisition of valuables. Most of the Frenchmen were armed with large clubs, and what they could not carry away, they smashed to atoms. In one room you would see several officers and men of all ranks with their heads and hands brushing and knocking together in the same box, searching and grasping its contents. In another a scramble was going on over a collection of handsome state robes. Some would be playing pitch and toss against the large mirrors; others would be amusing themselves by taking 'cock' shots at the chandeliers. Respect for position was completely lost sight of, and the most perfect dis-organization prevailed.[28]

There was little interpreting to be done. Swinhoe watched as men of distinguished rank donned imperial, silken robes and filled the pockets

---

[25] Wolseley, *A Soldier's Life*, 1:40.

[26] National Army Museum, Online Collection, https://collection.nam.ac.uk/detail.php?acc=1963-10-290-1 (accessed 18 June 2019).

[27] Apparently insurers will not protect museum pieces described as 'looted'. See James Scott, 'Chinese Gordon', in *Collecting and Displaying China's Summer Palace: The Yuanmingyuan in Britain*, ed. Louise Tythacott (London: Routledge, 2017), 90–4.

[28] Robert Swinhoe, *Narrative of the North China Campaign of 1860* (London: Smith, Elder, 1861), 305–6.

with gems, grabbing porcelain and precious metals. They struggled under larger vases and incense burners, and carried off anything they perceived as valuable. One Captain John Hart Dunne records his sole regret as not being *better* at looting: 'I own to being very green about the business.'[29] He notes that officers who had served in India tended, from practice, to be the most efficient at evaluating and seizing valuables. To Swinhoe, looting 'afforded a very good proof of the innate evil in man's nature when unrestrained'. As his account continues he ceases to use the word 'officers', preferring 'plunderers' and 'marauders'.[30] Having looted the Summer Palace, participants ransacked local villages. The proceeds must have been almost worthless compared to the Summer Palace treasures, but the looters were in a frenzy.

The potential for the Summer Palace looting to beget lasting chaos was immediately evident to the British commanders. It was not that looting was unprecedented on the China campaign, but that there was a dangerously unique detail to this incident. Here, officers had looted the Summer Palace while the rank-and-file were confined to camp. Not only had the officers failed as exemplars, but they had enriched themselves while their subordinates received nothing. Sir James Hope Grant (1808–75), Commander of the British Army, understood that even if the madness subsided, a dissatisfied soldiery might induce mutiny. He decided that items taken from the Summer Palace should be auctioned, and the proceeds divided between officers and men by rank:

The British share of the plunder was all arranged for exhibition in the hall of the large llama [*sic*] temple, where the Head-quarters' Staff were quartered, and a goodly display it was: white and green jade-stone ornaments of all tints, enamel-inlaid jars of antique shape, bronzes, gold and silver figures and statuettes, &c; fine collections of furs, many of which were of much value, such as sable, sea-otter, ermine, Astracan lamb, &c.; and court costume, among which were two or three of the Emperor's state robes of rich yellow silk, worked upon with dragons in gold thread, and beautifully woven with floss-silk embroidery on the skirts, the inside being lined with silver fur or ermine, and cuffed with glossy sable. . . . The sale continued over three whole days, and was largely attended both by officers and men. . . . Fancy the sale of an emperor's effects beneath the walls of the capital of his empire, and this by a people he despised as weak barbarians and talked of driving into the sea![31]

[29] John Hart Dunne, *From Calcutta to Pekin* (London: Sampson Low, 1861), 130.
[30] Swinhoe, *Narrative*, 306–7.   [31] Swinhoe, *Narrative*, 311–12.

The auction restored order to the army. A peculiar period of calm followed while the men awaited the arrival and fresh orders of Elgin and Hope Grant. In this time, they went shopping. Laurence Oliphant, secretary to Lord Elgin, records that the two indulged their passion for crockery and book stores. Swinhoe portrays the Britons as model tourists: 'All the army was desirous to purchase some memento of the great city of Cathay, and the six or seven shops which were well supplied with every kind of article *de luxe* that the empire produces, drove a flourishing trade during the period of our stay.'[32]

The jolly respite ended with news that Qing forces had executed eleven British, French, and Sikh prisoners. Ten days after the Summer Palace had been looted, Elgin ordered for the buildings to be incinerated in retaliation to the killings. Ringmar assesses this act in Burkean terms too. He claims that Elgin's real purpose was to destroy the awe that the Emperor effected, and so significantly to weaken a regime that ruled by fear.[33] To sack the Palace would undoubtedly be 'a blow to [the Emperor's] pride as well as to his feelings', but it would also demonstrate his helplessness. The question arises of whether Elgin struck out in vengeance simply in order to dismay the proud Emperor, or whether more complex political machinations were on his mind which required the Chinese public to interpret events at the Summer Palace in a particular way and to respond accordingly, perhaps by revolution.

Elgin set an arduous task: 3500 men spent three days reducing the Summer Palace to ruins. To some participants, the systematic arson was as senseless as the frenzy of looting. Swinhoe describes a hellish scene:

> The crackling and rushing noise of fire was appalling, and the sun shining through the masses of smoke gave a sickly hue to every plant and tree, and the red flame gleaming on the faces of the troops engaged made them appear like demons glorying in the destruction of what they could not replace. . . . It betokened to our minds a sad portent of the fate of this antique empire, its very entrails being consumed by internecine war.[34]

With 'demons', Swinhoe's diminishing epithets for the servicemen reach their nadir. Yet the attitude among participants in the arson

---

[32] Swinhoe, *Narrative*, 356.

[33] Erik Ringmar, *Liberal Barbarism: The European Destruction of the Palace of the Emperor of China* (New York: Palgrave Macmillan, 2013), 31–3. Ringmar drops the term *entheos* from the book-length study.

[34] Swinhoe, *Narrative*, 330.

was far from universally negative, as is evident from one officer's account that was frequently syndicated in British Asia: 'We . . . watched with pleasure. . . . "Revenge is sweet."'[35]

In a letter home, Captain Charles 'Chinese' Gordon (1833–85) documents his emotions on following Lord Elgin's orders. Gordon would become a secular martyr on his death in Khartoum. More immediately after the 1860 campaign, he won fame as an Old China Hand who assisted Qing forces against the Taiping Rebellion (1850–64). His account of Yuanmingyuan is intriguing not simply because of Gordon's fame, but because of his complicated response to the conflagration. It is as though Gordon recognized, while he set the Summer Palace aflame, that British civilization was imperilled:

We accordingly went out, and after pillaging it, burned the whole place, destroying in a Vandal-like manner most valuable property, which would not be replaced for four millions . . . . You can scarcely imagine the beauty and magnificence of the places we burnt. It made one's heart sore to burn them; in fact these palaces were so large, and we were so pressed for time, that we could not plunder them carefully. Quantities of gold ornaments were burnt, considered as brass. It was wretchedly demoralizing work for an army. Everybody was wild for plunder. You would scarcely conceive the magnificence of this residence, or the tremendous devastation the French have committed.[36]

'Vandal-like' with a capital 'V': it is obvious, in Gordon's version of events, that the barbarians are British. However, his regret at incinerating the Summer Palace is at least partly because the army might have robbed it more 'carefully' first. It is uncertain whether 'valuable property' refers to the buildings or their contents. One wonders whether Gordon would have withheld the term 'Vandals' had the army demonstrated good taste by removing all artworks before destroying the Palace. It is equally striking that Gordon has no sooner acknowledged culpability for barbaric behaviour than he shifts the blame to Britain's allies, the French.

In the aftermath of events at the Summer Palace, the British and French sides defended themselves by each alleging that the other had

---

[35] The same officer is casual about looting and destruction near Yuanmingyuan: 'Unfortunately the houses of the surrounding villages were not spared in the general destruction and thousands of unhappy subjects had to suffer for the sins of their rulers.' *The Friend of India*, 6 December 1860, 1162.

[36] Quoted in George Barnett Smith, *General Gordon: the Christian Soldier and Hero* (London: S.W. Partridge, 1896), 24.

behaved worse.[37] Maurice d'Hérisson's *Journal of an Interpreter* (1866) would become the dominant French version of events, in which the fault lay with Chinese trespassers for the initial outbreak of looting. French commentators were scandalized by the destruction of the Summer Palace, but not by the looting. This is probably because similar pillage had occurred in recent French history. In *Sentimental Education* (1869), Gustave Flaubert documents revolutionary violence at the Tuileries in 1848:

The people, less out of vengeance than a desire to assert its supremacy, tore up curtains, smashed mirrors, chandeliers, sconces, tables, chairs, stools—everything that was movable, right down to albums of drawings and needlework baskets. They were the victors, so surely they were entitled to enjoy themselves. . . . Then the frenzy took on a darker note. An obscene curiosity drove them to ransack all the closets, search all the alcoves, and turn out all the drawers. . . . All round, in the two arcades, the populace, after raiding the wine-cellars, had embarked upon a horrifying orgy.[38]

Of the fires at the Summer Palace, Swinhoe claims that 'the French refused to co-operate, as they condemned the measure as a piece of barbarism', despite their responsibility for the 'chief mischief' in looting the Palace.[39] Reports of the incineration provoked outrage in France: '*Every Frenchman* cries out against the sacking and burning of the Summer Palace.'[40]

British journalism on the Summer Palace was initially more positive than negative. Contemporary newspapers in the British Empire account for the Summer Palace booty with such vagaries as that 'articles . . . have been secured for the English army' and that 'it is a subject of congratulation that the English soldiers were not exposed to the same temptation as their neighbours.'[41] Contrarily, *The Lady's Newspaper* portrays the British troops producing wares from their pockets to sell and trade: 'every soldier who was present is replete with loot'.[42] Journalistic

---

[37] See for example *The London and China Telegraph*, 16 March 1874, 190–1.

[38] Gustave Flaubert, *Sentimental Education*, trans. Robert Baldick, rev. Geoffrey Wall (London: Penguin Classics, 2004), 313–15.

[39] Swinhoe, *Narrative*, 330.

[40] *Diplomatic Review*, 6 March 1861, 29.

[41] *The Belfast News-Letter*, 22 December 1860; *Freeman's Journal and Daily Commercial Advertiser*, 21 December 1860.

[42] *The Lady's Newspaper*, 19 January 1861, 39.

coverage remained ambivalent for years. When the French Captain Henri de Negroni's Summer Palace haul was exhibited at the Crystal Palace in 1865, *The Era* was sympathetic towards the looters: 'Soldiers, especially those who are sent thousands of miles to catch Tartars, deserve consolation, and it can take no more satisfactory form than the privilege of appropriating property called "looting."'[43] A quarter of a century later, and more immediately affected by the legacy of the Anglo-French campaign than were commentators at home, missionaries would lament the destruction of the Summer Palace,

An act which has so impressed the whole nation with a conviction that all foreigners are barbarous Vandals, that it is generally coupled with their determined pushing of the opium trade. These two crimes form the double-barrelled weapon of reproach wherewith Christian missionaries in all parts of the Empire are assailed, and their work grievously hindered.[44]

Chinese commentators viewed the Summer Palace incidents as beyond the occurrences of ordinary warfare. An essay attributed to diplomat and polyglot Zeng Jize (1839–90) adopts Keatsian classicism as it considers events of 1860 among several highly significant incursions, beginning with the Treaty of Tianjin in 1842. The essay was drafted on Zeng's instructions by the Counsellor to the Chinese Legation in London, Samuel Halliday Macartney (1833–1906). Halliday Macartney, who was related to the 1793 ambassador, and considered himself a poet, probably supplied the literary allusion himself:

This did something to rouse China from the Saturnian dreams in which she had been so long indulging; but more was wanting to make her wide awake. It required the fire of the Summer Palace to singe her eyebrows, the advance of the Russian in Kuldja and the Frenchman in Tong-King, to enable her to realise the situation in which she was being placed by the ever-contracting circle that was being drawn around her by the European.[45]

Keats's *Hyperion: A Fragment* (1819) recounts the myth in which 'Old Saturn lifted up | His faded eyes, and saw his kingdom gone' (89–90). The poem invites association with China where Thea performs a kowtow to the fallen Saturn: 'She touch'd her fair large forehead to the ground'

---

[43] *The Era*, 26 March 1865.   [44] *The Evening Telegraph*, 2 January 1885, 4.
[45] Zeng Jize, 'China: The Sleep and the Awakening', *The Chinese Recorder and Missionary Journal* 18 (April 1887): 148.

(8). The idea of a sleeping China would become commonplace; Zeng's essay elaborates the image in Keatsian terms. China is a fallen Titan, not merely asleep but deposed by a new order. We can only wonder whether Zeng and Macartney discussed Gibbon. The final metaphor above announces China's arrival at the very position of encirclement that the Qianlong Emperor dreaded, the position of defeat in the game of *weiqi*.

As a gesture intended to upset the Emperor, the ruin of the Summer Palace succeeded. The Xianfeng Emperor had fled to Chengde. He was unable to bear the thought of royal domains overrun by foreigners. Rather than witness such affronts, the Emperor and his entourage remained in the northern retreat, which had long been uninhabited, and was ill-equipped for the cold weather. Obstinacy took its toll on the Emperor, who died in 1861.

If Elgin intended to demonstrate the inferiority of the Qing army, it is arguable that he failed. For one thing, the despairing missionary reports tell us that much of the population focussed on the foreigners' barbarism rather than their display of military prowess, or the inadequacies of Chinese resistance. For Elgin to have made his statement clearly, he would need to have prevented looting. The manner in which events unfolded made arson appear a natural companion to pillage rather than a political statement; a further example of impulsiveness and not a measured response to the execution of prisoners. Furthermore, a story arose in China that the Summer Palace was burgled by locals while the Emperor and his retinue were unaccountably absent.[46] Undoubtedly locals stole from Yuanmingyuan too, but what is remarkable about this popular myth is that it purports to explain the pillage without acknowledging the presence of the allied powers. The tale of local robbers was presumably more palatable than the truth that Chinese forces had been overcome easily by foreigners. Surely this is the counterpart to David Porter's hypothesized 'instrumental amnesia', by which China was so obviously important to Britain that its relatively infrequent appearance in Anglophone literature should be attributed to embarrassment at earlier admiration, and avoidance of the diplomatic humiliations.[47]

---

[46] George Nathaniel Curzon, *Problems of the Far East: Japan—Korea—China*, 2nd ed. (London: Longmans, Green, and Co., 1894), 274.

[47] David Porter, *The Chinese Taste in Eighteenth-Century England* (Cambridge: Cambridge University Press, 2010), 158.

Accordingly, the British soldiers' final act at Yuanmingyuan was to bear off carriages, astronomical equipment, and two howitzer guns from the grounds. The Macartney delegation had gifted these items to the Qianlong Emperor in 1793. Now the soldiers reversed the process. Doubtless they were valuable, but the repossessed presents also enabled the British army to erase evidence of a painful history. Thus great statements were made, if not interpreted as intended, and cultures carefully edited the stories they would tell of themselves.

Elgin & Son: the Parthenon Sculptures, the Summer Palace Treasures, and Repatriation Debates

Objects can be used to tell very different stories in different contexts. An artefact crafted for an emperor's personal use might become loot, and then a commodity in an auction house, and finally a display item in a museum, serving whatever narrative of inter-cultural relations that institution told. To Qing officials, the Macartney delegation's gifts supported the interpretation of the Embassy that they needed; that it was a display of tribute from an inferior society. Removed nearly 70 years later, the same items corroborated accounts of British supremacy to some and barbarism to others. Certain objects from the Summer Palace are displayed in British military museums, where they communicate a history of success overseas. Other artefacts reside in the British Museum which, at the height of British Empire, projected the notion of possessing the world, but which nowadays assumes the more modest role of surveyor. The Great Exhibition of 1862 showed Chinese wares with imperialist overtones. Exhibitions in Bristol and Edinburgh in 1861, to which Elgin and Hope Grant loaned items, presented Summer Palace artefacts as evidence of an imperial Chinese aesthetic that had never been accurately communicated to Britain before, in the hope of stimulating domestic art. Some disingenuous stories arose about looted items. Nearly every Anglophone treatment of the wooden seat that Chinese Gordon donated to the Royal Engineers Museum, for instance, refers to it as *the* imperial throne.[48] However, the seat actually reassembled in England as 'throne'

---

[48] See for example Ringmar, *Liberal Barbarism* (2013), 73.

comprises wood from an assortment of objects, mostly from a garden chair.[49] Other commonplaces are debatable, such as the tale, perpetuated by Hugo and others, that the fate of the Summer Palace treasures re-enacts that of Elgin's Parthenon Sculptures.

A comparison of the two Elgins necessitates a decided position on the events that brought pieces of the Parthenon Sculptures to London. William St Clair's account remains the most persuasive treatment of Elgin Senior, who appears not to have believed his luck when the Ottoman forces proved willing to sell the relics. Elgin had initially hoped for no more than plaster casts of the Parthenon. He was oppor-tunistic, but he was not a thief.[50] Moreover, the removal of artefacts from the Summer Palace in 1860 had nothing to do with Elgin Junior, who arrived on the scene after the site had been looted. If he had ordered that the Summer Palace be disassembled and shipped to London—or if Elgin Senior had instigated the destruction of the Acropolis—the son's actions would be more closely comparable to his father's. The two Elgins behaved recklessly, and were inattentive to long-term consequences of their actions overseas. Otherwise, the resemblances between their stories are vague. To portray them as doubles in a tale of father-and-son plunderers may constitute entertaining storytelling, but not truthful history. Yet as with Hugo, the temptation to merge these figures often proves irresistible. 'Perhaps it was a family tradition, or a genetic dis-order', Richard Kraus says of the Elgins' behaviour towards Greek and Chinese sites.[51]

Consequently, each of the respective debates over repatriation of Parthenon and Summer Palace artefacts frequently invokes the other.

Perceived parallels between the Parthenon Sculptures and the Summer Palace episodes have been increasingly popular in recent dis-cussions of repatriation. Commonly, critics presume that resolution of one dispute would determine the other by establishing precedent. Some opponents of repatriation view it as an inconvenience so daunting that the effort involved substantiates a case against serious consideration of

---

[49] Scott, 'Chinese Gordon', 91.

[50] William St Clair, *Lord Elgin and the Marbles*, 3rd ed. (Oxford: Oxford University Press, 1998).

[51] Richard Kraus, 'When Legitimacy Resides in Beautiful Objects: Repatriating Beijing's Looted Zodiac Animal Heads', in *State and Society in 21st Century China: Crisis, Conten-tion, and Legitimation*, ed. Peter Gries and Stanley Rosen (London: Routledge, 2004), 197.

restoration.[52] The Parthenon Sculptures controversy has become a source text for discussions of Summer Palace treasures. Here the debates are more closely alike than were the actions of the Elgins. Some commentators, against repatriation of Summer Palace treasures, wonder whether the complex would have been destroyed during the Cultural Revolution (1966–76) if it had not been so already. Such arguments, as Kraus notes, commonly cite speculation over how well Elgin Senior's Greek acquisitions would have fared in the remainder of Ottoman rule.[53] That the systematic destruction of the Cultural Revolution had some resemblance to Elgin's methods at the Summer Palace problematizes the vision of the British soldiers as saviours of the Chinese treasures. Further to this conjecture over what might have befallen objects in their earlier homes is the argument that British institutions are better curators of artefacts than are those in their original locations. This claim is contestable in relation to the Summer Palace loot, as it is of the Parthenon Sculptures. The scandal that erupted in the 1930s over the mistreatment of the Parthenon Sculptures, scoured and bleached in appeal to tourists' visions of marmoreal antiquity, leads William St Clair to term the British Museum's declarations of conscientious stewardship a 'cynical sham'.[54] The uncertain identity of 'Chinese' Gordon's 'throne' demonstrates that Chinese objects, like the Parthenon Sculptures, could be altered to suit the host nation's aesthetic. Worse still, a considerable quantity of Chinese objects has been lost since arrival in Britain. The most significant damage occurred when the Surrey Infantry Museum was incinerated in 2015. The fire was caused by an electrical fault. This 'worst disaster ever to befall the National Trust' casts doubt over suggestions that Summer Palace artefacts are more responsibly curated in Britain than elsewhere.[55]

---

[52] For example Tiffany Jenkins, *Keeping Their Marbles: How the Treasures of the Past Ended Up in Museums—And Why They Should Stay There* (Oxford: Oxford University Press, 2016).

[53] Richard Kraus, 'The Politics of Art Repatriation: Nationalism, State Legitimation, and Beijing's Looted Zodiac Animal Heads', in *Chinese Politics: State, Society and the Market* ed. Peter Gries and Stanley Rosen (London: Routledge, 2010), 214.

[54] St Clair, *Lord Elgin*, 342ff.

[55] 'Battle of the Somme football among priceless artifacts lost in Clandon Park blaze', *Daily Telegraph*, 30 April 2015. https://www.telegraph.co.uk/news/uknews/11574829/Battle-of-the-Somme-football-among-priceless-artifacts-lost-in-Clandon-House-blaze.html (accessed 21 June 2019).

Although ancient objects are at stake, repatriation of things is a new kind of story which centres on young ideas. 'Cultural property', in reference to the 'material evidence' of a people, was a coinage of the 1970 UNESCO Convention. The Convention aimed to protect 'cultural property' from illicit transport overseas. Moreover, discussion of 'cultural property' assumes that the object in question has been reconceptualized. 'Cultural property' always refers to artefacts whose original function is obsolete. No ceremonial offerings are made, for instance, at the Victoria & Albert Museum's incense burner, taken from the Summer Palace by 'Chinese' Gordon. 'Cultural property' is old and symbolic, and is there for appearances. China has devised its own terminology in pursuit of the Summer Palace treasures, but this too revolves around neologism, reflecting a recent change in perspective on material culture. When twentieth-century Maoists spoke of China's 'cultural relics' (*wenwu*, 文物), they meant evidence of a decadent past that should be demolished. China's interest in retrieving objects this millennium has relied on a term derived from Japan, 'national treasures' (*guobao*, 国宝), the meaning of which is close to 'cultural property'. The Japanese loan-word exemplifies how China's own nationalist narratives are eclectic as well as recent.

The Chinese state has made a set of bronze animal heads representative of the Summer Palace treasures, although the reasons for this focus are elusive. The twelve heads, each a figure of the Chinese zodiac, were once affixed to anthropomorphic bodies. They were part of a fountain. Every two hours (that is, one traditional Chinese hour), a different head would spray water. Yet nobody is sure why the heads have been made to represent the Summer Palace loot as opposed to, say, the imperial seal, carved from jade, that is displayed at the British Museum. Never apparently favourites of any emperor, the heads fell into disrepair in the late eighteenth-century and were not fixed. Furthermore, there is no reference to the heads in nineteenth-century accounts of the Summer Palace either in English or in French. They may have been in storage during the 1860 campaign. There is actually no evidence that foreigners took the zodiac heads: Chinese thieves may have smuggled them overseas. As such, the objects that the Chinese government has chosen as symbols for the Summer Palace atrocity were neither prized by their original owners nor demonstrably part of the controversial 1860 loot.

Nor are they strictly Chinese. In a study of how classics exerts its presence on Anglophone treatments of China, the punchline is perhaps

Figure 7.1 Ai WeiWei's *Circle of Animals/Zodiac Heads* (2011) emulates the disfigured sculptures taken from the Yuanmingyuan fountain.
Carnegie Museum of Art (CMOA). Photo: Matt Nemeth.

that the zodiac heads, icons of Chinese art lost to Western barbarism, are as much European as Chinese. In 2011, Ai WeiWei made complete sets of twelve heads in both bronze- and gold-plate, imitating the sculptures taken from Yuanmingyuan. The artist refers to the un-Chinese qualities of his model in explanation of his *Circle of Animals/Zodiac Heads* (2011, see Figure 7.1): 'They were designed by an Italian, made by a Frenchman for a Qing dynasty emperor, which actually is somebody who invaded China. So if we talk about national treasure, what nation are we talking about?'[56]

In 1760 the zodiac heads at Yuanmingyuan were constructed by Qing craftsmen in collaboration with Michel Benoist, a French expert in hydraulics, to the plan of an Italian Jesuit priest, Giuseppe Castiglione (1688–1766). The use of anthropomorphic bodies was a remnant of Castiglione's original design, which featured naked nymphs. The

---

[56] *Ai WeiWei: Never Sorry*, directed by Alison Klayman, IFC Films, 2012.

execution of his sketches, although intricately detailed artwork, demonstrated Castiglione's un-Chinese aesthetics. Now on display in Nanjing, the tiger appears notoriously unlike either a tiger or a traditional representation of a tiger. The priest had no idea what a tiger looked like. Nor did he adopt traditional zodiac imagery for his designs. The bronze heads required Chinese labour, and treated a Chinese subject, but the aesthetic was entirely European. Perhaps, ironically, it is because the heads are so un-Chinese that they are useful as symbols. They are more easily identified than Summer Palace items that use traditional Chinese principles. Ai's zodiac animals are heads on stakes. He does not represent the original anthropomorphic bodies, but communicates decapitation. These zodiac heads are fragmentary. Belonging completely to no country, they are homeless—or they belong to everyone.

Meanwhile the Chinese Communist Party is adamant that the original zodiac heads belong to China. Its efforts to retrieve the heads demonstrate anxiety over governmental legitimacy on both domestic and international stages. Controversy over the heads has the power to unite Chinese people in outrage. A disgruntled art-dealer who declined to pay, having submitted a winning bid at auction for the rabbit and rat heads in 2009, claimed to act on behalf of the Chinese nation. Casino-owner Stanley Ho purchased and donated the horse head in 2009. The Chinese Communist Party welcomes such generosity as a display of patriotism, and has also taken action itself, as with the purchase of the boar head in 2003. Retrieval of the heads from overseas could authenticate the current government by confirming its place in an ancient Chinese succession. Anyone who suggests that the heads would be going home if sent to China implies that it is essentially the same place as when the objects were crafted. Old heads are discussed with reference to cultural longevity, but really at stake is a Chinese government that has overseen extraordinary political-change from socialism to capitalism.

By claiming the zodiac heads, the Chinese Communist Party reaches for the past, which might stabilize national identity amidst unrelenting change. This impulse is as Macaulay describes of ancient texts standing by us in new realms and, of course, is analogous to imperial Britain's use of classical models. Some episodes in China's ongoing attempts to repatriate the heads are self-conscious historical re-enactments. For example, the tiger, ox, and monkey heads were purchased in auctions at Christie's and Sotheby's by the Poly Group in 2000. With intimate ties to senior figures in the People's Liberation Army, the Poly Group's capture of the heads reverses the image of European soldiers carrying them off.[57] The national narrative is frequently revised. By mid-2008 the 'Never Forget National Humiliation' inscription was gone.[58] The Yuanmingyuan complex had changed into a monument to past grandeur, which celebrates achievement rather than lamenting devastation. With this new emphasis Yuanmingyuan is as suitable a model for a rising China as Rome was for Britain. No matter that a considerable amount of the Summer Palace architecture was, like the zodiac heads, executed in European aesthetics. This is what Hugo means by describing the site as 'chimerical'. National narratives that are indebted to classical models and dubious facts provoke questions about authenticity, but wonders can be made where cultures meet.

---

[57] Kraus, 'The Politics of Art Repatriation', 204–5.

[58] James L. Hevia, 'The Afterlives of a Ruin: The Yuanmingyuan in China and the West', in *Collecting and Displaying China's Summer Palace*, 29.

8

Coda: 'All Things Fall and Are Built Again'

Yeats's Daoist Optimism and the Fall of the Qing Dynasty

William Butler Yeats (1865–1939) was so pleased by a birthday gift he received in 1935 that he wrote a poem about it. 'Lapis Lazuli' (1938) begins with rumblings of the Second World War approaching, in response to which the poem's central message is that 'all things fall and are built again | And those that build them again are gay' (35–36). That lesson is intuitive to Yeats, yet he struggles for evidence. His context is public scepticism about art's relevance to crisis. Yeats's audience is tired of 'poets that are always gay', but Yeats feels that optimism remains appropriate in difficult times (3). He finds his opinion validated by the carved stone.

Now displayed at the National Library of Ireland, Yeats's lapis lazuli (Figure 8.1) is Chinese. The stone was carved in the mid-eighteenth century from a material with meditative associations. It is etched with images of ascetics climbing a mountain. Additionally, the stone is engraved with a poem in traditional Chinese characters which is attributed to the Qianlong Emperor. This text was originally inset with gold—now worn away—and would once have appeared prominent:

'春山訪友'
綠雲紅雨向清和
寂寂深山幽事多
曲徑苔封人跡絕
抱琴高士許相過

China from the Ruins of Athens and Rome: Classics, Sinology, and Romanticism, 1793–1938.
Chris Murray, Oxford University Press (2020). © Chris Murray.
DOI: 10.1093/oso/9780198767015.001.0001

Figure 8.1 Carved in the mid-eighteenth century, Yeats's lapis lazuli is etched with images of ascetics climbing a mountain.

Photo: Colin Smythe

> 'Visiting a Friend on Spring Mountain'
> Green clouds and red rain, late spring approaches.
> Quiet, quiet, deep mountains; secrets abound,
> On moss-sealed, winding paths, without human footprints,
> A hermit bears a zither, a promise to meet.[1]

The subject befits the author. Traditionally a new emperor toured the sacred mountains in order to secure the Mandate of Heaven (*tianming*, 天命). In this context, 'Heaven' (*tian*, 天) is akin to *natura naturans*. The Heavenly Mandate means, in essence, assurance that the Emperor will

---

[1] I am indebted to the scholarship of Jerusha McCormack, who acknowledges Zhang Xin's assistance, in 'The Poem on the Mountain: A Chinese Reading of Yeats's "Lapis Lazuli"', *Yeats Annual* 19 (2013): 71. See also Christina Han, 'Ekphrasis as a Transtextual and Transcultural Event: Revisiting "Lapis Lazuli"', *The Yeats Journal of Korea* 51 (2016): 73–96.

act in accordance with nature. Good governance is therefore a natural process like the cycle of seasons and the revolution of celestial bodies. A wicked ruler deviates from the way of nature. His consequent loss of the Mandate might be signalled by famine, drought, or another form of disaster. The Emperor's poem evokes family duties as well as attention to the natural order. The grave-sweeping festival, which occurs in late spring, is a time at which ancestral voices would call to the Emperor. He would clean their resting-places in an exemplary act of filial piety. In performance of ritual and adherence to the will of Heaven, the Emperor himself must become such a sage as entices Yeats in his reading of Daoism.

Mindful of these paradigms, Yeats's conclusive description of the lapis lazuli enables him to answer his critics on how culture might reconcile us to the devastation of war. To reach this point he considers the trajectory of tragedy and the rise and fall of civilizations. The pictures on the Chinese artefact offer him another perspective on catastrophe, literally: he imagines the men on his stone as watchers of human affairs, and attributes to them a wise resignation. 'On all the tragic scene they stare' but, we are told of the figures on the carved mountain, 'their ancient, glittering eyes are gay' (52–56). Because his interpretation of the stone is consistent with his Nietzschean reading of Greek tragedy as joyful, Yeats gains confidence that he has apprehended universal wisdom: that art should promote pragmatism and gaiety as the only worthwhile responses to crisis. Evidently, his thoughts are lapidary. The end of the Qing Dynasty in 1911 has enhanced the artefact's prophetic wisdom, and with Yeats's poem ends a Romantic mode of viewing China that has been central to this book. In Ezra Pound's reception of Ernest Francisco Fenollosa's work (especially in *The Cantos*, 1915–70), the curious relationship between classics and China begets a new kind of literature.[2] Yeats's poem also rounds off a particular lineage of thought in another way. The tableau on the lapis offers an opportunity to correct the pessimism of Matthew Arnold's *Empedocles on Etna: A Dramatic Poem* (1852), and so to insist that classical forebears are invoked in the right

---

[2] Yeats experimented with the Japanese Noh theatre in *Four Plays for Dancers* (1921) having introduced Pound's *Certain Noble Plays of Japan* (1916), which Pound based on a draft translation by Fenollosa.

spirit. Yeats's use of Daoism to this end reverses a pattern that has recurred in this book: here the Chinese material resolves what is incomplete in the classical. The dialogue between China and classics continues but has been changed, amongst other factors, by advances in Sinology. I interpret Yeats's encounter with China as Romantic in several senses, but it is a Romanticism supplemented both by recent history and by translations that had made aspects of Chinese culture newly accessible. Translation, of course, offers an imperfect experience of a text. But Yeats's most profound reading of classical works was—like his reading of Chinese texts—based on English versions, which is how most Anglophone readers approach classics nowadays. Hence, this coda examines a historical moment by which certain boundaries between classics and Chinese culture had dissolved to an extent; they co-existed thereafter in the context of a shared, global heritage, or world literature.

Before making it the subject of a poem, Yeats approached his stone in light of eighteenth- and nineteenth-century books on China. He owned several books on China that dated from the late eighteenth-century, including two different distillations of Jesuit Sinology. Of course, the stone itself is an eighteenth-century work. I presume that the iconography and the Chinese text were explained to Yeats by someone such as the illustrator Edmund Dulac, who offered to translate the characters. To take on the stone's associations with the Qianlong Emperor enriches our reading of 'Lapis Lazuli' as it relates to war, consolation, prophecy, and gift exchange. Literature roughly contemporary with the artefact influences Yeats's ekphrasistic treatment. We might consider 'Lapis Lazuli' in light of Yeats's self-applied label, 'last Romantic' in 'Coole Park and Ballylee, 1931':

> We were the last romantics – chose for theme
> Traditional sanctity and loveliness;
> Whatever's written in what poets name
> The book of the people; whatever most can bless
> The mind of man or elevate a rhyme.
>
> (41–45)

The fifth line echoes the elevation in Wordsworth's 'Tintern Abbey' (1798), but my focus is on 'sanctity and loveliness'. Such language befits a key influence on 'Lapis Lazuli', Keats's 'Ode on a Grecian Urn'. Like 'Lapis Lazuli', 'Grecian Urn' is an ekphrastic work in which the central artefact prompts reflections on mutability, and the immortality of art. The urn resists Keats's gaze, divorced from its original, ancient context and appearing in a society whose vision of the classical ranged from the high culture of the recently acquired Parthenon Sculptures to the fad for neoclassical designs in Wedgwood crockery. Comparably Yeats's stone is mysterious; his early attempts to read the object, as he documents them in letters, do so through a fog of Orientalist generalizations. 'Ascetic, pupil, hard stone, eternal theme of the sensual east': so Yeats described the stone to Dorothy Wellesley the day after he received it in July 1935.[3] The sages ascending a mountain on the lapis lazuli reminded Yeats of his introduction to *The Holy Mountain* (1934), a memoir by the Indian monk Bhagwan Shri Hamsa. Here Yeats says that Chinese and Japanese art is 'a celebration of mountains', because mountains are 'dwelling-places of the Gods'. In this treatment of Hindu meditation, in which the practitioner attempts to perceive universality, Yeats refers to 'all existence brought into the words "I am"'.[4] He pursues the Coleridgean phrasing by quoting from the short poem 'What is Life?' (1804), which begins,

> Resembles Life what once was deemed of Light,
> Too ample in itself for human Sight?

$$(1-2)$$

This analogue illustrates again that Yeats's conception of China is Romantic in the sense that it is often refracted, like his readings of Milton and Dante, through Romantic authors. His allusion to Coleridge's words on the ineffable exemplifies Yeats's explicit reliance on Romantic thought to examine Asian ideas. In 'Lapis Lazuli' Yeats reveals advancement from China viewed within the broad domain of the Orient to Sinology, or specific knowledge of China which is grounded in scholarship. The Yeats who composed 'Lapis Lazuli' in 1936 obviously knew a great deal more about the artefact than the Yeats who resorted to 'eternal themes of the sensual east' a year earlier.

His broad reading on Asia occurred within a lifelong quest for esoteric knowledge, which also encompassed Yeats's Philhellenism. He was a Neoplatonist, especially absorbed in the English texts of Plotinus that

---

[3] *The Letters of W.B. Yeats*, ed. Allan Wade (London: Rupert Hart-Davis, 1954), 837.
[4] W.B. Yeats, *Essays and Introductions* (London: Macmillan & Co Ltd, 1961), 454–5.

Stephen McKenna produced between 1917 and 1930. Yeats struggled with languages—he was mocked in *The Irish Times* for his poor Latin—but benefitted from the work of scholars such as E. R. Dodds. Yeats attempted to derive an idyll of Byzantium from Gibbon, whose own treatment of the city is dubious. In 'Sailing to Byzantium' (1927) he imagines that he might be dematerialized and refined 'into such a form as Grecian goldsmiths make' (4.3). The formal commitment to numbered stanzas of *ottava rima* in this poem aligns Yeats with the craftsmen, who might recast him as a mechanical bird that would sing wisdom 'Of what is passed, or passing, or to come' (4.8). The eclectic search for *gnosis* also shaped Yeats's reading of Chinese metaphysics. 'Lapis Lazuli' demonstrates that Yeats read diversely, but adapted literature to suit a philosophy that was instinctive. He claimed that in books we 'seek . . . clarification of what we already believe.'[5]

Yeats's account of the lapis lazuli encapsulates his thoughts on Daoism. The thinker most significant to this poem is Zhuangzi (369–286 BCE), the Chinese philosopher who, famously, is uncertain whether he dreamt of being a butterfly or whether a butterfly dreamt of being Zhuangzi.[6] The sole text attributed to this philosopher is the eponymous work *Zhuangzi*.[7] This occurs as a series of vignettes, some involving the man himself, others featuring mythical and historical figures; even Confucius appears, to show up his own flawed philosophy. The episodes are often humorous and, as such, offer a more accessible notion of the way of harmony than in Laozi's *Dao De Jing*, a densely symbolic work. Laozi encodes Daoism in natural images of potentiality which partake of the ineffable Way or *dao*, as where he characterizes great philosophers:

Timid were they, like one fording a stream in winter. Cautious were they, like a man [far] from home. Vanishing were they, like ice that is about to melt. Simple were they, like unwrought wood. Vacant were they, like a valley. Dim were they, like muddy water.[8]

---

[5] W. B. Yeats, *Explorations* (London: Macmillan & Co Ltd, 1962), 310.

[6] *Chuang Tzu: Mystic, Moralist, and Social Reformer*, trans. Herbert A. Giles (London: Bernard Quaritch, 1889), 32.

[7] Giles records the scholarly consensus that only the first seven or 'inner chapters' of the received recension's thirty-three chapters are likely to be authored by Zhuangzi himself. See *Chuang Tzu*, xiv.

[8] *Tau The King*, 10–11.

By contrast Laozi's follower, Zhuangzi, is the plain-speaking philosopher who advises us explicitly to cease strife. Zhuangzi claims that the world will be governed peacefully if we resign to the natural course of affairs.

Yeats's initial excitement over Daoism can be traced to a meeting with Oscar Wilde (1854–1900). He recalled the effect of Wilde's talk on their first encounter in 1888 with 'astonishment'.[9] When Yeats visited Wilde's London home early in 1890, Wilde was reviewing Herbert Giles's 1889 translation of *Zhuangzi*. In 1882 Wilde had found himself converted unexpectedly to Chinese aesthetics on a visit to Chinatown in San Francisco, as documented in the posthumous *Personal Impressions of America* (1906). The translation of Zhuangzi delighted him no less, and left an impression on his essays, such as the anarchic 'Soul of Man under Socialism' (1891). In his review of Giles's translation, Wilde rejoices in the anti-authoritarian Zhuangzi's 'great creed of Inaction', and his insistence on 'the uselessness of all useful things'.[10] The resemblance that the Daoist sage's way of inaction (*wuwei*, 无为) bears to eighteenth-century theories of poetic indolence exemplifies how his new interest in China stimulated Wilde. Exposure to Chinese culture also prompted Wilde to reconsider poverty, including the poor in Ireland. From his knowledge of Chinese ceramics, textiles, and Daoism, Wilde concluded, to his surprise, that high principles of aesthetics and philosophy prevailed among ordinary Chinese people, who 'will have nothing about them that is not beautiful'.[11] Wilde's admiration for the Chinese poor was followed by his increased attention to the disadvantaged in general. The learned Chinese taught him that poor people might be worthy of greater notice than Wilde first thought. In short, Daoism not only captured Wilde's and Yeats's imaginations as a novel philosophy, but it caused each of them to view important themes in new ways. Much later, Yeats pursued Daoism further to read a treatise on inner alchemy, *The Secret of the Golden Flower* (c. 1750), which Yeats described as an 'invaluable Chinease book [sic]'.[12] This treatise assimilates various Daoist and Buddhist works and offers instructions for meditation. The central teaching is attributed to

---

[9] W. B. Yeats, *Autobiographies* (London: Macmillan & Co Ltd, 1955), 130.

[10] Oscar Wilde, 'A Chinese Sage', *The Speaker* 1 (1890): 144.

[11] *Oscar Wilde in America: The Interviews*, ed. Matthew Hofer and Gary Scharnhorst (Urbana and Chicago: University of Illinois Press, 2010), 179.

[12] *Letters of W.B. Yeats*, 788. Wade corrects Yeats's spelling of 'Chinese' from the manuscript.

Lu Dongbin (whose lifespan is popularly dated 796–1016 CE): the blossoming flower represents the open mind. Probably unwittingly, Yeats's misspelling 'Chin*ease*' confirms the centrality of inaction to this philosophy (my emphasis). What Yeats represents of Daoism in 'Lapis Lazuli' can be summarized as 'gaiety', which tells us that he comprehended a fundamental Daoist principle which permeates Zhuangzi's advice on fear and hesitation:

> Now if you have a big tree and are at a loss what to do with it, why not plant it in the domain of non-existence, whither you might betake yourself to inaction by its side, to blissful repose beneath its shade? There it would be safe from the axe and from all other injury; for being of no use to others, itself would be free from harm.[13]

Yeats's piece of lapis lazuli was a gift from the poet Harry Clifton, but had longer-reaching associations with the act of presentation. The Qianlong Emperor's text connects the stone to the Irish-born Macartney and the 1793 Embassy, an occasion of elaborate ceremony and gift-exchange. Furthermore, the artefact represents both conflict and foreknowledge. It reminds the Anglophone reader of the Embassy's unhappy aftermath, as evident in Macartney's notorious journal entry, which historians view as prophetic of the Opium Wars: 'Can they be ignorant that a couple of British frigates would be an overmatch for the whole naval force of the empire . . . ?' As we saw in the previous chapter, the family name was kept in public debate in Yeats's lifetime by Halliday Macartney, who helped Zeng Jize articulate his thoughts on British barbarism during the Opium Wars. That the lapis could evoke thoughts of war explains the relevance of Yeats's opening to a poem in which the focus appears to shift abruptly:

> I have heard that hysterical women say
> They are sick of the palette and fiddle-bow,
> Of poets that are always gay,
> For everybody knows or else should know
> That if nothing drastic is done
> Aeroplane and Zeppelin will come out,
> Pitch like King Billy bomb-balls in
> Until the town lie beaten flat.
>
> (1–8)

---

[13] *Chuang Tzu*, 11.

The poets, 'always gay', have their counterpart in Yeats's final description of the Chinese sages, whose 'glittering eyes are gay'. Yeats will appeal to Daoist philosophy to justify the universal spirit of art, which has ever been gaiety. Historical associations also help to define the overall shape of the poem. A westerner who knew a few facts about the stone would associate Harry Clifton's gift with the landmark occasion of gift exchange in China, the Macartney Embassy. The unhappy encounter between Macartney and the Emperor, which originated the Opium Wars, corresponds to the foreboding that prevails at the start of 'Lapis Lazuli'. Yeats identifies Kaiser Wilhelm with William III—the English king who conquered Ireland in the seventeenth century—to communicate that history is cyclical.[14] 'Aeroplane and Zeppelin', an A to Z of warfare, also delineates a sequence of catastrophes, a shape to devastations which individually appear meaningless.

In 'Lapis Lazuli' art has been charged with some 'drastic' measure that could prevent the recurrence of war or reconcile us to it. The poem commences with hearsay in conversational language. The tone is prescriptive, but it is also vague: something should be done by art, by nobody appears to know precisely what. This vagueness is set up in opposition to the stark visions of carnage, indicating Yeats's Modernist turn. Romanticism and Modernism jostle in 'Lapis Lazuli'. The younger genre enacts the uncertainty of the early twentieth century; the older offers perspective founded on transcendent principles. Greek and Roman antiquity is the ultimate source of those ideas, but Yeats is mindful that they must be deployed correctly. He turns to tragedy as the obvious creative form to mediate crisis:

> All perform their tragic play,
> Black out; Heaven blazing into the head:
> Tragedy wrought to its uttermost.
> Though Hamlet rambles and Lear rages,
> And all the drop scenes drop at once
> Upon a hundred thousand stages,
> It cannot grow by an inch or an ounce.
>
> (9–24)

---

[14] Yeats explored this hypothesis amidst a revival of interest in Giambattista Vico's *The New Science* (1725).

Those who play their part in history are tragic actors and Yeats, resuming the matter that opened the poem, insists that the tragic cast is gay. This is his interpretation of Greek tragedy, even if the stage he describes is Shakespearean. The same year he introduced the *Oxford Book of Modern Verse* with similar, Nietzschean sentiments: 'In all the great tragedies, tragedy is a joy to the man who dies; in Greece the tragic chorus danced.'[15] In 'Lapis Lazuli', Yeats reasons that if the world is a stage, the real-life actors should likewise play their parts without cause for weeping, because the cycles of historic change are as inevitable as the passing acts of a play. As Yeats read in Plotinus' *Enneads*, the dead will return in a new form, much as actors take on new roles (3.2.15). 'Heaven blazing' aligns the air raids of wartime bombers with the lightning bolt of Zeus. The principles of performing one's duty remain the same despite the variations of 'a hundred thousand stages'. 'It cannot grow by an inch or an ounce' because tragedy is tragedy. Despite this firmness, a note of doubt occurs where 'Hamlet rambles and Lear rages'. A few lines earlier each was gay. This is the difference between a tragic actor and a tragic character. Yeats intimates that the audience suspends disbelief to experience staged tragedy emotionally, but that one must transcend involvement—ceasing to suspend disbelief—in order to comprehend the form, or tragedy as a ritual.

In this sequence, China becomes discernible in light of the letter Yeats wrote on receiving the lapis in 1935. He describes the stone thus: 'Ascetic, pupil, hard stone, eternal theme of the sensual east, the heroic cry in the midst of despair.' Next, Yeats corrects himself: 'But no, I am wrong; the east has its solutions always & therefore knows nothing of tragedy.'[16] The sage's persona that Yeats identifies on the stone in 'Lapis Lazuli' will not pose the problematic discord between actor and character. This sage is ideal precisely because he makes no 'heroic cry', no attempt to ennoble strife. The correct gaiety is not a response to the tragic action itself but is a kind of wise detachment. This disengagement from unhappy events is not avoidance of them, but pragmatic resistance to negative emotional-involvement. The wise viewer, to return to an earlier point, derives gaiety

---

[15] W. B. Yeats ed., *The Oxford Book of Modern Verse, 1892–1935* (Oxford: Clarendon Press, 1936), xxxiv.

[16] *Letters of W. B. Yeats*, 837.

from tragedy viewed as a natural process and not from the suspension of disbelief, which encourages emotion.

In the next verse paragraph Yeats takes a wider, historical perspective. Humble arrivals were the basis of great polities, which fell in time. But from the ruins of these came new developments. Hence the key realization of the poem:

> On their own feet they came, or on shipboard,
> Camel-back, horse-back, ass-back, mule-back,
> Old civilisations put to the sword.
> Then they and their wisdom went to rack:
> No handiwork of Callimachus
> Who handled marble as if it were bronze,
> Made draperies that seemed to rise
> When sea-wind swept the corner, stands;
> His long lamp chimney shaped like the stem
> Of a slender palm, stood but a day;
> All things fall and are built again
> And those that build them again are gay.
>
> (25–36)

While the opening section called for drastic action, Yeats affirms that to rebuild is all that can be done. As an example Yeats chooses Callimachus the sculptor, a perfectionist who fussed over details. Yet a lamp that Callimachus designed for the Temple of Athena (c. 432–08 BCE) 'stood' as Yeats puts it, 'but a day': even great art is not assured immortality. If destroyed, new art must be made. Callimachus' work was materially ruined but, like Kubla Khan's pleasure dome, built anew in air in the words of historical record and Yeats's poem.

As in the account of tragedy, there is Asian subtext to Yeats's account of Callimachus. In his introduction to Pound's *Certain Noble Plays of Japan*, Yeats declares that 'it may be well if we go to school in Asia' and cites Callimachus in 'half-Asiatic Greece'. Callimachus' Ionic aesthetic offered an alternative to the realism, or 'august formality', that dominated Greek sculpture.[17] The transcultural aspects of this mode appeal to Yeats. The Ionic method originated in Egypt, reaching Greece via an Ionia that was ruled by Persia. Yeats's key source on Callimachus is Adolf Furtwängler's *Masterpieces of Greek Sculpture* (1895), a book heavily

---

[17] Yeats, *Essays and Introductions*, 225.

reliant on Winckelmann's *Reflections*. But Yeats does not adopt Winckelmann's argument that a foreign idea serves only as the basis of a better, Greek idea. The Greeks' advantage, in Yeats's view, is that they remained 'but half-European'. The union of East and West in great art is ever-fertile because it is a continuous exchange. Yeats alleges a decline of 'naturalism' in European art and literature despite an 'illusion of progress'. He attributes this to a loss of scope: 'Only our lyric poetry has kept its Asiatic habit.'[18] Conversely in 'The Statues' (1939), Yeats considers how idols are remade when artists attempt to render visually what is ultimately inexpressible. He observes that the Greeks' conventional 'one image' of Apollo, brought to India by Alexander's men, influenced early carvings of Buddha (17). Yet each magnifies and reflects incomprehension:

> Empty eyeballs knew
> That knowledge increases unreality, that
> Mirror on mirror mirrored is all the show.
>
> (20–22)

Peoples that emerge and are eventually put to the sword, and half-Asiatic Greece, prompt reflections on identity, continuity, and consistency. Yeats knows that Manchu China has joined the number of lost empires. The Qing Dynasty fell in 1911. China had been carved up and impoverished by foreign powers. From within arose rebels, emboldened by Qing weakness. Puyi (1906–67), the Xuantong Emperor and last Emperor of China, abdicated in 1912 at five years of age. He resurfaced in 1931 in a new role, when Japan invaded and made Puyi ruler of its puppet state, Manchukuo. With the rise of Japan in the 1930s, Yeats witnessed another significant moment in the cycles of history.

Amidst such considerations, Yeats has thought of Greek sculpture in 'Lapis Lazuli' primarily because the object of his meditations is similar. In the Keatsian ekphrastic mode, the otherness of the object is central. The thing has made a journey across time and space, therefore the poet expects to derive some insight to those themes from examination of the artefact. The wisdom encoded on the stone might be brought to bear on the destruction of its own culture, giving the stone a prophetic air. It is as though the lapis has stepped outside of history, or has survived a siege to bear its knowledge overseas.

---

[18]   Yeats, *Essays and Introductions*, 225–6.

Sages on Mountains

The scene on Yeats's stone illustrates the Qianlong Emperor's poem. However, 'Lapis Lazuli' mediates no fewer than four images of sages ascending mountains with their disciples. These men must be spiritual adepts, as only masters can repel the tigers and dragons that keep mortals from the sacred peaks. Instead of dwelling on the scene before him on the lapis, Yeats envisions a sequel. He communicates another picture, of the figures at the end of their journey. Having climbed the mountain to a vantage point on human affairs, they sit and watch and are joyful.

I

Delight to imagine them seated there;
There, on the mountain and the sky,
On all the tragic scene they stare.

(49–51)

Third, Yeats documents that in a prelude to the main pilgrimage of *The Holy Mountain*, the master and follower are summoned to Mount Girnar by Dattatreya, the three-headed god incorporating Brahma, Vishnu, and Shiva. Purohit, the disciple, laments what appears to be a wasted journey, and threatens to fling himself from the precipice if Dattatreya remains hidden. The god responds by granting Purohit *samadhi* (enlightenment) when he falls asleep.[19] Presumably this episode supplies the 'cry' amidst 'despair' with which Yeats interprets similar imagery on the lapis.

A further analogue for the ascent of the mountain is Arnold's *Empedocles on Etna*, which portrays the philosopher's final hours and suicide. Yeats refers to Arnold's text in *The Oxford Book of Modern Verse*. He defends his decision to exclude war poetry thus: 'I have rejected these poems for the same reason that made Arnold withdraw his "Empedocles on Etna" from circulation; passive suffering is not a theme for poetry.'[20] To delineate the correct literary perspective on hardship, Yeats's reference to the dancing tragic-chorus follows his allusion to Arnold.

Undoubtedly Yeats sympathizes with Arnold's decision to suppress *Empedocles* a year after its publication, as that poem attempts to solve similar problems to those of 'Lapis Lazuli'. In each case a philosopher-

---

[19] Yeats, *Essays and Introductions*, 452.   [20] *The Oxford Book of Modern Verse*, xxxiv.

poet stands divided from society. Arnold conflates those roles by having Empedocles deliver a philosophical statement in verse. As in Yeats's poem, Empedocles addresses a social problem, although it is the nineteenth-century decline of spirituality rather than the twentieth-century prospect of war. While Yeats's world faces the threat of annihilation, Arnold's suffers the intellectual vacuity of too many things. This stuffication ensues the processes of accumulation examined in earlier chapters, both of objects and information. Empedocles deplores the proliferation of worthless knowledge:

> But still, as we proceed
> The mass swells more and more
> Of volumes yet to read,
> Of secrets yet to explore.
> Our hair goes grey, our eyes are dimm'd, our heat is tamed.
>
> (1.2.332–36)

In Arnold's poem the cry for remedy is individual rather than collective. What solution the philosopher prescribes is uncertain. This Empedocles' exact creed is obscure for two reasons. The first lies where the philosophy of Arnold's poem departs from the fragments of the historical Empedocles. It is unclear whether these deviations result from Arnold's intention or from errors in his source, Simon Karsten's *Philosophorum Graceorum Veterum* (1838).[21] Secondly, it is apparent from Act 2 of Arnold's work that his Empedocles does not believe the creed he expounds for Pausanias in Act 1.

The poem-within-a-poem is a performance. Empedocles accompanies himself on a harp as he instructs his fellow philosopher. Pausanias believes reports that Empedocles restored a dead girl to life. Hence Pausanias wants to learn miracles. Empedocles' exile relates to the rise of the Sophists, and he scorns ostentation. He offers Pausanias no advice on marvels, but instead delivers a doctrine on how to live. The philosopher's primary problem, Empedocles explains, is that knowledge is fragmentary:

> Hither and thither spins
> The wind-borne, mirroring soul,

---

[21] John Woolford demonstrates these inaccuracies. See 'Arnold on Empedocles', *The Review of English Studies* 50 ns., no. 197 (1999): 33–52.

> A thousand glimpses wins,
> And never sees a whole;
> Looks once, drives elsewhere, and leaves its last employ.
>
> (1.2.82–86)

Alienated from society by his powers of mind, Arnold's Empedocles is a Byronic figure, although more Manfred than Heathcliff. If this is a reasonable dramatization of the real Empedocles, it is surprising that Arnold makes him a Romantic Pantheist:

> All things the world which fill
> Of but one stuff are spun,
> That we who rail are still,
> With what we rail at, one.
>
> (1.2.287–90)

Empedocles tells Pausanias that to invent and blame gods for human unhappiness is foolish because they are the same substance. The attitude to misfortune that he prescribes is Stoic in sentiment:

> Since life teems with ill,
> Nurse no extravagant hope;
> Because thou must not dream, thou needs't not then despair!
>
> (1.2.424–26)

These are strong words, but in Act 2 the reader learns that Empedocles does not live by his own advice. The Pantheism that he professes (while the real Empedocles hypothesized four elements) may be a facile and insincere lesson for Pausanias, who is incapable of higher philosophy. Privately, and true to his real-life counterpart, Empedocles reveals that reflection has driven him to despair. Excessive thought has made him unnatural:

> thou art
> A living man no more, Empedocles!
> Nothing but a devouring flame of thought –
> But a naked, eternally restless mind!
>
> (2.1.327–30)

Mind is isolating; it leaves us 'prisoners of our consciousness' (2.1.352). Suicide offers Empedocles temporary respite. He knows that he will suffer again in a series of punitive reincarnations, but he is desperate for a moment of relief. Into the volcano he jumps.

Callicles the harpist, the third of three characters in *Empedocles on Etna*, has the last words. On the loss of a mentor, he answers bereavement with song. 'What forms are these coming?' he asks, describing a procession of Apollo and the Muses (2.437). The forms are not coming but going. Their purpose is not to lament Empedocles; 'they bathe on this mountain' and are returning to Olympus (2.453). Thus Apollo and his troupe turn their back on misfortune. Callicles outlines a hierarchy of divine concern, in which humanity lies bottom:

> First hymn they the Father
> Of all things; and then,
> The rest of immortals,
> The action of men.
>
> The day in his hotness,
> The strife with the palm;
> The night in her silence,
> The stars in their calm.
>
> (2.461–68)

'Strife', associated with humanity by the articulate 'palm', belongs to a separate realm from that of the gods. This is, like the conclusion to Tennyson's revised 'Lotos-Eaters', a Lucretian image of distant and dispassionate gods, based—problematically, as I shall discuss—on Book 3 of *On the Nature of Things*. Callicles' song reflects that although the late Empedocles recognized the mind as divine, he did not achieve the Lucretian gods' serenity by accumulating knowledge. The pursuit of wisdom is an arduous waste of time in this text.

The allusion to Lucretius may help to explain the inconsistent philosophical vision of *Empedocles on Etna*. Arnold intended to write a tragedy on Lucretius, and used some of the material in his poem about Empedocles. He uses the same language to characterize the two. Callimachus describes Empedocles as 'moody' (1.1.74), and Pausanias laments his 'settled gloom' (1.1.84). In the lecture 'On the Modern Element in Literature', Arnold says that Lucretius possesses 'a rigid, a moody gloom' which he contrasts with Virgil's 'melancholy'.[22] A further complication is the Victorian insistence that Lucretius' gods are real

---

[22] *Arnold: Poetry and Prose*, 282.

rather than cognitive. Victorian interpretations of Lucretius' gods tend to focus on the famous lines which Tennyson paraphrases in his poem 'Lucretius' (1868), which portray blissful deities in a realm untouched by winds and rain, where nothing disturbs their peace (*On the Nature of Things*, 3.18–25). Atheism is untenable to Arnold. In his misreading of Lucretius, the gods exist and must therefore be cruelly indifferent to the lives of mortals. Little wonder that Arnold found his *Empedocles* simply 'painful, not tragic'.[23] The dialogue with Empedocles in 'Lapis Lazuli' hints at an alternate reading of Lucretius that is close in meaning to Yeats's Daoism.

Yeats answers Arnold explicitly in 'The Gyres' (1938), in which he reflects on interpenetrating cycles of history:

> For beauty dies of beauty, worth of worth,
> And ancient lineaments are blotted out.
> Irrational streams of blood are staining earth;
> Empedocles has thrown all things about;
> Hector is dead and there's a light in Troy;
> We that look on but laugh in tragic joy.

(3–8)

Across distances of time and space Empedocles' turmoil appears childish, Hector's death insignificant, and the conflagration at Troy but a 'light'. 'Past "beauty" will destroy the possibility of further "beauty", unless its own destruction is accepted.' The poet 'is a creature of the very culture he is consigning to the void,' much as the lapis stands in relation to its Qing origins.[24] The world of 'Lapis Lazuli' poses a different problem from what Yeats belittles in 'The Gyres'. In 'Lapis Lazuli' violence cannot be dismissed as remote and 'irrational'; it is imminent. Yeats would associate inexorable catastrophe with a favourite fragment attributed to Empedocles: 'Wretched race of mortals, miserable race! From such kinds of strife and such groans are you born!'[25]

---

[23] *The Poems of Matthew Arnold*, ed. Kenneth Allott, 2nd ed. rev. Miriam Allott (New York: Longman Group Limited, 1979), 656.

[24] Michael O'Neill, *The All-Sustaining Air: Romantic Legacies and Renewals in British, American, and Irish Poetry since 1900*, repr. (Oxford: Oxford University Press, 2012), 57.

[25] André Laks and Glenn W. Most ed. and trans., *Early Greek Philosophy*, Loeb Classical Library 528, 9 vols (Cambridge, Massachusetts: Harvard University Press, 2016), 5:373.

The sages live to hear the music in 'Lapis Lazuli'. Arnold's Empedocles avoids sorrow by suicide, and the gods by their distance, but Yeats's Daoists court it:

> There, on the mountain and the sky,
> On all the tragic scene they stare.
> One asks for mournful melodies;
> Accomplished fingers begin to play.
> Their eyes mid many wrinkles, their eyes,
> Their ancient, glittering eyes, are gay.
>
> (51–56)

Thus Yeats returns to address the main problem of the poem, the suggestion that gaiety is unsuitable for art in the grim realities of the twentieth century. Yeats replies by observing that art should be joyful; tragedy is externally a display of dire events, but internally is a joyously performed ritual of a natural cycle, creation and destruction. This cycle has been in effect for the course of human history, it is a universal truth and as such is the subject of a Chinese stone as much as it is evident in Greek sculpture. Art is gay, Yeats insists, but not because it is an escape from reality: in fact, art never takes its eyes off atrocity and hardship, it is ever watchful, emphasized in the repetition of 'eyes'. Here not only does art not hide from misfortune, but chooses to mediate it: the sages request 'mournful melodies' in which the musician will respond to sorrow. Yet, in language that twice reminds us of another possible reaction to disaster in Coleridge's 'Ancyent Marinere', their 'ancient, glittering eyes are gay'. Art teaches us that gaiety, and the knowledge that we can rebuild, are the only pragmatic attitudes we can have when we look upon the tragic scenes of life. Throughout the poem Yeats has developed faith in this perspective by identifying analogues, and I think that Lucretius has an anonymous presence in 'Lapis Lazuli' too. There is evidence of Yeats interpreting *On the Nature of Things* differently from Arnold, and truer to Lucretian philosophy. Undoubtedly Lucretius offers material to predicate Arnold's opinion of his 'gloom'. But, although it is not the religious assurance that Arnold wants, Lucretius also urges his reader to conquer the fear of death. As we do not miss ourselves in sleep, so is it in death, Lucretius tells us. To him too, all things fall and are built again, as one generation eternally gives rise to another; this is the best we can hope for as mere tenants in life (3.970–71). Perhaps such consolations are trite.

Yet their comfort is genuine to Yeats, whose anger at 'the beating down of wise men | And great art beaten down' in 'The Fisherman' (1917, 23–24) recalls the complaint that 'great qualities are trodden down' in Arnold's *Empedocles* (2.92). From similar artistic crises and comparable literary influences they reach dissimilar conclusions. Daoism provides Yeats with the decisive evidence for optimism, and the stone reifies the lesson that he has encountered in authors from Aeschylus to Zhuangzi, by way of Romanticism.

APPENDIX

Sara Coleridge, 'Tennyson's "Lotos-Eaters" With a New Conclusion' (1842/43)

This poem was first published in Sara Coleridge's *Collected Poems*, edited by Peter Swaab (2007). In the text below, Roman typeface denotes Tennyson's original text, as retained by Sara Coleridge. Strikethrough denotes Coleridge's cuts and italics her additions. Text is underlined where Coleridge repeats Tennyson's words so that certain lines, if Coleridge's text were appended to Tennyson's, would appear twice.

'The Lotos blooms below the ~~barren~~ *flowery* peak:
The Lotos blows by every winding creek:
All day the wind breathes low with mellower tone:
Thro' every hollow cave and alley lone
Round and round the spicy downs the yellow Lotos-dust is blown.
We have had enough of motion,
Weariness and wild alarm,
Tossing on the ~~tossing~~ restless Ocean',
Here are a thousand charms
One best of all, that every pang disarms,
Th'enchanted lotos bloom o'er all our senses reigning
~~Where the tuskèd seahorse walloweth~~
~~In a stripe of grassgreen calm,~~
~~At noon—tide beneath the lee,~~
~~And the monstrous narwhale swalloweth~~
~~His foamfountains in the sea.~~
~~Long enough the winedark wave our weary bark did carry.~~
~~This is lovelier and sweeter,~~
~~Men of Ithaca, this is meeter,~~
~~In the hollow rosy vale to tarry,~~
~~Like a dreamy Lotos—eater, a delirious Lotos—eater!~~
~~We will eat the Lotos, sweet~~
~~As the yellow honeycomb,~~
~~In the valley some, and some~~
~~On the ancient heights divine;~~
~~And no more roam,~~
~~On the loud hoar foam,~~
~~To the melancholy home~~

~~At the limit of the brine,~~
~~The little isle of Ithaca, beneath the day's decline.~~
'*Then* ~~We'll~~ lift no more the shattered oar,
No more unfurl the straining sail;
~~With the blissful Lotos—eaters pale~~
We will abide in the golden vale
~~Of the Lotos—land, till the Lotos fail,~~
~~We will not wander more.~~
One radiant smile our tranced gaze detaining
Of one calm lake out of whose bosom ever,
Drawn from many a shadowy fountain,
In yon far distant boundary mountain
Softly flows the travelled river
Just heard above the stock dove's plaining:
Or, borne upon the wave, with lilies float,
Tranquil as they amid the slumb'rous gleam,
Or, in the zephyr-wafted boat,
As though we flew unpinioned in a dream
From fragrant bank to bank pass lightly o'er.
Hark! how sweet the horned ewes bleat
On the solitary steeps,
And the merry lizard leaps,
And the foam—white waters pour;
And the dark pine weeps,
And the lithe vine creeps,
And the heavy melon sleeps
On the level of the shore:
Oh! islanders of Ithaca, we will not wander more,
~~Surely, surely, slumber is more sweet than toil, the shore~~
~~Than labour in the ocean, and rowing with the oar.~~
~~Oh! islanders of Ithaca, we will return no more.~~

'We have had enough of motion,
<u>Weariness and wild alarm,</u>
<u>Tossing on the restless ocean,'</u>
<u>'Long enough the wine-dark wave our weary bark did carry.'</u>
Here are a thousand charms
One best of all that every pang disarms,
The Lotos-bloom that woos us in the vale to tarry.

<u>We will abide in the golden vale</u>
And never launch into the boundless plain,
The watery waste where threat'ning billows roar,
But nigh the sapphire lake remain
In whose deep hospitable breast
Derived from many a shadowy fountain
In yon far distant sky-commingled mountain
The travelled waters sink to rest,
And there beside th'untroubled lilies float.

References

Aarne, Antti. *The Types of the Folktale: A Classification and Bibliography*. Translated by Stith Thompson. Rev. ed. Helsinki: Suomalainen Tiedeakatemia, 1964.

Aeschylus. Edited and translated by Alan H. Sommerstein. The Loeb Classical Library 145, 146, and 505. 3 vols. Cambridge, Massachusetts, and London: Harvard University Press, 2008.

Alighieri, Dante. *The Vision; or, Hell, Purgatory, and Paradise.* Translated by Henry Francis Cary. 3 vols. London: Taylor and Hessey, 1819.

Allen, Christopher. 'Ovid and Art'. In *The Cambridge Companion to Ovid*, edited by Philip Hardie, 336–67. Cambridge: Cambridge University Press, 2002.

Anderson, Aeneas. *A Narrative of the British Embassy to China, in the Years 1792, 1793, and 1794.* London: J. Debrett, 1795.

The Arabian Nights Entertainments: Consisting of One Thousand and One Stories, Told by the Sultaness of the Indies. 4 vols. Edinburgh: D. Schaw, 1802.

Arkins, Brian. *Builders of my Soul: Greek and Roman Themes in Yeats.* Gerrards Cross: Colin Smythe, 1990.

Armstrong, Isobel, ed. *Victorian Scrutinies: Reviews of Poetry, 1830–1870.* London: The Athlone Press, 1972.

Arnold, Matthew. *Matthew Arnold: Poetry and Prose.* Edited by John Bryson. London: Rupert Hart-Davis, 1954.

Arnold, Matthew. *The Poems of Matthew Arnold.* Edited by Kenneth Allott. 2nd ed. Revised by Miriam Allott. New York: Longman Group Limited, 1979.

Barbeau, Jeffrey W. *Sara Coleridge: Her Life and Thought.* New York: Palgrave Macmillan, 2014.

Barnes Stevenson, Catherine. 'The Shade of Homer Exorcises the Ghost of De Quincey: Tennyson's "The Lotos-Eaters"'. *Browning Institute Studies* 10 (1982): 117–41.

Barrow, John. *Travels in China.* London: T. Cadell and W. Davies, 1804.

Barrow, John, ed. *Some Account of the Public Life, and a Selection from the Unpublished Writings, of the Earl of Macartney.* 2 vols. London: Cadell and Davies, 1807.

Bell, John. *Travels from St. Petersburg in Russia to Diverse Parts of Asia.* 2 vols. Glasgow: Foulis, 1763.

Bennett, George. *Wanderings in New South Wales, Batavia, Pedir Coast, Singapore, and China.* London: Richard Bentley, 1834.

Bhabha, Homi K. *The Location of Culture.* New York: Routledge, 1994.

Bickers, Robert. 'Paul Cohen, the Boxers, and Alfred, Lord Tennyson'. *The Chinese Historical Review* 14:2 (2007): 192–5.

Bickers, Robert. *The Scramble for China: Foreign Devils in the Qing Empire, 1832–1914.* Oxford: Oxford University Press, 2011.

Black, Jeremy. 'Responding to the Outside World'. *Eighteenth-Century Studies* 45, no. 1 (2012): 319–20.

Blunden, Edmund. *Charles Lamb and His Contemporaries.* London: Hogarth Press, 1934.

Bowden, Brett. 'The Ideal of Civilisation: Its Origins and Socio-Political Character'. *Critical Review of International Social and Political Philosophy* 7, no. 1 (2004): 25–50.

Bradley, Mark, ed. *Classics and Imperialism in the British Empire.* Oxford: Oxford University Press, 2010.

[Bruce, James]. *Letters and Journals of James, Eighth Earl of Elgin.* Edited by Theodore Walrond. London: John Murray, 1872.

Brylowe, Thora. *Romantic Art in Practice: Cultural Work and the Sister Arts, 1760–1820.* Cambridge: Cambridge University Press, 2019.

[Burnett, James, Lord Monboddo]. *Of the Origins and Progress of Language.* Vol. 6. London: T. Cadell, 1792.

Burton, Robert. *The Anatomy of Melancholy.* Edited by Nicolas K. Kiessling et al. Oxford Scholarly Editions. 6 vols. Oxford: Oxford University Press, 1994.

Burton, Sarah. *A Double Life: A Biography of Charles and Mary Lamb.* London: Penguin Books, 2003.

Burwick, Frederick. 'Greek Drama: Coleridge, de Quincey, A.W. Schlegel'. *The Wordsworth Circle* 44:1 (2013): 3–12.

Cain, Peter J. 'Character, "Ordered Liberty", and the Mission to Civilise: British Moral Justification of Empire, 1870–1914'. *The Journal of Imperial and Commonwealth History* 40, no. 4 (2012): 557–78.

Cavendish, Lady Frederick. *The Diary of Lady Frederick Cavendish.* Edited by John Bailey. 2 vols. London: John Murray, 1927.

Chen, Song-Chuan. *Merchants of War and Peace: British Knowledge of China in the Making of the Opium War.* Hong Kong: Hong Kong University Press, 2017.

Christensen, Allan C., ed. *The Challenge of Keats: Bicentenary Essays 1795–1995.* Amsterdam: Rodopi, 2000.

Clarke, Abel. *Narrative of a Journey in the Interior of China.* London: Longman, Hurst, Rees, Orme, and Brown, 1818.

Clarke, Charles Cowden. *Recollections of Writers.* London: Sampson Low, Marston, Searle, and Rivington, 1878.

Cleary, Thomas, trans. *Classics of Buddhism and Zen.* 5 vols. Boston: Shambhala, 2005.

Coffman, Ralph J. *Coleridge's Library: A Bibliography of Books Owned or Read by Samuel Taylor Coleridge*. Boston: G.K. Hall & Co., 1987.

Coleridge, Samuel Taylor. *Biographia Literaria, or, Biographical Sketches of My Literary Life and Opinions*. Edited by Sara Coleridge. 2 vols. London: William Pickering, 1847.

Coleridge, Samuel Taylor. *Collected Letters of Samuel Taylor Coleridge*. Edited by Earl Leslie Griggs. 6 vols. Oxford: Oxford University Press, 1956–71.

Coleridge, Samuel Taylor. *The Notebooks of Samuel Taylor Coleridge*. Edited by Kathleen Coburn and Anthony John Harding. 5 vols in 10 parts. London: Routledge & Kegan Paul, 1957–2002.

Coleridge, Samuel Taylor. *The Collected Works of Samuel Taylor Coleridge*. Edited by Kathleen Coburn et al. Bollingen Series 75. 16 vols in 34 parts. Princeton: Princeton University Press, 1969–2003.

Coleridge, Sara. *Collected Poems*. Edited by Peter Swaab. Manchester: Fyfield Books, 2007.

Coleridge, Sara. *The Regions of Sara Coleridge's Thought: Selected Literary Criticism*. Edited by Peter Swaab. Nineteenth-Century Major Lives and Letters. New York: Palgrave Macmillan, 2012.

Conington, John, trans. *The Æneid of Virgil*. New York: W.J. Middleton, 1867.

Cronin, Richard, Alison Chapman, and Anthony H. Harrison, ed. *A Companion to Victorian Poetry*. Oxford: Blackwell, 2002.

Cudworth, Ralph. *The True Intellectual System of the Universe: The First Part*. London: Richard Royston, 1678.

Curzon, George Nathaniel. *Problems of the Far East: Japan—Korea—China*. 2nd ed. London: Longmans, Green, and Co., 1894.

Davies, Simon, Daniel Sanjiv Roberts, and Gabriel Sánchez Espinosa, ed. *India and Europe in the Global Eighteenth Century*. Oxford: Oxford University Press, 2014.

Davis, John F. *The Chinese: A General Description of the Empire of China and its Inhabitants*. 3 vols. Rev. ed. London: Charles Knight & Co., 1844.

D'Hérisson, Maurice. *Journal d'un Interprète en Chine*. 3rd ed. Paris: Paul Ollendorf, 1886.

Dickens, Charles. *The Pickwick Papers: The Posthumous Papers of the Pickwick Club*. Edited by Mark Wormald. London: Penguin Classics, 2000.

Dickens, Charles. *Nicholas Nickleby*. Edited by Paul Schlike, Oxford World's Classics. Oxford: Oxford University Press, 2009.

Dike, Clarence S. 'The Humor of "Roast Pig."' *The English Journal* 11, no. 5 (1922): 288–92.

Douglas, John. *The Criterion or, Miracles Examined with a view to Expose the Pretensions of Pagans and Papists*. London: A. Millar, 1754.

Dove, John. *An Essay on Inspiration*. London: E. Withers, 1756.

Du Halde, Jean-Baptiste. *The General History of China*. Translated by R. Brookes. 3rd ed. 4 vols. London: J. Watt, 1741.

Dunne, John Hart. *From Calcutta to Pekin*. London: Sampson Low, 1861.

Eastlake, Laura. *Ancient Rome and Victorian Masculinity*. Classical Presences. Oxford: Oxford University Press, 2018.

Eckerman, Chris. 'Lucretius on the Divine.' *DRN* 3.17–30, 5.1161–93, and 6.68–79'. *Mnemosyne* 72, no. 2 (2019): 284–99.

Ellis, Henry. *Journal of the Proceedings of the Late Embassy to China*. London: John Murray, 1817.

Engelfriet, Peter M. *Euclid in China: The Genesis of the First Chinese Translation of Euclid's Elements*. Leiden: Brill, 1988.

Fang, Karen. *Romantic Writing and the Empire of Signs: Periodical Culture and Post-Napoleonic Authorship*. Charlottesville: University of Virginia Press, 2010.

Farrell Brodie, Janet, and Marc Redfield, ed. *High Anxieties: Cultural Studies in Addiction*. Berkeley: University of California Press, 2002.

Felicity and Margot. *Bo-bo and the Pig*. Tiny Tots Tales. Sydney: Juvenile Publications Co., 1948.

Feng Menglong. *Stories to Caution the World: A Ming Dynasty Collection*. Translated by Shuhui Yang and Yunqin Yang. 3 vols. Seattle and London: Washington University Press, 2000–09.

Flaubert, Gustave. *Sentimental Education*. Translated by Robert Baldick. Revised by Geoffrey Wall. London: Penguin Classics, 2004.

Forman, Ross G. *China and the Victorian Imagination: Empires Entwined*. Cambridge Studies in Nineteenth Century Literature and Culture. Cambridge: Cambridge University Press, 2013.

Fortune, Robert. *Three Years' Wanderings in the Northern Provinces of China*. London: John Murray, 1847.

Fortune, Robert. *A Residence among the Chinese*. London: John Murray, 1857.

Fotopoulos, Annetta. 'Understanding the Zodiac Saga in China: World Cultural Heritage, National Humiliation, and Evolving Narratives'. *Modern China* 41, no. 6 (2015): 603–30.

Fulweiler, Howard W. '"The Argument of the Ancient Sage": Tennyson and the Christian Intellectual Tradition'. *Victorian Poetry* 21, no. 3 (1983): 203–16.

Gibbon, Edward. *Miscellaneous Works of Edward Gibbon*. Edited by John Holroyd, Earl of Sheffield. 3 vols. Dublin: P. Wogan, 1796.

Gibbon, Edward. *The History of the Decline and Fall of the Roman Empire*. Edited by David Womersley. 3 vols. Rev. ed. London: Penguin Classics, 1995–2005.

Gigante, Denise. *Taste: A Literary History*. New Haven: Yale University Press, 2006.

Gladstone, William Ewert. *War in China*. London: Rivingtons, 1857.

Goldhill, Simon. *Who Needs Greek? Contests in the Cultural History of Hellenism.* Cambridge: Cambridge University Press, 2002.

Goldhill, Simon. *Victorian Culture and Classical Antiquity: Art, Opera, Fiction, and the Proclamation of Modernity.* New Jersey: Princeton University Press, 2011.

Golvers, Noël. *Libraries of Western Learning for China, vol. 1, Logistics of Book Acquisition and Circulation.* Leuven: Ferdinand Verbiest Institute KUL, 2012.

Gregory, Lady. *Lady Gregory's Journals 1916–1930.* Edited by Lennox Robinson. London: Putnam, 1946.

Gries, Peter, and Stanley Rosen, ed. *Chinese Politics: State, Society and the Market.* London: Routledge, 2010.

Gu, Ming Dong. *Sinologism.* London: Routledge, 2013.

Gutzlaff, Charles. *Journal of Three Voyages along the Coast of China in 1831, 1832, & 1833.* London: Thomas Ward & Co., 1834.

Haddad, John R. 'Imagined Journeys to Distant Cathay: Constructing China with Ceramics, 1780–1920'. *Winterthur Portfolio* 41, no. 1 (Spring 2007): 53–80.

Hagerman, C. A. *Britain's Imperial Muse: The Classics, Imperialism, and the Indian Empire, 1784–1914.* New York: Palgrave Macmillan, 2013.

Hale, W. P. *The Mandarin's Daughter!* London: Thomas Hailes Lacy, 1851.

[Hallam, Arthur Henry]. 'On Some of the Characteristics of Modern Poetry, and on the Lyrical Poems of Alfred Tennyson'. *The Englishman's Magazine* 1 (1831): 616–28.

[Hallam, Arthur Henry]. *Remains in Verse and Prose.* Edited by H. Hallam. London: W. Nicol, 1834.

Han, Christina. 'Ekphrasis as a Transtextual and Transcultural Event: Revisiting "Lapis Lazuli"'. *The Yeats Journal of Korea* 51 (2016): 73–96.

Haw, Stephen G. *Marco Polo's China: A Venetian in the Realm of Khubilai Khan.* London: Routledge, 2006.

Hawks, Francis L. *Narrative of the Expedition of an American Squadron to the China Seas and Japan 1852–54.* New York: D. Appleton, 1856.

Hazlitt, William. *The Spirit of the Age, or, Contemporary Portraits.* 2nd ed. London: Henry Colburn, 1825.

Hegel, G. W. F. *Lectures on the Philosophy of World History.* Translated by H. B. Nisbet. Cambridge: Cambridge University Press, 1975.

Hevia, James L. *Cherishing Men from Afar: Qing Guest Ritual and the Macartney Embassy of 1793.* Durham, NC and London: Duke University Press, 1995.

Hofer, Matthew, and Gary Scharnhorst, ed. *Oscar Wilde in America: The Interviews.* Urbana and Chicago: University of Illinois Press, 2010.

Hole, Richard. *Remarks on the Arabian Nights' Entertainments.* London: Cadell & Davies, 1797.

Hone William, ed. *The Every Day Book*, or, a Guide to the Year. 2 vols. London: William Tegg, 1825.

Honour, Hugh. *Chinoiserie: The Vision of Cathay.* London: John Murray, 1961.

Hood, Basil. *The Willow Pattern.* London: Chappell, 1901.

Hopkins, David. 'Ovid'. In *The Oxford History of Classical Reception in English Literature III: 1660–1790.* Edited by David Hopkins and Charles Martindale, 197–216. Oxford: Oxford University Press, 2012.

Hugo, Victor 'The Sack of the Summer Palace'. Translated. *The UNESCO Courier: A Window Open on the World* 38, no. 11 (1985): 15.

Hunt, Leigh. *Lord Byron and some of his Contemporaries.* 2nd ed. London: Henry Colburn, 1828.

Idema, Wilt L., trans. *The White Snake and Her Son.* Indianapolis: Hackett Publishing Company, 2009.

Inglis, Lucy. *The Milk of Paradise.* London: Macmillan, 2018.

Irwin, Robert. *For Lust of Knowing: The Orientalists and their Enemies.* Reprinted, London: Penguin Books, 2007.

Jacques, Martin. *When China Rules the World: The Rise of the Middle Kingdom and the End of the Western World.* 2nd ed. London: Penguin Books, 2012.

Jardine Proudfoot, William. *Biographical Memoir of James Dinwiddie.* Liverpool: Edward Howell, 1868.

Jenkins, Tiffany. *Keeping Their Marbles: How the Treasures of the Past Ended Up in Museums—And Why They Should Stay There.* Oxford: Oxford University Press, 2016.

Jocelyn, Robert. *Six Months with the Chinese Expedition.* London: John Murray, 1841.

Johnson, W. R. *Darkness Visible: A Study of Vergil's Aeneid.* Berkeley: University of California Press, 1976.

Jones, Joseph. *A Series of Important Facts, Demonstrating the Truth of Christian Religion.* London: Rowland Hunter, 1820.

Jones, William, trans. *The Moallakát, or Seven Arabian Poems, which were Suspended on the Temple at Mecca.* London: Elmsly, 1782.

Jones, William. *The Works of Sir William Jones.* Edited by John Shore, Baron Teignmouth. 13 vols. London: Stockdale, 1807.

Keats, John. *The Letters of John Keats.* Edited by Hyder Edward Rollins. 2 vols. Cambridge, Massachusetts: Harvard University Press, 1958.

Keats, John. *The Poems of John Keats.* Edited by Jack Stillinger. Cambridge, Massachusetts: Harvard University Press, 1978.

Keay, John. *The Honourable Company: A History of the English East India Company.* London: HarperCollins, 1993.

King, Charles William. *Opium Crisis: A Letter Addressed to Charles Elliot.* London: E. Suter, 1839.

Kissinger, Henry. *On China.* Reprinted, London: Penguin Books, 2012.

Kitson, Peter J. *Forging Romantic China: Sino-British Cultural Exchange 1760–1840.* Cambridge Studies in Romanticism 105. Cambridge: Cambridge University Press, 2013.

Kitson, Peter J. 'The Strange Case of Dr White and Mr De Quincey: Manchester, Medicine and Romantic Theories of Biological Racism'. *Romanticism* 17, no. 3 (2011): 278–87.

Kitson, Peter J. and Robert Markley, ed. *Writing China: Essays on the Amherst Embassy (1816) and Sino-British Cultural Relations.* Rochester: Boydell & Brewer, 2016.

Kowaleski-Wallace, Beth. 'Women, China and Consumer Culture in Eighteenth-Century England'. *Eighteenth-Century Studies* 29, no. 2 (1995): 153–67.

Krishnan, Sanjay. *Reading the Global: Troubling Perspectives on Britain's Empire in Asia.* New York: Columbia University Press, 2007.

Kumar, Krishan. 'Greece and Rome in the British Empire: Contrasting Role Models'. *Journal of British Studies* 51, no. 1 (2012): 76–101.

[Laozi], *Tau The King: The Speculations on Metaphysics, Polity, and Morality of 'The Old Philosopher', Lau-Tsze.* Translated by John Chalmers. London: Trübner & Co., 1868.

Laks, André, and Glenn W. Most, ed. and trans. *Early Greek Philosophy.* Loeb Classical Library 528. 9 vols. Cambridge, Massachusetts: Harvard University Press, 2016.

Lamb, Charles. *The Adventures of Ulysses.* London: The Juvenile Library, 1808.

Lamb, Charles and Mary. *The Letters of Charles and Mary Lamb.* Edited by E. V. Lucas. 3 vols. London: Methuen & Co., 1935.

Lamb, Charles and Mary. *The Works of Charles and Mary Lamb.* Edited by E. V. Lucas. 7 vols. London: Methuen & Co., 1903.

Lardner, Nathaniel. *Works of Nathaniel Lardner.* 10 vols. London: T. Bensley, 1815.

Lau, Beth, ed. *Keats's Paradise Lost.* Gainesville: University Press of Florida, 1998.

Leask, Nigel. *British Romantic Writers and the East: Anxieties of Empire.* Cambridge Studies in Romanticism. Cambridge: Cambridge University Press, 1992.

Leask, Nigel. *Curiosity and the Aesthetics of Travel Writing, 1770–1840.* Oxford: Oxford University Press, 2002.

Lemon, Mark. 'A True History of the Celebrated Wedgewood Hieroglyph, Commonly Called the Willow Pattern'. *Bentley's Miscellany* 3 (1838): 61–5.

Lemprière, John. *Bibliotheca Classica; or, A Classical Dictionary.* Reading: T. Cadell, 1788.

Leung, K. C., 'Chinese Courtship: The *Huajian Ji* in English Translation'. *CHINOPERL* 20, no. 1 (1997): 269–88.

Levinson, Marjorie. *Keats's Life of Allegory*. Oxford and New York: Basil Blackwell, 1988.

Liebregts, P. Th. M. G. *Centaurs in the Twilight: W.B. Yeats's use of the Classical Tradition*. Amsterdam and Atlanta: Rodopi, 1993.

Lindsay, H. Hamilton. *Letter to the Right Honourable Viscount Palmerston on British Relations with China*. 2nd ed. London: Saunders and Otway, 1836.

Livingston, James C. 'Tennyson, Jowett, and the Chinese Buddhist Pilgrims'. *Victorian Poetry* 27, no. 2 (1989): 157–68.

Lovell, Julia. *The Opium War: Drugs, Dreams and the Making of China*. London: Picador, 2011.

Lucian. *The Private History of Peregrinus Proteus*. Translated by William Tooke. 2 vols. London: J. Johnson, 1796.

Lucretius. *De Rerum Natura*. Edited and translated by W. H. D. Rouse. Revised by Martin Ferguson Smith. Loeb Classical Library 181. Reprinted, Cambridge, Massachusetts: Harvard University Press, 2002.

M'Ghee, R. J. L. *How We Got into Pekin: A Narrative of the Campaign in China of 1860*. London: Richard Bentley, 1862.

Macartney, Lord. *An Embassy to China: Being the Journal kept by Lord Macartney*. Edited by J. L. Cranmer-Byng. London: Longmans, Green, and Co Ltd, 1962.

Macaulay, Thomas Babington. *Critical and Miscellaneous Essays: Contributed to the Edinburgh Review*. 3 vols. London: Longman, Brown, Green, and Longman, 1843.

Makdisi, Saree. *Romantic Imperialism: Universal Empire and the Culture of Modernity*. New York: Cambridge University Press, 1998.

Makdisi, Saree and Felicity Nussbaum, ed. *The Arabian Nights in Historical Context: Between East and West*. Oxford: Oxford University Press, 2008.

Manning, Thomas. *Thomas Manning Archive*. Royal Asiatic Society Online Collections, 2015. https://royalasiaticcollections.org/thomas-manning-archive/ (accessed 31 October 2019).

Mao, Haijian. *The Qing Empire and the Opium War*. The Cambridge China Library. Cambridge: Cambridge University Press, 2016.

Markley, A. A. *Stateliest Measures: Tennyson and the Literature of Greece and Rome*. Toronto: University of Toronto Press, 2004.

Marsden, William. *A Dictionary of the Malayan Language*. London: Cox and Baylis, 1812.

[Mathias, Thomas James]. *The Imperial Epistle from Kien Long: Emperor of China, to George the Third*. 4th ed. London: T. Becket, 1794.

McCormack, Jerusha. 'From Chinese Wisdom to Irish Wit: Zhuangzi and Oscar Wilde'. *Irish University Review* 37, no. 2 (2007): 302–21.

McCormack, Jerusha. 'The Poem on the Mountain: A Chinese Reading of Yeats's "Lapis Lazuli"'. *Yeats Annual* 19 (2013): 261–88.

McFarland, Thomas. *The Masks of Keats: The Endeavour of a Poet.* New York: Oxford University Press, 2000.

McKitterick, Rosamond, and Roland E. Quinault, ed. *Edward Gibbon and Empire.* New York: Cambridge University Press, 1997.

Meadows, Thomas Taylor. *The Chinese and their Rebellions: Viewed in Connection with Their National Philosophy, Ethics, Legislation, and Administration.* London: Smith, Elder & Company, 1856.

Medhurst, Walter Henry. *China, its State and Prospects.* London: John Snow, 1838.

Middleton, Charles. *A New and Complete System of Geography.* 2 vols. London: J. Cooke, 1778–79.

Mill, James. *The History of British India.* 3rd ed. 6 vols. London: Baldwin, Craddock, and Joy, 1826.

Mill, John Stuart. *Essays on Poetry by John Stuart Mill.* Edited by F. Parvin Sharpless. Columbia: University of South Carolina Press, 1976.

Millward, James A. et al., eds. *New Qing Imperial History: The Making of Inner Asian Empire at Qing Chengde.* London and New York: Routledge, 2004.

Morrison, Robert. *A View of China for Philological Purposes.* Macao: East India Company Press, 1817.

Morrison, Robert. *The English Opium Eater: A Biography of Thomas de Quincey.* London: Weidenfeld & Nicolson, 2009.

Morrison, Robert and S. J. Roberts, ed. *Thomas de Quincey: New Theoretical and Critical Directions.* London: Routledge, 2007.

O'Gorman, Francis. 'Tennyson's "The Lotos-Eaters" and the Politics of the 1830s'. *Victorian Review* 30, no. 1 (2004): 1–18.

O'Neill, Michael. *The All-Sustaining Air: Romantic Legacies and Renewals in British, American, and Irish Poetry since 1900.* Reprinted, Oxford: Oxford University Press, 2012.

Pamuk, Orhan. 'Love, Death and Storytelling'. *New Statesman* 135, no. 4823–25 (2006): 34–6.

Paolo, Charles De. 'Coleridge and Gibbon's Controversy over *The Decline and Fall of the Roman Empire.*' *CLIO: A Journal of Literature, History, and the Philosophy of History* 20, no. 1 (Fall 1990): 13–22.

Philostratus. *The Life of Apollonius.* Translated by Edward Berwick. London: T. Payne, 1809.

Philostratus. *Apollonius of Tyana.* Edited and translated by Christopher P. Jones. 2 vols. Loeb Classical Library 16–17. Cambridge, Massachusetts: Harvard University Press, 2005.

Pindar, Peter [John Wolcot]. *A Pair of Lyric Epistles to Lord Macartney and his Ship*. London: H.D. Symonds, 1792.

Pocock, J. G. A. *Barbarism and Religion*, 6 vols. Cambridge: Cambridge University Press, 1999–2015.

Polo, Marco. *The Travels of Marco Polo*. Translated by William Marsden. London: Longman, 1818.

Polo, Marco. *The Travels of Marco Polo*. Translated by William Marsden. Revised by Manuel Komroff. Reprinted, New York: Norton, 2003.

Pomeranz, Kenneth. *The Great Divergence: China, Europe, and the Making of the Modern World Economy*. Princeton, New Jersey: Princeton University Press, 2000.

Porphyry. *Selected Works of Porphyry*. Translated by Thomas Taylor. Vol. 2 of The Thomas Taylor Series. Reprinted, Lydney, Gloucestershire: The Prometheus Trust, 1999.

Porter, David. *The Chinese Taste in Eighteenth-Century England*. Cambridge: Cambridge University Press, 2010.

Porter, David. *Ideographia: the Chinese Cipher in Early Modern Europe*. Stanford: Stanford University Press, 2001.

Potter, John. *Archaeologia Graeca, or the Antiquities of Greece: A New Edition*. Edited by G. Dunbar. 2 vols. London: Stirling & Slade, 1818.

Qian, Zhaoming, ed. *Ezra Pound and China*. Ann Arbor: University of Michigan Press, 2003.

De Quincey, Thomas. *The Works of Thomas de Quincey*. Edited by Grevel Lindop et al. 21 vols. London: Pickering & Chatto, 2000–03.

Raffles, Thomas Stamford. *The History of Java*. 2 vols. London: Black, Parbury and Allen, 1817.

Ricci, Matteo. *China in the Sixteenth Century: The Journals of Matteo Ricci, 1583–1610*. Translated by Louis Gallagher. New York: Random House, 1953.

Ringmar, Erik. *Liberal Barbarism: The European Destruction of the Palace of the Emperor of China*. New York: Palgrave Macmillan, 2013.

Ringmar, Erik. 'Liberal Barbarism and the Oriental Sublime: The European Destruction of the Emperor's Summer Palace'. *Millennium: Journal of International Studies* 34, no. 3 (2006): 917–33.

Roberts, Charlotte. *Edward Gibbon and the Shape of History*. Oxford: Oxford University Press, 2014.

Robinson, Dwight E. 'Imprint of Wedgwood in the Longer Poems of Keats'. *Keats-Shelley Journal* 16 (1967): 23–8.

Rosenthal, Jean-Laurent, and R. Bin Wong. *Before and Beyond Divergence: The Politics of Economic Change in China and Europe*. Cambridge, Massachusetts: Harvard University Press, 2011.

Said, Edward W. *Orientalism: Western Perceptions of the Orient*. Rev. ed. London: Penguin Classics, 2003.

Schiller, Friedrich. *The Armenian; or, the Ghost Seer*. Translated by Wilhelm Render. 4 vols. London: H.D. Symonds, 1800.

Schofield, Robin. *The Vocation of Sara Coleridge: Authorship and Religion*. London: Palgrave Macmillan, 2018.

Shils, Edward. *Tradition*. Chicago: University of Chicago Press, 1981.

Simmons, Diane. *The Narcissism of Empire: Loss, Rage and Revenge in Thomas de Quincey, Robert Louis Stevenson, Arthur Conan Doyle, Rudyard Kipling and Isak Dinesen*. Eastbourne: Sussex Academic Press, 2006.

Slade, John. *Narrative of the Late Proceedings and Events in China*. Canton: Canton Register Press, 1839.

Smith, George Barnett. *General Gordon: the Christian Soldier and Hero*. London: S.W. Partridge, 1896.

Southey, Robert. *The Collected Letters of Robert Southey*. Edited by Lynda Pratt, Tim Fulford, and Ian Packer. 9 vols. Romantic Circles, 2009–. https://romantic-circles.org/editions/southey_letters (accessed 7 July 2019).

Spence, Joseph. *Polymetis*. 2nd ed. London: R. and J. Dodsley, 1755.

Stackhouse, Thomas. *A Defence of the Christian Religion from Several Objections of Modern Antiscripturists*. 2nd ed. London: Edward Symon, 1733.

Standen, Edith A. 'Ovid's "Metamorphoses": A Gobelins Tapestry Series'. *Metropolitan Museum Journal*, 23 (1988): 149–91.

Staunton, George. *An Authentic Account of an Embassy from the King of Great Britain to the Emperor of China*. 2 vols. London: W. Bulmer, 1797.

Staunton, George. *An Historical Account of the Embassy to the Emperor of China*. London: J. Stockdale, 1797.

Staunton, George Thomas, trans. *Ta Tsing Leu Lee: Being the Fundamental Laws and a Selection of the Supplementary Statutes of the Penal Code of China*. London: Cadell and Davies, 1810.

Staunton, George Thomas. *Miscellaneous Notices Relating to China*. Rev. ed. London: John Murray, 1850.

Swinhoe, Robert. *Narrative of the North China Campaign of 1860*. London: Smith, Elder, 1861.

Sypher, F.J. 'Politics in the Poetry of Tennyson.' *Victorian Poetry* 14, no. 2 (1976): 101–12.

Teng, Ssu-yü, and John Fairbank, ed. *China's Response to the West: A Documentary Survey, 1839–1923*. Cambridge, MA: Harvard University Press, 1954.

Tennyson, Lord Alfred. *The Poems of Tennyson: in Three Volumes*. Edited by Christopher Ricks. Longman Annotated English Poets. 2nd ed. London: Longman, 1987.

Tennyson, Hallam. *Alfred Lord Tennyson: a Memoir by his Son.* 4 vols. London: Macmillan, 1897.

Thelwall, Algernon Sydney. *The Iniquities of the Opium Trade with China.* London: H. Allen & Co., 1839.

Thesleff, Holger. *An Introduction to the Pythagorean Writings of the Hellenistic Period.* Abo: Abo Akademi, 1961.

Thirlwall, Connop. *A History of Greece.* 8 vols. London: Longman, Rees, Orme, Brown, Green, & Longman, 1835–44.

Thoms, Peter Perring, trans. 花箋: *Chinese Courtship in Verse; to which is added an Appendix, treating of the Revenue of China.* London: Parbury, Allen, and Kingsbury, 1824.

Ting, Nai-tung. 'The Holy Man and the Snake-Woman. A Study of a Lamia Story in Asian and European Literature'. *Fabula* 8, no. 1 (January 1966): 145–91.

Toner, Jerry. *Homer's Turk: How Classics Shaped Ideas of the East.* Cambridge, Massachusetts: Harvard University Press, 2013.

Trevelyan, Charles. *On the Education of the Peoples of India.* London: Longman, Orme, Brown, Green & Longmans, 1838.

Tythacott, Louise, ed. *Collecting and Displaying China's Summer Palace: The Yuanmingyuan in Britain.* London: Routledge, 2017.

Vasunia, Phiroze. *The Classics and Colonial India.* Classical Presences. Oxford: Oxford University Press, 2013.

Virgil. Edited and translated by H. Rushton Fairclough. Revised by G.P. Goold, Loeb Classical Library 63–64. 2 vols. Reprinted, Cambridge, Massachusetts: Harvard University Press, 2006.

Walker Camehl, Ada, ed. *The Blue-China Book.* New York: E.P. Dutton, 1916.

Watson, Robert. *An Apology for Christianity.* Cambridge: T. & J. Merrill, 1776.

Wilde, Oscar. 'A Chinese Sage'. *The Speaker* 1 (1890): 144–6.

Wilkins, Charles, trans. *The Bhagvat-geeta, or Dialogues of Kreeshna and Arjoon.* London: C. Nourse, 1785.

Winckelmann, Johann Joachim. *Reflections on the Painting and the Sculpture of the Greeks.* Translated by Henry Fuseli. London: A. Millar, 1765.

Wingrove Cooke, George. *China: Being 'The Times' Special Correspondence from China in the Years 1857–58.* London: G. Routledge & Co., 1858.

Witchard, Anne Veronica. *Thomas Burke's Dark Chinoiserie: Limehouse Nights and the Queer Spell of Chinatown.* Farnham: Ashgate, 2009.

Wolseley, Garnet. *The Story of a Soldier's Life.* 2 vols. Reprinted, New York: Charles Scribner's Sons, 1904.

Woolford, John. 'Arnold on Empedocles'. *The Review of English Studies* n.s. 50, no. 197 (1999): 33–52.

Yeats, W. B., ed. *The Oxford Book of Modern Verse, 1892–1935.* Oxford: Clarendon Press, 1936.

Yeats, W. B. *The Letters of W.B. Yeats.* Edited by Allan Wade. London: Rupert Hart-Davis, 1954.

Yeats, W. B. *Autobiographies.* London: Macmillan & Co Ltd, 1955.

Yeats, W. B. *Essays and Introductions.* London: Macmillan & Co Ltd, 1961.

Yeats, W. B. *Explorations.* London: Macmillan & Co Ltd, 1962.

Yeats, W. B. *The Poems.* Edited by Daniel Albright. Everyman's Library 103. London: J.M. Dent & Sons Ltd, 1990.

Young, G.M. *Gibbon.* Edinburgh: Peter Davies Limited, 1932.

Zhang Longxi. *Unexpected Affinities: Reading across Cultures.* Toronto: University of Toronto Press, 2007.

Zhmud, Leonid. *Pythagoras and the Early Pythagoreans.* Translated by Kevin Windle and Rosh Ireland. Oxford: Oxford University Press 1994.

[Zhuangzi]. *Chuang Tzu: Mystic, Moralist, and Social Reformer.* Translated by Herbert A. Giles. London: Bernard Quaritch, 1889.

Zuroski Jenkins, Eugenia. *A Taste for China: English Subjectivity and the Prehistory of Orientalism.* New York: Oxford University Press, 2013.

Index